Mastering Groovy Programming

From Basics to Expert Proficiency

Contents

1 **Introduction to Groovy** **11**
1.1 What is Groovy? 11
1.2 History and Evolution of Groovy 14
1.3 Key Features and Benefits 16
1.4 Groovy vs. Java: A Comparison 19
1.5 Groovy Ecosystem and Tools 21
1.6 Real-world Applications of Groovy 24
1.7 Getting Started with Groovy Scripts 27
1.8 First Groovy Program 30

2 **Groovy Installation and Setup** **33**
2.1 System Requirements 33
2.2 Installing Groovy on Windows 36
2.3 Installing Groovy on macOS 38
2.4 Installing Groovy on Linux 40
2.5 Setting Up Groovy in an IDE 42
2.6 Using Groovy with Command Line 44
2.7 Setting Up Groovy with Maven 46
2.8 Setting Up Groovy with Gradle 49
2.9 Verifying the Installation 52
2.10 Troubleshooting Common Issues 53

3 Groovy Language Basics **59**

3.1 Groovy Syntax Overview 59
3.2 Variables and Data Types 62
3.3 Operators in Groovy 64
3.4 Control Structures: if, else, switch 68
3.5 Loops: for, while, and do-while 71
3.6 Defining and Using Functions 74
3.7 Exception Handling 77
3.8 Groovy Script Structure 79
3.9 Using Annotations 82
3.10 Comments and Documentation 84

4 Working with Collections **89**

4.1 Introduction to Collections 89
4.2 Working with Lists 92
4.3 Working with Sets 94
4.4 Working with Maps 97
4.5 Collection Operators and Methods 99
4.6 Iterating Over Collections 101
4.7 Filtering and Searching Collections 104
4.8 Transforming Collections 106
4.9 Sorting Collections 109
4.10 Advanced Collection Techniques 111

5 Closures and Functional Programming **115**

5.1 Introduction to Closures 115
5.2 Defining and Using Closures 117
5.3 Closure Parameters and Return Values 120
5.4 Closures in Collections 122
5.5 Delegate and Owner in Closures 125

5.6 Using Currying in Closures 128
5.7 Groovy's Built-in Higher Order Functions 129
5.8 Functional Programming Techniques 132
5.9 Combining Closures and DSLs 135
5.10 Practical Examples of Functional Programming 137

6 Object-Oriented Programming in Groovy 141

6.1 Introduction to Object-Oriented Programming (OOP) . . 141
6.2 Classes and Objects in Groovy 145
6.3 Attributes and Methods 148
6.4 Constructors and Initializers 151
6.5 Inheritance and Polymorphism 154
6.6 Encapsulation and Access Modifiers 156
6.7 Abstract Classes and Interfaces 159
6.8 Traits and Mixins 161
6.9 Using Groovy's @CompileStatic 166
6.10 Best Practices for OOP in Groovy 169

7 Groovy and Java Integration 173

7.1 Introduction to Groovy and Java Integration 173
7.2 Calling Java from Groovy 177
7.3 Calling Groovy from Java 180
7.4 Interoperability: Data Types and Collections 183
7.5 Using Java Libraries in Groovy 186
7.6 Mixing Groovy and Java Classes 189
7.7 Annotations and Groovy's @Grab 191
7.8 Java Development Kit (JDK) Compatibility 193
7.9 Performance Considerations 196
7.10 Practical Examples of Groovy-Java Integration 199

8 Metaprogramming in Groovy 203

8.1 Introduction to Metaprogramming 203
8.2 Dynamic Method Invocation 206
8.3 ExpandoMetaClass and MetaClass 208
8.4 Method Missing and Property Missing 210
8.5 Using Categories 213
8.6 AST Transformations 215
8.7 Compile-time Metaprogramming 218
8.8 MetaObject Protocol (MOP) 220
8.9 Intercepting Method Calls 222
8.10 Practical Examples of Metaprogramming 225

9 Working with XML and JSON **229**
9.1 Introduction to XML and JSON in Groovy 229
9.2 Reading XML with XmlSlurper 232
9.3 Reading XML with XmlParser 234
9.4 Writing XML with MarkupBuilder 237
9.5 Reading JSON with JsonSlurper 240
9.6 Writing JSON with JsonBuilder 243
9.7 Navigating and Querying XML 247
9.8 Manipulating JSON Data 249
9.9 Transforming XML and JSON 252
9.10 Real-world Examples 256

10 Groovy Testing and Debugging **261**
10.1 Introduction to Testing in Groovy 261
10.2 Unit Testing with JUnit 264
10.3 Behavior-Driven Development (BDD) with Spock 268
10.4 Mocking and Stubbing 270
10.5 Integration Testing 273
10.6 Test Coverage Tools 276

10.7 Test Automation Techniques 278
10.8 Debugging Groovy Applications 282
10.9 Using the Groovy Console for Debugging 285
10.10Best Practices for Testing and Debugging 288

Introduction

Groovy is a powerful, optionally typed and dynamic language that is capable of working seamlessly with Java. It offers a flexible syntax and a rich feature set that provides developers with a comprehensive toolkit for a wide variety of programming tasks. Designed with simplicity and power in mind, Groovy can be used both as a scripting language and for building sophisticated applications. This book, "Mastering Groovy Programming: From Basics to Expert Proficiency," is intended to guide readers from the foundational concepts to the advanced features of Groovy, ensuring a well-rounded understanding of the language.

The early chapters of this book will cover the fundamental elements of Groovy, starting with its installation and setup. A thorough grounding in how to get Groovy up and running on different operating systems, as well as integration with various Integrated Development Environments (IDEs), ensures that readers have a solid base from which to start coding.

Following the basic setup, the book will introduce the core language syntax. Readers will learn about variables, data types, operators, control structures, and loops. This section is vital for establishing a clear understanding of how Groovy scripts are structured and how they execute.

Groovy's collections framework is indispensable for efficient data manipulation. We will cover a comprehensive range of topics on lists, sets, and maps, as well as the numerous methods Groovy provides for interacting with collections. Detailed examples will illustrate how to filter, search, transform, and sort collections, providing readers with practical skills for their coding endeavors.

Closures in Groovy allow for elegant and concise code, especially in conjunction with functional programming paradigms. The book will delve into the creation and application of closures, discussing key concepts such as parameters, return values, and advanced techniques like currying and using built-in higher-order functions. This will prepare readers to write more modular and maintainable code using functional programming techniques.

Object-Oriented Programming (OOP) is a cornerstone of Groovy, just as it is for Java. This book will cover the essential OOP principles as they apply to Groovy, including class definitions, inheritance, polymorphism, encapsulation, traits, and mixins. By understanding OOP in Groovy, readers will be able to design robust and scalable applications.

An important feature of Groovy is its seamless integration with Java. This allows developers to augment existing Java applications with Groovy's dynamic capabilities or simply use Java libraries within Groovy code. We will explore the interoperability between Groovy and Java, including calling methods, handling collections, and leveraging Java libraries from Groovy.

Metaprogramming in Groovy provides powerful tools for dynamic code generation and modification. Readers will learn about invoking methods dynamically, the use of ExpandoMetaClass, metaClass, method missing, and property missing, as well as compile-time and runtime metaprogramming techniques. These advanced capabilities enable developers to create highly flexible and dynamic systems.

Furthermore, the book will cover the techniques for working with XML and JSON, which are ubiquitous in modern software development. Groovy's facilities for parsing, querying, and generating XML and JSON will be discussed in detail, enabling readers to handle structured data effectively.

Finally, we will address testing and debugging in Groovy. A section dedicated to unit testing with JUnit and Behavior-Driven Development (BDD) with Spock will highlight the importance of reliable code. Strategies for mocking, stubbing, integration testing, and ensuring test coverage will be outlined, alongside methods for effective debugging of Groovy applications.

By the end of this book, readers will have gained a deep understanding of both the basics and advanced features of Groovy. The goal is not merely to expose the syntax and features of the language but to enable the reader to apply them effectively in practical scenarios. This comprehensive guide thus serves as both a learning resource and a long-term reference for mastering Groovy programming.

Chapter 1

Introduction to Groovy

Groovy is a dynamic language that builds upon the strengths of Java, offering enhanced productivity and a more concise syntax. This chapter provides a detailed overview of what Groovy is, its history and evolution, key features, and benefits. It also includes a comparison with Java to highlight Groovy's distinct advantages, an introduction to the Groovy ecosystem and tools, and real-world applications. Additionally, it covers the basics of getting started with Groovy scripts and demonstrates writing your first Groovy program.

1.1 What is Groovy?

Groovy is a powerful, dynamic language that operates on the Java Virtual Machine (JVM). It is designed to enhance productivity and offer a more concise syntax compared to Java, while maintaining compatibility with Java code and libraries. Groovy incorporates many features from other programming languages, notably Python, Ruby, and Smalltalk, resulting in a modern programming experience that emphasizes ease of use and expressiveness.

At its core, Groovy syntax is a superset of Java, meaning that all Java code is valid Groovy code. This allows Java developers to gradually transition to Groovy without a steep learning curve. Groovy introduces several new language constructs and operational efficiencies, such as dynamically-typed variables, closures, operator overloading, and native syntax for lists, maps, and ranges.

To illustrate, consider a simple Java code snippet:

```
public class HelloWorld {
    public static void main(String[] args) {
        System.out.println("Hello, World!");
    }
}
```

The equivalent Groovy code is notably more concise:

```
println 'Hello, World!'
```

This example encapsulates Groovy's capability to simplify and streamline common programming tasks.

One of Groovy's notable features is its ability to interact seamlessly with existing Java code. This interoperability means that Groovy can use Java libraries and frameworks directly, making it particularly useful for projects that require integration with prevailing Java infrastructure. As a dynamically typed language, Groovy allows developers to write more flexible and less verbose code than its statically typed counterpart.

Groovy supports the following attributes:

- **Static and Dynamic Typing:** Groovy supports both static and dynamic typing. You may declare a variable with a specific type or opt for loosened type constraints using the "def" keyword.
- **Closures:** Groovy introduces closures, which are anonymous blocks of code that can be assigned to variables, passed as arguments to methods, or executed directly.
- **Native Syntax for Collections and Ranges:** Groovy includes literal notation for common collections (lists and maps) and introduces the concept of ranges, making collection manipulation intuitive and expressive.
- **Operator Overloading:** Through operator overloading, Groovy allows custom behavior for standard operators, enabling a more natural and readable interaction with objects.
- **Domain-Specific Languages (DSLs):** Groovy's syntax and runtime metaprogramming capabilities make it an excellent choice for creating domain-specific languages.
- **Simplified I/O Operations:** Reading from and writing to files is

more straightforward in Groovy, significantly lowering the boilerplate code required for common I/O tasks.

Dynamic typing in Groovy can be demonstrated through the following code example:

```
def a = 10 // dynamic typing
String b = "Hi" // static typing
def c = [1,2,3] // list
def d = [name: "Alice", age: 24] // map
```

Closures are pivotal in Groovy's functional programming capabilities:

```
def square = { it * it }
assert square(4) == 16
```

To illustrate Groovy's handling of collections and ranges:

```
def nums = [1, 2, 3, 4, 5]
def squares = nums.collect { it * it }
def range = 'a'..'z'
assert range.size() == 26
```

Operator overloading allows for custom and more streamlined code interactions:

```
class Complex {
    def real, imag
    Complex plus(Complex other) {
        new Complex(real: real + other.real, imag: imag + other.imag)
    }
}
def z1 = new Complex(real: 1, imag: 2)
def z2 = new Complex(real: 3, imag: 4)
def sum = z1 + z2
assert sum.real == 4 && sum.imag == 6
```

Here is an example demonstrating I/O operations with fewer lines of code:

```
def file = new File('example.txt')
file.eachLine { line -> println line }
file.withWriter('UTF-8') { writer -> writer.writeLine('New Content') }
```

Groovy's combination of brevity, flexibility, and powerful features positions it as a versatile tool for a variety of programming tasks, ranging from simple scripting to the development of complex, scalable applications.

1.2 History and Evolution of Groovy

Groovy is a dynamic programming language for the Java platform. It was created by James Strachan and Bob McWhirter as a means to blend the strengths of the Java language with features often found in other dynamic scripting languages, notably those in the Python and Ruby ecosystems. The purpose of Groovy was to provide a Java-compatible language with a more succinct, flexible, and productive syntax.

The creation of Groovy began in August 2003, with the version 1.0 release in January 2007 serving as the language's official introduction to the public. This first stable release adhered closely to Java's design principles, providing seamless integration with Java classes and libraries while also enhancing user productivity through a more streamlined syntax.

One of the significant milestones in Groovy's evolution was its standardization through the Java Community Process (JCP). This resulted in the establishment of the JSR 241 specification: "The Groovy Programming Language." This formal acknowledgment further solidified Groovy's position in the Java ecosystem, granting it widespread recognition and adoption.

Groovy's evolution continued with subsequent versions incorporating language enhancements, library updates, and performance improvements. Version 1.5 introduced comprehensive support for the Java 5 language features, including annotations and generics. This was a crucial update as it allowed developers to leverage modern Java paradigms directly within Groovy.

The release of Groovy 2.0 in July 2012 represented a significant leap forward. A critical feature introduced in this version was the Groovy static compiler, which provided developers the option to compile Groovy code into Java bytecode in a more type-safe manner. This could offer optimizations and performance improvements similar to those available in statically-typed languages. Additionally, Groovy 2.0 brought support for modularity with invokedynamic, making it faster and more versatile on the Java Virtual Machine (JVM).

```
@groovy.transform.CompileStatic
def add(int x, int y) {
    return x + y
}
println add(1, 2)
```

Groovy 2.3 later introduced traits, an improvement on Java's support for inheritance and composition. Traits allowed for more flexible object composition, providing reusable method implementations that could be mixed into classes without the limitations of multiple inheritance.

```
trait FlyingAbility {
    String fly() {
        "I'm flying!"
    }
}

class Bird implements FlyingAbility {}

def b = new Bird()
println b.fly()
```

In 2015, Groovy underwent another significant transformation when it moved under the umbrella of the Apache Software Foundation, thus becoming Apache Groovy. This transition ensured that Groovy would benefit from the Foundation's governance and infrastructure, leading to enhanced community engagement and project sustainability.

Groovy's design emphasizes several core principles that have steered its development over the years. It remains dynamically typed and employs a similar syntax to Java, but includes features inspired by other programming languages designed to simplify everyday coding tasks. These features include:

- Closure: A critical feature that allows for the creation of anonymous blocks of code that can be passed around and executed.
- Metaprogramming: The ability to modify or extend the program's behavior at runtime.
- Operator Overloading: Allows for more natural expressions of operations on objects.
- GDK: Groovy Development Kit extends the standard JDK with additional convenience methods.

Groovy continues to evolve with an active community contributing to its development. Its versioning follows semantic procedures, with major versions signaling significant additions or changes to the language and libraries. Current releases focus on maintaining backward compatibility while introducing new features and optimizations aligned with advancements in the Java ecosystem.

Proceeding versions have continued to build on Groovy's strengths, with enhancements in performance, support for the latest Java versions, and integration improvements with various ecosystems and tools. Groovy's capacity for leveraging the full potential of the Java platform, combined with its own unique features, positions it as an invaluable asset for developers seeking both brevity and expressive power in their code.

1.3 Key Features and Benefits

Groovy, as a dynamic programming language for the Java Platform, presents numerous features that enhance developer productivity while providing seamless integration with existing Java codebases. Understanding these features is imperative for leveraging Groovy effectively in various software development projects.

Dynamic Typing - Groovy allows dynamic typing, meaning variables do not need to have their types explicitly declared. This facilitates a more flexible and less verbose code, enhancing developer productivity. For example:

```
def myVariable = "Hello, Groovy"
println myVariable
myVariable = 42
println myVariable
```

In this example, myVariable is initially assigned a string and later reassigned an integer without causing any type errors. The dynamic typing in Groovy reduces the boilerplate code associated with static type declarations, enabling a more streamlined coding experience.

Optional Typing - Although Groovy supports dynamic typing, it also allows optional static typing. This flexibility means developers can specify types when needed for added clarity, type safety, or performance optimizations:

```
int myNumber = 10
String greeting = "Hello, Groovy"
```

The ability to toggle between dynamic and static typing offers the best of both worlds in terms of flexibility and control over type checking.

Closures - Groovy incorporates closures, which are anonymous blocks of code that can be assigned to variables, passed to methods, and executed at a later time. Closures bring functional programming capabilities into Groovy. Example usage:

```
def square = { int number -> number * number }
println square(5) // Outputs: 25
```

Closures offer powerful ways to handle iterative processes, enabling the use of constructs like .each, .collect, and .findAll, simplifying collection manipulations.

String Interpolation - Groovy provides a more convenient way to concatenate strings using string interpolation. Using the $ symbol within double-quoted strings or the slashy strings:

```
def name = "World"
println "Hello, ${name}!"
```

This results in the output:

Hello, World!String interpolation eliminates the need for cumbersome concatenation, making the code more readable and concise.

Native Syntax for Lists and Maps - Groovy simplifies working with collections through native syntax for lists and maps:

```
def myList = [1, 2, 3, 4]
def myMap = [name: "Groovy", age: 3]
```

This syntactic sugar helps in creating and accessing collections with minimal code, improving readability and development speed.

Enhanced Markup Processing - Groovy provides built-in support for constructing and manipulating XML and JSON. This feature is particularly useful for applications that require extensive data interchange and configuration. Example of creating XML:

```
def writer = new StringWriter()
def xml = new groovy.xml.MarkupBuilder(writer)
xml.person {
    name "John Doe"
    age 30
}
println writer.toString()
```

The resulting XML:

```
<person>
    <name>John Doe</name>
    <age>30</age>
</person>
```

These capabilities simplify working with widely-used data formats.

Meta-programming - Groovy supports Meta-programming, where the program can modify its own structure and behavior at runtime. This is achieved using the MetaClass, which allows adding or altering methods dynamically:

```
String.metaClass.doSomething = { ->
    return delegate.toUpperCase()
}
println "hello groovy".doSomething()
```

This mechanism fosters adaptive and flexible code architectures, which can adapt to various needs dynamically.

Operator Overloading - Groovy allows customizing the behavior of operators for user-defined types, increasing the intuitiveness of the code. For instance, one can override the plus operator:

```
class Complex {
    double real, imaginary
    Complex plus(Complex other) {
        return new Complex(real: this.real + other.real, imaginary: this.imaginary +
                other.imaginary)
    }
}
```

This facilitates more natural and expressive DSL (Domain-Specific Language) creation.

Domain-Specific Languages (DSLs) - Groovy excels at creating concise and readable DSLs. The syntax and flexibility of Groovy allow for tailoring mini-languages that are specific to different problem domains, enhancing expressiveness and reducing boilerplate code.

Compatibility with Java - One of Groovy's most significant advantages is its compatibility with Java. Groovy code can call Java methods, inherit from Java classes, and implement Java interfaces:

```
import java.util.ArrayList

def list = new ArrayList()
list.add("Groovy")
println list.get(0)
```

This seamless interoperability enables developers to incrementally adopt Groovy in an existing Java project, promoting a smooth transition without requiring substantial rewrites.

Rapid Prototyping - Groovy's dynamic nature, combined with its succinct syntax, makes it highly suitable for rapid prototyping and scripting. Developers can quickly test and iterate on their ideas with less boilerplate code and faster turnaround times.

Built-in Testing - Groovy includes modules such as GroovyTestCase and Spock for testing. These tools provide a rich set of features to write expressive and easy-to-maintain tests, ensuring the reliability and robustness of the code.

Utilizing these key features, Groovy provides significant benefits that enhance development productivity, code maintainability, and flexibility, making it an excellent tool for modern software development.

1.4 Groovy vs. Java: A Comparison

Groovy and Java share a deep integration since they both run on the Java Virtual Machine (JVM) and leverage the existing Java ecosystem. However, Groovy differentiates itself from Java through various enhancements that aim to improve developer productivity and provide more flexibility in scripts and programs. This section explores several aspects where Groovy and Java either align or diverge, thus highlighting the strengths and differences of Groovy.

Syntax and Readability

One of the most noticeable differences between Groovy and Java is syntax. Groovy's syntax is designed to be more concise and expressive. For example, semicolons are optional in Groovy, which can make the code cleaner.

```
public class HelloWorld {
    public static void main(String[] args) {
        System.out.println("Hello, World!");
    }
}
```

The equivalent Groovy code is significantly shorter, providing the same functionality with fewer lines and simpler syntax:

```
println "Hello, World!"
```

Type System

Java is statically typed, meaning that type checking is enforced at compile-time. This helps in catching errors early but may require verbose code.

```
int number = 10;
String message = "Hello, Java!";
```

In contrast, Groovy is dynamically typed, allowing developers to declare variables without explicitly specifying their types. This can reduce boilerplate code, although Groovy also supports optional static typing:

```
def number = 10
def message = "Hello, Groovy!"
```

Groovy's dynamic typing can speed up development, but developers must be cautious about potential runtime errors.

Closures

Groovy introduces closures, which are code blocks that can be assigned to variables, passed as method parameters, or returned from methods. Closures enhance the ability to create more dynamic and flexible code structures:

```
def greet = { name -> println "Hello, $name" }
greet("World")
```

Java, prior to version 8, did not have an equivalent feature. With Java 8, lambda expressions were introduced, which provide similar, albeit less powerful, functionality compared to Groovy closures:

```
Consumer<String> greet = name -> System.out.println("Hello, " + name);
greet.accept("World");
```

Collections and Ranges

Groovy extends and simplifies Java's collection framework and includes a native syntax for creating and manipulating lists, maps, and ranges:

```
def list = [1, 2, 3, 4, 5]
def map = [name: "Groovy", type: "Language"]
def range = 1..5 // Range from 1 to 5
```

In Java, creating and initializing collections and ranges is more verbose:

```
List<Integer> list = Arrays.asList(1, 2, 3, 4, 5);
Map<String, String> map = new HashMap<>();
map.put("name", "Java");
map.put("type", "Language");
```

Metaprogramming

Groovy provides powerful metaprogramming capabilities, allowing developers to modify or extend classes and methods at runtime. This feature is not natively supported by Java:

```
class Car {
    String make
    String model
```

```
}

Car.metaClass.getDetails = { -> "$make $model" }
def car = new Car(make: 'Tesla', model: 'Model S')
println car.getDetails() // Outputs "Tesla Model S"
```

Compatibility and Interoperability

Despite their differences, Groovy maintains seamless interoperability with Java. Groovy code can call Java methods and use Java libraries without any special configuration, making it possible to incrementally adopt Groovy in existing Java projects:

```
import java.util.Date

def currentDate = new Date()
println "Current Date: $currentDate"
```

Compile Time and Performance

Java, being statically typed, can optimize code better at compile time, potentially offering better runtime performance. Groovy, while flexible and concise, sometimes incurs additional overhead due to dynamic typing.

Overall, the choice between Groovy and Java depends on the specific needs of a project. Developers might prefer Java for large-scale, performance-critical applications where early error detection and type safety are crucial. Groovy shines in scenarios that benefit from reduced verbosity, rapid development, and dynamic features.

When the strengths of both languages are combined, leveraging Groovy for scripting and Java for performance-intensive tasks, a balance can be struck to harness the capabilities of both languages effectively.

1.5 Groovy Ecosystem and Tools

Groovy is not merely a programming language; it is part of a vibrant and extensive ecosystem that offers a robust suite of tools and libraries. Understanding these tools is pivotal for leveraging Groovy to its fullest potential. This section elucidates various components of the Groovy ecosystem, detailing their functionality and application.

Groovy Console The Groovy Console is an interactive tool that provides a graphical user interface (GUI) for writing, testing, and running

Groovy scripts. It is an excellent environment for experimenting with Groovy code, debugging, and learning the nuances of the language. To open the Groovy Console, execute the following command:

```
groovyConsole
```

This command launches a window where users can write Groovy code and execute it in real-time. The Groovy Console is particularly useful for iterative development as it allows for immediate feedback on code execution.

Groovysh Groovysh is a command-line shell that offers an alternative to the Groovy Console for executing Groovy code interactively. It is useful for users who prefer working within a terminal environment. To start Groovysh, use the following command:

```
groovysh
```

Within Groovysh, you can execute Groovy code line by line, inspect variables, and test expressions. It also supports code completion, history, and other features to improve productivity.

Grape Grape (Groovy Adaptable Packaging Engine) is a built-in dependency management system in Groovy. It allows developers to add external libraries to their Groovy scripts easily. Grape simplifies the process of specifying and resolving dependencies, similar to how Maven or Gradle operates for Java projects. To use Grape, annotate your Groovy script with the @Grab annotation, as demonstrated below:

```
@Grab(group='org.apache.commons', module='commons-lang3', version='3.12.0')
import org.apache.commons.lang3.StringUtils

println StringUtils.capitalize('hello grapes')
```

When the script is executed, Grape automatically downloads and includes the specified library, enabling seamless integration of third-party dependencies.

Groovy CLI Builder The Groovy CLI Builder is a powerful utility for parsing command-line options and arguments. It provides a convenient approach to handling various input parameters in a script. An example of using the CLI Builder is as follows:

```
def cli = new CliBuilder(usage: 'groovyScript -f <filename>')
cli.with {
    f longOpt: 'file', args: 1, argName: 'filename', 'Specify the file name'
}

def options = cli.parse(args)
```

```
if (!options?.f) {
    cli.usage()
    System.exit(1)
}
println "File name specified: ${options.f}"
```

In the example above, the CLI Builder is employed to parse a command-line option -f for specifying a filename. The parsed option can be accessed using the options object.

Groovydoc Groovydoc generates documentation for Groovy projects in a manner similar to Javadoc for Java. It extracts documentation comments from the source code and produces HTML files that provide an organized and navigable view of the project's API. To generate documentation, execute the following command:

```
groovydoc -d docs src/*.groovy
```

This command tells Groovydoc to generate documentation in the docs directory for all Groovy source files in the src directory.

IDE Support Modern Integrated Development Environments (IDEs) such as IntelliJ IDEA, Eclipse, and Visual Studio Code offer excellent support for Groovy. They provide features such as syntax highlighting, code completion, refactoring, and debugging tailored specifically for Groovy. Configuring an IDE to support Groovy generally involves installing a plugin or enabling Groovy support in the IDE settings.

Build Tools Groovy integrates seamlessly with several build tools, with Gradle being the most prominent. Gradle uses a Groovy-based DSL (Domain Specific Language) to define build scripts, making it a natural choice for Groovy projects. A simple Gradle build script for a Groovy project might look like this:

```
apply plugin: 'groovy'

repositories {
    mavenCentral()
}

dependencies {
    implementation 'org.codehaus.groovy:groovy-all:3.0.8'
    testImplementation 'junit:junit:4.13.2'
}
```

This Gradle script applies the Groovy plugin, specifies Maven Central as the repository, and declares dependencies for the Groovy library and JUnit for testing.

Continuous Integration For continuous integration, tools like Jenkins and Travis CI support Groovy pipelines and scripts. Jenkins, for instance, allows the use of Groovy for defining build and deployment pipelines via Jenkins Pipeline DSL. Here is an example of a simple Jenkins pipeline written in Groovy:

```
pipeline {
   agent any

   stages {
      stage('Build') {
         steps {
            sh 'gradlew build'
         }
      }
      stage('Test') {
         steps {
            sh 'gradlew test'
         }
      }
      stage('Deploy') {
         steps {
            echo 'Deploying...'
         }
      }
   }
}
```

This Groovy-based pipeline script defines three stages: build, test, and deploy. The sh steps execute shell commands to build and test the project using Gradle.

These tools and components collectively enrich the Groovy ecosystem, enhancing developer productivity and application quality.

1.6 Real-world Applications of Groovy

Groovy has established itself as a powerful and versatile language within various domains, benefiting from its dynamic nature, easy integration with Java, and concise syntax. This section delves into the diverse real-world applications of Groovy, emphasizing its use in web development, scripting, testing, data science, and dev-ops automation.

One prominent area where Groovy excels is in web development. Groovy, combined with frameworks like Grails, simplifies the development of web applications by leveraging the convention-over-configuration paradigm and providing a robust environment for building scalable and maintainable systems. The seamless integration with the Spring ecosystem allows developers to quickly build RESTful web services, manage databases, and implement security features.

For scripting tasks, Groovy offers a highly expressive and readable syntax, making it an ideal choice for writing build scripts and automating repetitive tasks. For instance, Gradle, a popular build automation system, is built on Groovy. Gradle allows fine-grained control over the build process, integrates with multiple languages, including Java, Kotlin, and Scala, and provides a flexible model for dependency management and task execution.

```
apply plugin: 'java'
apply plugin: 'application'

mainClassName = 'com.example.Main'

repositories {
    mavenCentral()
}

dependencies {
    implementation 'org.springframework:spring-context:5.3.8'
    testImplementation 'junit:junit:4.13.2'
}

task runApp(type: JavaExec) {
    main = mainClassName
    classpath = sourceSets.main.runtimeClasspath
}
```

In testing, Groovy's concise and readable syntax, along with its dynamic features, make it a powerful tool for writing and maintaining tests. Spock, a testing and specification framework for Java and Groovy applications, leverages Groovy's expressive syntax to create readable and powerful tests. Spock integrates easily with popular build tools (like Gradle and Maven) and supports mocking, stubbing, and behavior-driven development (BDD).

```
import spock.lang.Specification

class SimpleMathTest extends Specification {
    def "addition works correctly"() {
        expect:
        1 + 1 == 2
    }
}
```

In the context of data science and analytics, Groovy's succinct notation and ability to interact seamlessly with Java libraries make it a useful language for data manipulation and analysis. Libraries like Apache Commons Math, Groovy's built-in JSON handling, and the availability of third-party APIs facilitate data processing tasks. Scripts can be quickly written to parse large datasets, perform statistical computations, and generate visualizations.

```
import groovy.json.JsonSlurper

def json = '''{
  "students": [
    {"name": "John", "score": 90},
    {"name": "Jane", "score": 87},
    {"name": "Doe", "score": 82}
  ]
}'''

def jsonSlurper = new JsonSlurper()
def data = jsonSlurper.parseText(json)

data.students.each { student ->
  println "${student.name} scored ${student.score}"
}
```

Automation in dev-ops is another field where Groovy demonstrates its capabilities. Groovy scripting is widely used to automate tasks in continuous integration (CI) and continuous deployment (CD) pipelines. Jenkins, a popular automation tool, allows the use of Groovy for scripting complex workflows in Jenkins Pipelines. This ensures a streamlined process for code integration, automated testing, and deployment.

```
pipeline {
  agent any
  stages {
    stage('Build') {
      steps {
        sh 'mvn clean package'
      }
    }
    stage('Test') {
      steps {
        sh 'mvn test'
      }
    }
    stage('Deploy') {
      steps {
        sshPublisher(publishers: [
          sshPublisherDesc(
            configName: 'my-server',
            transfers: [
              sshTransfer(
                sourceFiles: 'target/*.jar',
                removePrefix: 'target',
                remoteDirectory: '/opt/app'
              )
            ]
          )
        ])
      }
    }
  }
}
```

Real-world applications of Groovy highlight its versatility and capability to integrate with various tools and frameworks. This extensive applicability makes Groovy a valuable tool for developers in multiple domains, offering solutions that enhance productivity and streamline development processes.

1.7 Getting Started with Groovy Scripts

Groovy scripts provide a powerful and flexible way to write succinct and efficient code with minimal setup. Leveraging Groovy's dynamic capabilities, developers can quickly iterate and execute tasks that would be more verbose in Java. This section explores the initial steps required to start writing Groovy scripts, from setting up the environment to understanding the basic structure of a Groovy script.

Setting Up the Environment

Before writing and executing Groovy scripts, it is necessary to have the Groovy SDK installed on your system. The recommended approach is to use the Software Development Kit Manager (SDKMAN!). SDKMAN! allows developers to easily install and switch between multiple versions of Groovy. Here are the steps to install SDKMAN! and subsequently Groovy:

```
# Install SDKMAN!
curl -s "https://get.sdkman.io" | bash
source "$HOME/.sdkman/bin/sdkman-init.sh"

# Install the latest version of Groovy
sdk install groovy
```

Once installed, verify the installation by checking the Groovy version:

```
groovy -version
```

The expected output should resemble:

```
Groovy Version: 3.0.8 JVM: 11.0.8 Vendor: AdoptOpenJDK OS: Mac OS X
```

Writing Your First Groovy Script

A Groovy script is a file with the .groovy extension containing Groovy code. Unlike Java, Groovy scripts do not require an explicit class definition or main method. Create a file named HelloGroovy.groovy and open it in your preferred text editor. Add the following code to the file:

```
println 'Hello, Groovy!'
```

This script uses the println method to print "Hello, Groovy!" to the console. Execute the script from the command line:

```
groovy HelloGroovy.groovy
```

The expected output is:

```
Hello, Groovy!
```

Basic Groovy Syntax

Groovy's syntax is designed to be concise yet expressive. Here are some basic constructs and idioms:

- def keyword: Used to define variables without specifying their type explicitly.
- GString: Groovy's implementation of string interpolation.
- Optional semicolons: Semicolons are optional at the end of statements.

Consider the following example demonstrating these features:

```
def name = "Groovy"
def greeting = "Hello, ${name}!"
println greeting
```

Executing the script will yield:

```
Hello, Groovy!
```

Comments in Groovy Scripts

Groovy supports both single-line and multi-line comments. Single-line comments start with //, while multi-line comments are enclosed within /* */. Example:

```
// This is a single-line comment
println 'Single-line comment example'

/*
 This is a multi-line comment
 spanning multiple lines
 */
println 'Multi-line comment example'
```

Variables and Data Types

Groovy is dynamically typed by default, but it also supports static typing. The def keyword is used to declare a variable without specifying its type. However, you can also declare typed variables:

```
def number = 42
String message = "The answer is ${number}"

println message

int intValue = 10
boolean isTrue = true
```

Functions in Groovy Scripts

Functions in Groovy are defined using the def keyword, followed by the function name and parameters in parentheses. Here is an example of a function and its invocation:

```
def add(int a, int b) {
    return a + b
}

def result = add(5, 3)
println "The sum is ${result}"
```

The script will output:

```
The sum is 8
```

Control Structures

Groovy supports standard control structures such as conditionals and loops. For conditionals, use if, else if, and else statements. Loops include for and while loops. Examples of both:

```
def number = 10

if (number > 5) {
    println "Number is greater than 5"
} else {
    println "Number is 5 or less"
}

for (int i = 0; i < 5; i++) {
    println "Iteration ${i}"
}

def count = 0
while (count < 3) {
    println "Count is ${count}"
    count++
}
```

This section provided a detailed guide on getting started with Groovy scripts, covering environment setup, basic syntax, and essential features such as variables, functions, and control structures. By following these steps, you can effectively begin writing and executing Groovy scripts, leveraging Groovy's powerful and concise capabilities for various programming tasks.

1.8 First Groovy Program

To solidify our understanding of Groovy, writing and executing our first Groovy program will be instrumental. This section will walk through the creation, execution, and analysis of a basic Groovy script. This exercise aims to provide a practical foundation on which further Groovy concepts may be built.

A Groovy script is a plain text file with the .groovy extension. Such files can be executed directly without the need for explicit compilation, thanks to the interpreted nature of Groovy. Let us start by creating a simple script that prints a message to the console.

```
println("Hello, Groovy World!")
```

The println method in Groovy is used to output text to the console. This script, when executed, prints the string "Hello, Groovy World!" to the standard output.

To execute this Groovy script, ensure you have Groovy installed on your system and the groovy command is accessible from your terminal or command prompt. Save the above script in a file named HelloWorld.groovy and run the following command:

```
groovy HelloWorld.groovy
```

The output will be:

```
Hello, Groovy World!
```

Now, let us explore some of the fundamental aspects of Groovy syntax and features by expanding our basic example.

Variable Declaration and Data Types

In Groovy, variables can be dynamically typed or statically typed. Dynamic typing allows the variable types to be inferred at runtime, whereas static typing requires the explicit declaration of variable types. Variables in Groovy can be defined using the def keyword for dynamic typing or an explicit type for static typing.

```
def dynamicVariable = "I'm dynamic!"
String staticVariable = "I'm static!"

println(dynamicVariable)
```

```
println(staticVariable)
```

Executing the above code will produce:

```
I'm dynamic!
I'm static!
```

Groovy supports numerous data types, including integers, floats, strings, lists, maps, and more. Here is an example demonstrating the assignment and printing of various data types:

```
def number = 42
def floatingPoint = 3.14
def string = "Groovy Language"
def list = [1, 2, 3, 4]
def map = ["key1": "value1", "key2": "value2"]

println(number)
println(floatingPoint)
println(string)
println(list)
println(map)
```

The expected output will be:

```
42
3.14
Groovy Language
[1, 2, 3, 4]
[key1:value1, key2:value2]
```

Control Structures

Groovy utilizes control structures similar to those found in Java but often with more concise syntax. Consider the following example that demonstrates the use of an if-else statement:

```
def number = 10

if (number > 0) {
    println("$number is positive")
} else if (number == 0) {
    println("$number is zero")
} else {
    println("$number is negative")
}
```

This script evaluates the value of number and prints an appropriate message. When executed, this will output:

```
10 is positive
```

Using loops in Groovy is straightforward. Here is an example of a for loop:

```
for (i in 1..5) {
    println("Iteration: $i")
```

```
}
```

```
Iteration: 1
Iteration: 2
Iteration: 3
Iteration: 4
Iteration: 5
```

Functions

Defining functions in Groovy is simple and can be done with or without explicitly specifying the return type. Consider the following example where we define and call a function to add two numbers:

```
def add(int a, int b) {
    return a + b
}

int result = add(5, 10)
println("The result of addition is: $result")
```

```
The result of addition is: 15
```

This foundation acquaints us with Groovy's syntactical elegance and capability. As we progress through more advanced topics, the fundamentals covered here will serve as essential building blocks.

Chapter 2

Groovy Installation and Setup

This chapter outlines the necessary steps to install and configure Groovy on various operating systems including Windows, macOS, and Linux. It covers setting up Groovy in popular Integrated Development Environments (IDEs), using Groovy with command-line tools, and configuring it with build tools like Maven and Gradle. The chapter also includes guidance on verifying the installation and troubleshooting common issues to ensure a smooth setup process.

2.1 System Requirements

Prior to installing Groovy, it is essential to ensure that your system meets the prerequisite requirements. This section delineates the necessary software and hardware specifications. Confirming these requirements can avoid common installation and runtime issues.

Operating System

Groovy is cross-platform and can be installed on various operating systems including:

- Windows 7 or later
- macOS 10.9 (Mavericks) or later

- Linux kernel 2.6.32 or later

Java Development Kit (JDK)

Groovy is a Java-syntax-compatible language and requires the Java Development Kit (JDK) to run. Ensure that you have JDK version 7 or higher installed. Preferably, JDK 8 or above should be used to leverage enhanced performance and features.

You can verify the installed JDK version by executing the following command in the terminal:

```
$ java -version
```

An example of a valid response indicating a compatible JDK version would be:

```
java version "1.8.0_281"
Java(TM) SE Runtime Environment (build 1.8.0_281-b09)
Java HotSpot(TM) 64-Bit Server VM (build 25.281-b09, mixed mode)
```

Memory and CPU Requirements

While Groovy itself is efficient in terms of resource usage, the development environment and associated tools may have higher demands. The following baseline specifications are recommended:

- **Memory:** At least 4 GB of RAM. For larger projects or more demanding environments, 8 GB or more is advisable.
- **CPU:** Multi-core processor (at least dual-core). Modern processors (Intel i3/i5/i7, AMD Ryzen) are preferable for development ease.

Disk Space

Sufficient disk space is necessary to accommodate the Groovy binaries, libraries, and any associated tools. Ensure that you have at least 500 MB of free space available. Additional disk space will be required for storing projects and dependencies.

Additional Software

Depending on your development workflow, you might need additional software tools:

- **Integrated Development Environment (IDE):** Tools like IntelliJ IDEA, Eclipse, or Visual Studio Code enhance productivity with

Groovy. Ensure that your IDE is compatible with the Groovy language.

- **Build Tools:** If you plan to integrate Groovy with build tools such as Maven or Gradle, ensure that these are installed and configured appropriately. Verify Maven by running:

```
$ mvn -version
```

A sample response showing a proper Maven installation is:

```
Apache Maven 3.6.3
Maven home: /usr/local/apache-maven/apache-maven-3.6.3
Java version: 1.8.0_281, vendor: Oracle Corporation, runtime: /usr/local/java/jdk1.8.0_281
```

Network Requirements

While Groovy itself can function offline after installation, certain features and dependencies may require internet access. Ensure that your system has reliable internet connectivity for downloading dependencies and accessing documentation.

Permissions and Privileges

Administrative privileges may be required to install Groovy and related tools, particularly on Windows systems. Make sure you have the necessary permissions to install software.

Environment Variables

Certain environment variables need to be set for Groovy to work effectively. These include:

- JAVA_HOME: Points to the root directory of the JDK installation.
- GROOVY_HOME: Should be set to the root directory of the Groovy installation.
- PATH: Should include the bin directory of both the JDK and Groovy installations.

An exemplary way to set these variables on a Unix-like system is by appending the following lines to the .bashrc or .zshrc file:

```
export JAVA_HOME=/path/to/jdk
export GROOVY_HOME=/path/to/groovy
export PATH=$PATH:$JAVA_HOME/bin:$GROOVY_HOME/bin
```

For Windows, these variables can be set in the System Properties under Environment Variables.

These system requirements ensure a stable and efficient setup for Groovy development, enabling a smooth installation process and optimal runtime performance.

2.2 Installing Groovy on Windows

The installation of Groovy on Windows can be achieved through several methods, each catering to different preferences and requirements. This section details the steps required to download, install, and configure Groovy on a Windows platform using the Windows Installer and manual installation methods. We also cover verifying the installation to ensure Groovy functions correctly.

Prerequisites:

- Windows 7, 8, 10, or later.
- Java Development Kit (JDK) 8 or later installed and properly configured. Groovy requires the JAVA_HOME environment variable to be set to the JDK installation path.

Verifying Java Installation:

To verify Java is installed and properly configured:

```
C:\> java -version
C:\> echo %JAVA_HOME%
```

Ensure that the Java version is 1.8 or higher and that %JAVA_HOME% outputs the JDK installation path.

Option 1: Using the Windows Installer:

1. Visit the official Groovy website at http://groovy-lang.org/download.html. 2. Download the latest Windows Installer (the .msi file). 3. Run the downloaded installer.

The installation wizard guides you through the installation process. Follow these steps:

- Welcome Screen: Click Next.
- License Agreement: Read and accept the terms, then click Next.

- Destination Folder: Choose the installation directory or use the default, then click Next.
- Ready to Install: Click Install to start the installation.
- Completion: Click Finish once the installation is complete.

Option 2: Manual Installation:

1. Download the ZIP file from the official Groovy download page. 2. Extract the contents of the ZIP file to a suitable directory, for example, C:\Groovy.

Set up the environment variables:

1. Open the Start Menu, search for Environment Variables, and select Edit the system environment variables. 2. In the System Properties window, click Environment Variables. 3. Under the System Variables section, click New and add GROOVY_HOME with the path to the Groovy directory, e.g., C:\Groovy. 4. Find the Path variable, select it, and click Edit. Add %GROOVY_HOME%\bin to the list.

Option 3: Using SDKMAN!:

SDKMAN! is a tool for managing parallel versions of multiple Software Development Kits on most Unix-based systems. It can also be used on Windows through a compatible terminal like Git Bash or the Windows Subsystem for Linux (WSL).

Installation steps for SDKMAN!:

```
$ curl -s "https://get.sdkman.io" | bash
$ source "$HOME/.sdkman/bin/sdkman-init.sh"
```

After installing SDKMAN!, install Groovy using:

```
$ sdk install groovy
```

Verifying the Installation:

To verify that Groovy has been correctly installed, open the Command Prompt and run the following command:

```
C:\> groovy -version
```

The output should resemble:

```
Groovy Version: 3.0.7 JVM: 1.8.0_252 Vendor: Oracle Corporation OS: Windows 10
```

If the version information is displayed correctly, Groovy is successfully installed on your system.

If any issues arise during installation, refer to the "Troubleshooting Common Issues" section for possible solutions. Proper installation of Groovy on Windows allows for seamless scripting and build automation, promoting enhanced developer productivity.

2.3 Installing Groovy on macOS

To install Groovy on macOS, follow these meticulous steps to ensure a precise and smooth setup. The Groovy programming environment can be installed using several methods, primarily through Homebrew, SDKMAN!, or by downloading the binaries directly. This section details each method.

System Requirements

Ensure your macOS meets the following prerequisites before proceeding:

- macOS version 10.10 (Yosemite) or higher.
- Java Development Kit (JDK) 8 or higher installed. Verify JDK installation with:

  ```
  java -version
  ```

  The output should display the Java version installed:

  ```
  java version "1.8.0_xxx"
  Java(TM) SE Runtime Environment (build 1.8.0_xxx-bxx)
  Java HotSpot(TM) 64-Bit Server VM (build 25.xx-bxx, mixed mode)
  ```

Method 1: Using Homebrew

Homebrew is a popular package manager for macOS, making the installation process straightforward.

1. Open the Terminal application.
2. Update Homebrew to the latest version:

   ```
   brew update
   ```

3. Install Groovy using Homebrew:

   ```
   brew install groovy
   ```

4. Verify the installation:

```
groovy -version
```

   You should see an output indicating the Groovy version installed:

   Groovy Version: 3.0.x JVM: x.x.x Vendor: Oracle Corporation OS: Mac OS X

Method 2: Using SDKMAN!

SDKMAN! (Software Development Kit Manager) is another convenient tool for managing multiple versions of development kits.

1. Open the Terminal application.
2. Install SDKMAN! by running:

```
curl -s "https://get.sdkman.io" | bash
```

3. Follow the on-screen instructions to initialize SDKMAN!:

   source "$HOME/.sdkman/bin/sdkman-init.sh"

4. Install Groovy using SDKMAN!:

```
sdk install groovy
```

5. Verify the installation:

```
groovy -version
```

   You should see an output indicating the Groovy version installed:

   Groovy Version: 3.0.x JVM: x.x.x Vendor: Oracle Corporation OS: Mac OS X

Method 3: Direct Binary Download

This method involves downloading the Groovy binaries directly from the official Groovy website.

1. Visit the official Groovy website: https://groovy.apache.org/download.html
2. Download the binary distribution (zip or tar.gz file) for the latest stable release.
3. Extract the downloaded archive to a desired location. For instance:

```
tar -xzf groovy-3.0.x.zip -C /usr/local/groovy
```

4. Set the GROOVY_HOME environment variable and update the PATH. Add the following lines to your /.bash_profile or /.zshrc file:

```
export GROOVY_HOME=/usr/local/groovy/groovy-3.0.x
export PATH=$PATH:$GROOVY_HOME/bin
```

5. Apply the changes:

```
source ~/.bash_profile # for Bash shell
source ~/.zshrc # for Zsh shell
```

6. Verify the installation:

```
groovy -version
```

   You should see an output indicating the Groovy version installed:

```
Groovy Version: 3.0.x JVM: x.x.x Vendor: Oracle Corporation OS: Mac OS X
```

All the above methods achieve the same result: a working Groovy installation on macOS. Choose the method that best fits your environment and preferences.

2.4 Installing Groovy on Linux

Installing Groovy on a Linux system involves a series of steps that ensure the language is correctly set up and functioning properly. This section will guide you through installing Groovy using the SDKMAN! tool, which is highly recommended for its simplicity and effectiveness.

Step 1: Install SDKMAN!

SDKMAN! is a tool for managing parallel versions of multiple Software Development Kits (SDKs) on most Unix-based systems. To install SDKMAN!, open your terminal and execute the following commands:

```
$ curl -s "https://get.sdkman.io" | bash
```

This command fetches the installation script and executes it using the bash shell. Follow the on-screen instructions to complete the installation. After SDKMAN! is installed, you need to load the sdk in the current shell session by running:

```
$ source "$HOME/.sdkman/bin/sdkman-init.sh"
```

Verify the installation by checking SDKMAN! version:

```
$ sdk version
```

Step 2: Install Groovy

With SDKMAN! set up, installing Groovy is straightforward. Use the following command to install the latest stable version of Groovy:

```
$ sdk install groovy
```

You will see output similar to the following, indicating the successful installation of Groovy:

```
Downloading: groovy 3.0.8
In progress...
\#\#\############################################################### 100.0%
...
Setting groovy 3.0.8 as default.
```

To verify the Groovy installation, you can check the version of Groovy installed by running:

```
$ groovy --version
```

```
Groovy Version: 3.0.8 JVM: 11.0.11 Vendor: AdoptOpenJDK OS: Linux
```

This command confirms that Groovy is correctly installed and available in your path.

Step 3: Configuring Environment Variables

Although SDKMAN! usually takes care of setting up environment variables automatically, you might want to manually verify or add them to your .bashrc or .zshrc file for persistence across sessions.

Edit your profile script (.bashrc or .zshrc) to include the following lines:

```
export GROOVY_HOME="$HOME/.sdkman/candidates/groovy/current"
export PATH="$GROOVY_HOME/bin:$PATH"
```

After editing the file, apply the changes by sourcing it:

```
$ source ~/.bashrc
```

Step 4: Running a Simple Groovy Script

To ensure that Groovy is properly installed and configured, you can run a simple Groovy script. Create a new file called HelloWorld.groovy and add the following code:

```
println 'Hello, Groovy!'
```

Execute the script using the Groovy command-line tool:

```
$ groovy HelloWorld.groovy
```

You should see the output:

```
Hello, Groovy!
```

This confirms that Groovy is successfully installed and operational on your Linux system.

Throughout the Groovy installation process on Linux using SDKMAN!, we ensure all steps are carefully executed to achieve an effective setup. This method is preferred due to its ease of use and management of Groovy versions. Any deviations or issues encountered can often be checked and corrected with relative ease, especially when leveraging the flexibility offered by SDKMAN!.

2.5 Setting Up Groovy in an IDE

Integrated Development Environments (IDEs) facilitate software development by providing a comprehensive environment equipped with essential tools for coding, debugging, and testing. For Groovy development, several popular IDEs such as IntelliJ IDEA, Eclipse, and Visual Studio Code offer robust support. This section will detail the steps to set up Groovy in these three widely-used IDEs.

Setting Up Groovy in IntelliJ IDEA

IntelliJ IDEA provides excellent support for Groovy through its built-in plugins. The steps to configure Groovy in IntelliJ IDEA are as follows:

- Download and install IntelliJ IDEA from the JetBrains website.
- Upon launching IntelliJ IDEA, navigate to File → New → Project.
- In the New Project window, select Groovy from the list on the left.
- Name your project and specify the project location.
- If prompted, configure the JDK. IntelliJ IDEA requires a JDK setup, which you can either download and install or point to an already installed JDK on your system.
- Select Create to set up the new Groovy project.

To verify the setup:

```
println 'Hello, Groovy!'
```

Run the file by right-clicking and selecting Run. The output should display in the Run window.

```
Hello, Groovy!
```

Setting Up Groovy in Eclipse

Eclipse requires the Groovy Development Tools (GDT) plugin to be installed. Follow these steps to configure Groovy in Eclipse:

- Download and install Eclipse IDE from the Eclipse Foundation website.
- Start Eclipse and navigate to Help → Eclipse Marketplace.
- In the Eclipse Marketplace, search for Groovy Development Tools and install the plugin.
- Restart Eclipse after the installation is complete to enable the plugin.
- To create a new Groovy project, go to File → New → Groovy Project.
- Enter a project name and click Finish.

To verify the setup:

```
println 'Hello, Eclipse Groovy!'
```

Run the script by selecting Run → Run As → Groovy Script. The console should display:

```
Hello, Eclipse Groovy!
```

Setting Up Groovy in Visual Studio Code

Visual Studio Code (VS Code) supports Groovy through the Code Groovy extension. The steps to set up Groovy in VS Code are:

- Download and install Visual Studio Code from the Visual Studio Code website.
- Open VS Code and navigate to the Extensions view by clicking the Extensions icon in the Activity Bar on the side of the window or by pressing Ctrl+Shift+X.

- Search for Groovy and select the Code Groovy extension from Vscjava.
- Click Install to add the Groovy extension.
- Open the Groovy script file or create a new file with the extension .groovy.

To verify the setup:

```
println 'Hello, VS Code Groovy!'
```

Run the script by clicking the Run button on the top-right corner or by using a terminal integrated within VS Code.

```
Hello, VS Code Groovy!
```

To ensure a smooth development experience, it is recommended to familiarize yourself with the IDE's debugging, code completion, and other utilities which enhance Groovy programming productivity. The specific IDE's documentation and user community offer valuable resources and support for optimizing your development environment.

2.6 Using Groovy with Command Line

Using Groovy through the command line interface provides a robust way to perform quick scripting tasks, automate processes, and test Groovy scripts outside of an Integrated Development Environment (IDE). This section details the steps required to execute Groovy scripts from the command line and utilize the associated tools like groovysh, a command-line shell for interactive Groovy scripting.

First, ensuring that the Groovy executable is correctly added to your system's PATH is crucial. This allows you to invoke Groovy commands from any terminal window. Once Groovy is installed and set up, the following command should verify that the installation is successful:

```
groovy -version
```

Executing the command above should produce an output similar to the following, which verifies the installed version of Groovy:

```
Groovy Version: 3.0.9 JVM: 1.8.0_292 Vendor: Oracle Corporation OS: Mac OS X
```

groovy command is used to execute Groovy scripts directly. Suppose you have a Groovy script file named HelloWorld.groovy with the following content:

```
println 'Hello, World!'
```

To run this script from the command line, navigate to the directory containing HelloWorld.groovy and execute:

```
groovy HelloWorld.groovy
```

This command should output:

```
Hello, World!
```

Groovy also provides an interactive shell, groovysh, which allows for immediate execution and testing of Groovy commands. Start the Groovy shell by entering:

```
groovysh
```

In the interactive shell, you will be presented with a prompt, where you can execute Groovy expressions directly:

```
groovy:000> println 'Hello from Groovy Shell!'
```

The shell will compile and run the command, outputting:

```
Hello from Groovy Shell!
```

groovysh supports multiple lines of input, allowing for more complex expressions and the definition of functions and other constructs, like so:

```
groovy:001> int square(int x) {
groovy:002> return x * x
groovy:003> }
groovy:004> println square(5)
```

Resulting in:

```
25
```

For scripting tasks requiring resource imports or external libraries, include the -cp (or -classpath) option to specify additional libraries. For example:

```
groovy -cp /path/to/lib/* MyScript.groovy
```

Compiling Groovy scripts into bytecode is possible using groovyc, the Groovy compiler. This process generates .class files that can be executed on any JVM. Consider the following script saved as Example.groovy:

```
class Example {
    static void main(String[] args) {
        println 'Compiled and Executed!'
    }
}
```

Compile this script using:

```
groovyc Example.groovy
```

This command produces Example.class. Run this compiled class using:

```
groovy Example
```

The output will be:

```
Compiled and Executed!
```

For scripting tasks needing argument parsing or more complex interactions, leverage Groovy's powerful command-line argument handling traits. Below is an example script ArgsExample.groovy that processes and prints command-line arguments:

```
if (args.length == 0) {
    println 'No arguments provided.'
} else {
    println "Arguments: ${args.join(', ')}"
}
```

Execute this from the command line with:

```
groovy ArgsExample.groovy arg1 arg2 arg3
```

The expected output would be:

```
Arguments: arg1, arg2, arg3
```

Utilizing command-line capabilities effectively can significantly expand Groovy's applicability to various scripting and automation tasks.

2.7 Setting Up Groovy with Maven

To integrate Groovy with Maven, you must configure your Maven project to use the Groovy-Eclipse plugin or the GMavenPlus plugin. This section will guide you through the detailed steps required to set up Groovy using the GMavenPlus plugin, which is widely used and maintained.

Step 1: Install Maven

Ensure Maven is installed on your system. You can verify this by running:

```
mvn -version
```

If Maven is not installed, download and install it from the official website: https://maven.apache.org/.

Step 2: Create a Maven Project

You can create a Maven project by using the command line. Navigate to the directory where you want to create your project, and execute:

```
mvn archetype:generate -DgroupId=com.example -DartifactId=groovy-demo -
    DarchetypeArtifactId=maven-archetype-quickstart -DinteractiveMode=false
```

This command will create a basic Maven project with the groupId set to com.example and the artifactId set to groovy-demo.

Step 3: Modify the pom.xml File

Open the pom.xml file in your newly created project directory. Add the GMavenPlus plugin to the build section. Below is a sample pom.xml configuration integrating Groovy:

```
<project xmlns="http://maven.apache.org/POM/4.0.0" xmlns:xsi="http://www.w3.
    org/2001/XMLSchema-instance" xsi:schemaLocation="http://maven.apache.org/
    POM/4.0.0 http://maven.apache.org/xsd/maven-4.0.0.xsd">
    <modelVersion>4.0.0</modelVersion>
    <groupId>com.example</groupId>
    <artifactId>groovy-demo</artifactId>
    <version>1.0-SNAPSHOT</version>
    <properties>
        <project.build.sourceEncoding>UTF-8</project.build.sourceEncoding>
        <groovy.version>3.0.9</groovy.version>
        <maven.compiler.source>1.8</maven.compiler.source>
        <maven.compiler.target>1.8</maven.compiler.target>
    </properties>
    <dependencies>
        <dependency>
            <groupId>org.codehaus.groovy</groupId>
            <artifactId>groovy-all</artifactId>
            <version>${groovy.version}</version>
        </dependency>
        <dependency>
            <groupId>junit</groupId>
            <artifactId>junit</artifactId>
            <version>4.13.1</version>
            <scope>test</scope>
        </dependency>
    </dependencies>
    <build>
        <plugins>
            <plugin>
                <groupId>org.codehaus.gmavenplus</groupId>
```

```
                <artifactId>gmavenplus-plugin</artifactId>
                <version>1.12.1</version>
                <executions>
                    <execution>
                        <goals>
                            <goal>addSources</goal>
                            <goal>addTestSources</goal>
                            <goal>generateStubs</goal>
                            <goal>compile</goal>
                            <goal>generateTestStubs</goal>
                            <goal>compileTests</goal>
                            <goal>removeStubs</goal>
                            <goal>removeTestStubs</goal>
                        </goals>
                    </execution>
                </executions>
            </plugin>
        </plugins>
    </build>
</project>
```

This configuration ensures that Maven can handle Groovy source files within your project. The version of Groovy specified here is 3.0.9, which is the stable version at the time of writing. Adjust this version as needed to match the latest Groovy release.

Step 4: Create Groovy Source Files

Maven expects the source files to be placed within specific directories. Create directories src/main/groovy for main Groovy source files and src/test/groovy for Groovy test files.

Example Groovy file structure:

```
groovy-demo/
|-- src/
    |-- main/
        |-- groovy/
            |-- com/
                |-- example/
                    |-- Demo.groovy
    |-- test/
        |-- groovy/
            |-- com/
                |-- example/
                    |-- DemoTest.groovy
```

Create a Groovy class, Demo.groovy:

```
package com.example

class Demo {
    static void main(String[] args) {
        println 'Hello, Groovy with Maven!'
    }
}
```

Create a corresponding test class, DemoTest.groovy:

```
package com.example

import org.junit.Test

class DemoTest {

    @Test
    void testDemo() {
        assert 1 + 1 == 2
    }
}
```

Step 5: Build and Run the Project

To build the project, navigate to the project directory and run:

```
mvn clean install
```

If the configuration is correct, Maven will compile the Groovy sources, execute the tests, and build the project without errors.

To run the compiled Groovy class, use:

```
mvn exec:java -Dexec.mainClass="com.example.Demo"
```

Expected output in the console:

```
Hello, Groovy with Maven!
```

This process ensures a seamless integration of Groovy with Maven, allowing you to leverage the features of Groovy in your Maven-based projects. Ensure all dependencies and configurations in the pom.xml file are correctly specified to avoid build issues.

2.8 Setting Up Groovy with Gradle

Gradle is a powerful build automation tool that supports Groovy as one of its scripting languages. This section details the steps required to set up a Groovy project using Gradle, covering both basic configuration and more advanced settings.

To begin, ensure you have both Groovy and Gradle installed on your system. Verify the installation by running the following commands in your terminal:

```
groovy -version
gradle -version
```

The above commands should display the versions of Groovy and Gradle installed. If either command fails, refer to earlier sections for installation guidance.

Create a new directory for your project and navigate to it. You can name your project directory as appropriate. Here, we will name it MyGroovyProject:

```
mkdir MyGroovyProject
cd MyGroovyProject
```

Initialize a new Gradle project using the gradle init command. Follow the prompts to configure the project. Choose the application type and Groovy as the language:

```
gradle init
```

Gradle will generate a basic project structure:

```
MyGroovyProject
  build.gradle
  gradle
    wrapper
  gradlew
  gradlew.bat
  settings.gradle
  src
    main
      groovy
      resources
    test
      groovy
      resources
```

Open the generated build.gradle file in your preferred text editor or IDE. The following configuration ensures your project supports Groovy:

```
plugins {
    id 'application'
    id 'groovy'
}

repositories {
    mavenCentral()
}

dependencies {
    implementation 'org.codehaus.groovy:groovy-all:3.0.8'
    testImplementation 'org.spockframework:spock-core:2.0-groovy-3.0'
}

application {
    mainClassName = 'com.example.App'
}
```

In the dependencies block, implementation configures the Groovy library, and testImplementation adds the Spock framework for testing. Adjust the versions of the dependencies as needed.

Next, create the App.groovy file in the src/main/groovy/com/example directory:

```
package com.example

class App {
    static void main(String[] args) {
        println 'Hello, Groovy with Gradle!'
    }
}
```

This file contains the main class of your Groovy application. The println statement verifies that the setup is correct when you run the application.

Build and run your project using the Gradle wrapper:

```
./gradlew run
```

For Windows, use:

```
gradlew.bat run
```

The console should display the output:

```
> Task :run
Hello, Groovy with Gradle!
```

To add more tasks or customize the build process, modify or extend the build.gradle file accordingly. For example, to include code quality tools like Checkstyle, add the following plugin and configuration:

```
plugins {
    id 'checkstyle'
}

checkstyle {
    toolVersion = '8.41'
    configFile = file('config/checkstyle/checkstyle.xml')
}

tasks.withType(Checkstyle) {
    reports {
        xml.required = false
        html.required = true
    }
}

check.dependsOn 'checkstyleMain', 'checkstyleTest'
```

Ensure you download or create a checkstyle.xml configuration file and place it in the config/checkstyle directory.

Gradle's flexibility allows for extensive customization of the Groovy development environment. Additional plugins, tasks, or dependency management can be introduced to tailor the project to specific needs. Refer to the Gradle documentation for advanced capabilities and best practices.

2.9 Verifying the Installation

After completing the installation process, it is crucial to verify that Groovy has been correctly installed and configured. This ensures that all environmental variables are correctly set up and that the Groovy executables are accessible from the command line. The verification process involves several steps, including checking the version of Groovy, running a simple Groovy script, and verifying the configuration within an Integrated Development Environment (IDE).

Checking the Groovy Version

The first step in verifying the installation is to check the installed version of Groovy. This can be accomplished by opening a terminal or command prompt and executing the following command:

```
groovy -version
```

If Groovy has been correctly installed and the GROOVY_HOME environment variable is set, you should see output similar to the following:

```
Groovy Version: 3.0.9 JVM: 1.8.0_292 Vendor: Oracle Corporation OS: Windows 10
```

The version number may differ based on the version of Groovy installed. The key point is that the command should execute without errors, and it should display the Groovy version, JVM version, and information about the operating system.

Running a Simple Groovy Script

Next, confirm that Groovy can execute scripts correctly. Create a simple Groovy script named HelloWorld.groovy with the following content:

```
println 'Hello, Groovy!'
```

Navigate to the directory containing the HelloWorld.groovy file using the terminal or command prompt. Execute the script using the Groovy command:

```
groovy HelloWorld.groovy
```

The expected output should be:

```
Hello, Groovy!
```

This indicates that Groovy can execute scripts correctly. If there are any errors, ensure that the file path is correct and that the Groovy installation directory is included in the system's PATH variable.

Verifying Groovy in IDE

For developers using an Integrated Development Environment (IDE) like IntelliJ IDEA or Eclipse, verifying the IDE configuration is an essential step. Here, we will go through the process for IntelliJ IDEA:

1. Open IntelliJ IDEA and navigate to File > Project Structure. 2. Select the SDKs option from the Platform Settings. 3. Ensure that an appropriate JDK is listed. If not, add a JDK via the + button and by specifying the JDK home path. 4. Navigate to File > Settings > Plugins, and ensure that the Groovy plugin is installed. If it is not, click on the Marketplace tab, search for "Groovy," and install the plugin. 5. Create a new project via File > New > Project. 6. Select Groovy from the left-hand pane, and configure the project SDK and Groovy library. 7. Create a new Groovy script by right-clicking on the src directory, selecting New > Groovy Script, and name it HelloIDEGroovy. 8. In the newly created script file, write the following code:

```
println 'Hello, Groovy from IDE!'
```

9. Run the script by right-clicking on the script file and selecting Run 'HelloIDEGroovy.main()'.

The console in the IDE should display:

```
Hello, Groovy from IDE!
```

This confirms the Groovy setup in the IDE and verifies that the scripting environment is functioning as expected.

These steps ensure that the Groovy environment is setup correctly and that it operates smoothly across both the command line and within an IDE environment, enabling the development of Groovy applications.

2.10 Troubleshooting Common Issues

Understanding common issues that may arise during the installation and setup of Groovy is essential for a smooth development experience. This section addresses frequent problems and provides detailed solutions.

1. Environment Variable Not Set Correctly

One common issue is that the GROOVY_HOME environment variable is not set correctly. This can lead to errors when attempting to run Groovy scripts or access Groovy commands from the command line. To resolve this:

For Windows:

```
setx GROOVY_HOME "C:\path\to\groovy"
setx PATH "%PATH%;%GROOVY_HOME%\bin"
```

For macOS and Linux:

```
export GROOVY_HOME=/path/to/groovy
export PATH=$PATH:$GROOVY_HOME/bin
```

After setting the environment variable, restart your terminal or command prompt to apply the changes. Verify the settings by running:

```
groovy -v
```

This command should print the version of Groovy installed, confirming that the environment variable is set correctly.

2. Command Not Recognized

Occasionally, the Groovy command might not be recognized by the system. This can indicate that the PATH variable does not include the Groovy binary directory. Follow these steps to correct the PATH variable:

For Windows:

```
setx PATH "%PATH%;C:\path\to\groovy\bin"
```

For macOS and Linux:

```
export PATH=$PATH:/path/to/groovy/bin
```

Verify the update by reopening your terminal or command prompt and typing:

```
groovy -v
```

3. Incorrect or Multiple Java Versions

Groovy requires a Java Development Kit (JDK) to run. If Groovy is not functioning correctly, it could be due to an incorrect, unsupported, or conflicting Java version. Verify the installed Java version with:

```
java -version
```

Ensure that the reported version is compatible with Groovy. If multiple versions of Java are installed, ensure the correct version is prioritized in the PATH.

For Windows: Open the System Properties dialog, navigate to Environment Variables, and adjust the PATH variable to prioritize the appropriate JDK bin directory.

For macOS and Linux: Edit your .bashrc, .zshrc, or .profile file to ensure the PATH correctly points to the desired JDK:

```
export PATH=/path/to/correct/jdk/bin:$PATH
```

4. Groovy Console Fails to Start

If the Groovy Console does not start, it may be due to missing or incompatible dependencies. Ensure that all required dependencies are installed and compatible with the installed Groovy version. Verify by checking for missing libraries or conflicting versions.

On Unix-like systems, use:

```
groovyConsole
```

Ensure that JAVA_HOME is set correctly:

```
echo $JAVA_HOME
```

If JAVA_HOME is not set, configure it accordingly.

For Windows:

```
setx JAVA_HOME "C:\path\to\jdk"
```

For macOS and Linux:

```
export JAVA_HOME=/path/to/jdk
```

5. IDE Integration Issues

When integrating Groovy with IDEs such as IntelliJ IDEA or Eclipse, misconfigurations can lead to errors. Ensure that the Groovy plugin is correctly installed and enabled.

For IntelliJ IDEA:

- Navigate to File → Settings → Plugins.

- Search for and install the Groovy plugin if not already installed.
- Make sure the JDK version and the Groovy SDK are correctly configured.

For Eclipse:

- Navigate to Help → Eclipse Marketplace.
- Search for and install the Groovy Development Tools.
- Verify that the installed Groovy version is correctly set up in the Preferences under Groovy → Compiler.

6. Build Tool Configuration Errors

When using build tools such as Maven or Gradle with Groovy, ensure that the project is configured correctly.

For Maven, update the pom.xml with the appropriate plugin:

```
<plugin>
    <groupId>org.codehaus.gmavenplus</groupId>
    <artifactId>gmavenplus-plugin</artifactId>
    <version>1.10.1</version>
    <executions>
        <execution>
            <goals>
                <goal>addSources</goal>
                <goal>addTestSources</goal>
                <goal>generateStubs</goal>
                <goal>compile</goal>
                <goal>generateTestStubs</goal>
                <goal>compileTests</goal>
                <goal>removeStubs</goal>
                <goal>removeTestStubs</goal>
            </goals>
        </execution>
    </executions>
</plugin>
```

For Gradle, update the build.gradle file to include the Groovy plugin:

```
plugins {
    id 'groovy'
}

repositories {
    mavenCentral()
}

dependencies {
    implementation 'org.codehaus.groovy:groovy-all:3.0.9'
    testImplementation 'junit:junit:4.13.1'
}
```

By ensuring these configurations, Groovy should integrate seamlessly with your chosen build tool.

These troubleshooting steps address the most commonly encountered issues during the installation and setup of Groovy, ensuring a stable and efficient development environment.

Chapter 3

Groovy Language Basics

This chapter covers the foundational elements of Groovy's syntax, including variables, data types, and operators. It introduces control structures such as if-else statements, switch cases, and looping constructs like for, while, and do-while loops. Additionally, it discusses the definition and usage of functions, exception handling, script structure, the utilization of annotations, and documentation through comments. This comprehensive overview equips readers with the essential building blocks for writing Groovy programs.

3.1 Groovy Syntax Overview

Groovy is an object-oriented programming language that seamlessly integrates with the Java ecosystem. It aims to improve Java through an expressive syntax and enhanced runtime performance. Understanding its syntax is key to leveraging its full potential.

Groovy scripts can be written in files with the extension .groovy. A script in Groovy is usually run with the groovy command, but it can also be compiled into Java bytecode.

Basic Structure:

A Groovy script resembles a Java class with a default main method. However, it allows for more concise expressions and can include standalone executable code outside of classes.

```
println 'Hello, Groovy'
```

The above line of code, when executed, prints the string 'Hello, Groovy' to the standard output.

Variables:

Variables in Groovy are typically declared using def, which infers the type dynamically. However, explicit type declaration is also supported.

```
def a = 1 // inferred type is Integer
String name = 'Groovy'
int x = 42
```

Groovy supports both primitive types and their corresponding wrapper classes, enhancing type safety while maintaining the ease of dynamic typing.

Data Types:

Groovy's data types include:

- Numeric types: Byte, Short, Integer, Long, Float, Double
- Character and Boolean types
- Wrapper classes equivalent to Java's
- Strings, which can be defined using single quotes, double quotes, or triple quotes for multiline strings

```
def flag = true
String singleQuote = 'single-quoted string'
String doubleQuote = "double-quoted string"
String tripleQuote = """This is
a multi-line string"""
```

Comments:

Single-line comments use //, while multi-line comments are enclosed in /* */.

```
// This is a single-line comment
/*
 This is a multi-line comment
*/
```

Operators:

Groovy supports conventional arithmetic and logical operators, including some specific to the language like the Elvis operator (?:) and spaceship operator (<=>).

```
def sum = 5 + 3 // addition
def diff = 5 - 3 // subtraction
def prod = 5 * 3 // multiplication
def quotient = 5 / 3 // division
def remainder = 5 % 3 // modulus
def isTrue = (5 > 3) // relational operator
def elvis = null ?: 'default' // Elvis operator
def comparison = 5 <=> 3 // spaceship operator
```

Control Structures:

Control structures, including if-else, switch, and looping constructs (for, while, do-while) in Groovy have a syntax similar to Java but are more flexible with their conditional expressions.

```
if (a > b) {
    println 'a is greater than b'
} else if (a == b) {
    println 'a equals b'
} else {
    println 'a is less than b'
}
```

Switch statements can handle a variety of types, including String and Enum:

```
def x = 'foo'
switch (x) {
    case 'foo':
        println 'found foo'
        break
    case 'bar':
        println 'found bar'
        break
    default:
        println 'not found'
}
```

Looping Constructs:

For loops in Groovy can iterate over ranges, collections, maps, and more:

```
for (i in 0..5) {
    println i
}

def list = [1, 2, 3, 4, 5]
for (item in list) {
    println item
}
```

While and do-while loops function similarly:

```
def count = 5
```

```
while (count > 0) {
    println count
    count--
}

count = 5
do {
    println count
    count--
} while (count > 0)
```

Groovy's flexible syntax, efficient integration with the JVM, and powerful features make it a practical language for various programming tasks. The ease of transitioning from Java, compounded with its additional features, facilitates rapid development while retaining robustness. Groovy's utility extends beyond scripting; it thrives in domains requiring agility and resilience.

3.2 Variables and Data Types

In Groovy, like many other programming languages, variables and data types are fundamental building blocks for writing scripts and applications. Understanding how to declare and use variables, as well as the different types of data they can hold, is crucial for effective programming.

Variables in Groovy do not require an explicit type declaration, making it a dynamically typed language. This flexibility allows developers to write more concise and readable code. However, Groovy also supports optional type checking, which can be useful for certain applications requiring stricter type enforcement.

To declare a variable in Groovy, the def keyword is commonly used:

```
def name = "Groovy"
def version = 2.5
def isDynamic = true
```

In the example above, name is assigned a string value, version is assigned a numeric value, and isDynamic is assigned a boolean value. Groovy infers the type of these variables at runtime.

Groovy supports a variety of data types, including both primitive and complex types. The primary data types are as follows:

- **Numbers:** Groovy provides an extensive range of numeric types, including Integer, Long, Double, BigDecimal, and BigInteger.

Groovy numbers can be declared without explicitly specifying the type.

- **Strings:** Similar to Java, Groovy uses String to represent sequences of characters. Strings can be created using single or double quotes.
- **Booleans:** Groovy uses the Boolean type to represent true or false values.
- **Collections:** Groovy offers several collection types, including List, Map, and Set, which are highly useful for managing groups of objects.
- **Closures:** A closure is essentially an anonymous block of code that can be passed around as a first-class object. Closures are powerful tools for functional programming in Groovy.

When working with numbers in Groovy, you can perform arithmetic operations seamlessly. Groovy supports the same arithmetic operators as Java, such as +, -, *, /, and %. Groovy also has operator overloading for addition (+) and subtraction (-), which simplifies concatenation operations.

```
def sum = 1 + 2 // Result: 3
def difference = 5 - 3 // Result: 2
def product = 4 * 2 // Result: 8
def quotient = 10 / 2 // Result: 5.0
def remainder = 10 % 3 // Result: 1
```

String handling in Groovy is both versatile and powerful. You can use single quotes to define a plain string, double quotes for strings that may contain escaped characters, and triple single quotes or triple double quotes for multi-line strings. Groovy supports string interpolation using the $ symbol within double-quoted strings.

```
def singleQuoteString = 'Hello, World!'
def doubleQuoteString = "Hello, \"Groovy\"!"
def multiLineString = '''This is a
multi-line string.'''
def interpolatedString = "Groovy version is ${version}"
```

Boolean expressions in Groovy can leverage typical logical operators such as && (AND), || (OR), and ! (NOT).

```
def isTrue = true
def isFalse = false
def result = isTrue && isFalse // Result: false
def inverted = !isTrue // Result: false
```

Groovy's collection types allow for efficient data management. Lists can be declared using square brackets, maps using curly braces, and sets can be created using the Groovy Set class.

```
def list = [1, 2, 3, 4]
def map = ['key': 'value', 'number': 123]
def set = [1, 2, 3] as Set
```

Closures provide a way to encapsulate blocks of code to be executed later or passed as arguments to methods. Closures can take parameters, and their syntax is straightforward.

```
def closure = { param -> println "Hello, ${param}" }
closure.call("World") // Output: Hello, World
```

Groovy's dynamic nature and powerful type system make it an ideal language for both simple scripts and complex applications, providing flexibility without sacrificing performance or readability. Understanding these basic building blocks will significantly enhance your ability to write efficient and elegant Groovy code.

3.3 Operators in Groovy

Operators are fundamental components in Groovy, enabling both simple and complex computations. They act on variables and values to form expressions. Groovy supports a number of operators including arithmetic, relational, logical, bitwise, assignment, and other special operators. This section will detail each operator class, showing their usage through examples.

Arithmetic Operators: These operators perform mathematical operations on numeric values. The table below lists the primary arithmetic operators available in Groovy:

- + (Addition)
- - (Subtraction)
- * (Multiplication)
- / (Division)
- % (Modulus)
- ++ (Increment)

- -- (Decrement)

Example usage:

```
def a = 10
def b = 3

println(a + b) // Addition
println(a - b) // Subtraction
println(a * b) // Multiplication
println(a / b) // Division
println(a % b) // Modulus
println(a++) // Increment
println(--b) // Decrement
```

```
13
7
30
3.3333333333333335
1
10
2
```

Relational Operators: These operators compare two values and return a Boolean result. They are essential for control flow in Groovy programs.

- == (Equal to)
- != (Not equal to)
- > (Greater than)
- < (Less than)
- >= (Greater than or equal to)
- <= (Less than or equal to)

Example usage:

```
def x = 5
def y = 10

println(x == y) // Equal to
println(x != y) // Not equal to
println(x > y) // Greater than
println(x < y) // Less than
println(x >= y) // Greater than or equal to
println(x <= y) // Less than or equal to
```

```
false
true
false
true
false
true
```

Logical Operators: These operators are used to perform logical operations on Boolean values. They help in creating complex logical expressions.

- && (Logical AND)
- || (Logical OR)
- ! (Logical NOT)

Example usage:

```
def a = true
def b = false

println(a && b) // Logical AND
println(a || b) // Logical OR
println(!a) // Logical NOT
```

```
false
true
false
```

Bitwise Operators: These operators perform bit-level operations on integer operands. Using bitwise operators allows for high-performance computation in certain applications.

- & (Bitwise AND)
- | (Bitwise OR)
- ^ (Bitwise XOR)
- ~ (Bitwise NOT)
- « (Left shift)
- » (Right shift)
- »> (Unsigned right shift)

Example usage:

```
def a = 4 // 0100 in binary
def b = 5 // 0101 in binary

println(a & b) // Bitwise AND
println(a | b) // Bitwise OR
println(a ^ b) // Bitwise XOR
println(~a) // Bitwise NOT
println(a << 1) // Left shift
println(a >> 1) // Right shift
println(a >>> 1) // Unsigned right shift
```

```
4
5
1
-5
8
2
2
```

Assignment Operators: Groovy provides several compound assignment operators that combine a basic operator with assignment, simplifying code.

- = (Simple assignment)
- += (Add and assign)
- -= (Subtract and assign)
- *= (Multiply and assign)
- /= (Divide and assign)
- %= (Modulus and assign)
- &= (Bitwise AND and assign)
- |= (Bitwise OR and assign)
- ^= (Bitwise XOR and assign)
- «= (Left shift and assign)
- »= (Right shift and assign)
- »>= (Unsigned right shift and assign)

Example usage:

```
def a = 10
a += 5
println(a) // Add and assign

a -= 2
println(a) // Subtract and assign

a *= 3
println(a) // Multiply and assign

a /= 4
println(a) // Divide and assign

a %= 3
println(a) // Modulus and assign
```

```
15
13
39
9
0
```

Other Special Operators: Groovy has several other operators which are useful in various scenarios.

- ?. (Safe navigation operator, avoids NullPointerException)
- ?.[] (Safe index operator)
- ?.() (Safe method call operator)
- :: (Method reference operator)
- . (Member access operator)

Example usage:

```
def person = null
println(person?.name) // Safe navigation operator

def list = [1, 2, 3, null]
println(list?.[3]) // Safe index operator

def greet() { return "Hello" }
def message = null
println(message?.greet()) // Safe method call operator

def methodRef = this.&greet
println(methodRef()) // Method reference operator

def map = ['Key': 'Value']
println(map.Key) // Member access operator
```

```
null
null
null
Hello
Value
```

Operators in Groovy provide a powerful toolkit that enhances the language's versatility and expressiveness. By understanding and utilizing these operators, programmers can write more efficient and readable code.

3.4 Control Structures: if, else, switch

Control structures are fundamental components in any programming language, enabling conditional execution of code segments based on

Boolean logic. In Groovy, the primary control structures used for conditional logic are if, else if, and else statements, as well as switch statements. These constructs allow for branching, thus empowering developers to control the flow of execution based on varying conditions.

The if statement evaluates a Boolean expression enclosed in parentheses. If the expression evaluates to true, the block of code within the braces is executed. Otherwise, execution continues with the next statement following the if block.

```
if (condition) {
    // code block to be executed if condition is true
}
```

The else statement can be used to define an alternative block of code that executes when the if condition evaluates to false.

```
if (condition) {
    // code block to be executed if condition is true
} else {
    // code block to be executed if condition is false
}
```

It is also possible to chain multiple conditions using else if.

```
if (condition1) {
    // code block to be executed if condition1 is true
} else if (condition2) {
    // code block to be executed if condition2 is true
} else {
    // code block to be executed if both condition1 and condition2 are false
}
```

Consider an example where we assign grades based on a score value.

```
int score = 85
String grade

if (score >= 90) {
    grade = 'A'
} else if (score >= 80) {
    grade = 'B'
} else if (score >= 70) {
    grade = 'C'
} else if (score >= 60) {
    grade = 'D'
} else {
    grade = 'F'
}
println grade
```

B

The flexibility of the if construct permits the handling of a wide range of scenarios, from simple decisions to complex nested logic. However, as the number of conditions grows, the code can become increasingly difficult to manage. In such situations, the switch statement offers a more structured approach to handle multiple conditions.

The switch statement compares the value of an expression against a series of potential matches, executing the block of code associated with the first successful match. Each potential match is defined using a case label, followed by a colon and the corresponding block of code. A default case is optionally included to handle situations where none of the specified cases match.

```
switch(expression) {
    case value1:
        // code block to be executed if expression evaluates to value1
        break
    case value2:
        // code block to be executed if expression evaluates to value2
        break
    default:
        // code block to be executed if none of the cases match
}
```

The break statement is essential to prevent the fall-through behavior, where subsequent case blocks execute sequentially until a break is encountered. Here's an example using the switch statement to assign grades based on a score value:

```
int score = 85
String grade

switch (score / 10) {
    case 10:
    case 9:
        grade = 'A'
        break
    case 8:
        grade = 'B'
        break
    case 7:
        grade = 'C'
        break
    case 6:
        grade = 'D'
        break
    default:
        grade = 'F'
}
println grade
```

B

In this example, the score is divided by 10 to simplify the range checks. The case statement accommodates the possibility of multiple values yielding the same result, as demonstrated with case 10 and case 9, both resulting in a grade of 'A'.

Groovy enhances the switch statement with additional capabilities beyond the strict equality checks found in many other languages. For instance, Groovy's switch statement supports matching with regular expressions, types, and even ranges. This flexibility allows for dynamic and expressive branching logic.

```
def value = 'home'

switch(value) {
    case 'home':
        println "Value is home"
        break
    case ~/.*o.*/ (regex):
        println "Regular expression match"
        break
    case java.util.List:
        println "Value is a List"
        break
    case [1..10]:
        println "Value is in the range 1 to 10"
        break
    default:
        println "No match found"
}
```

```
Value is home
```

In this example, the switch statement demonstrates diverse matching criteria: a string match, a regular expression match, a type match, and a range match. This enhanced flexibility of Groovy's switch statement enables more succinct and understandable code.

Understanding and mastering if, else if, else, and switch statements facilitate writing robust Groovy programs capable of making dynamic decisions based on input values or runtime conditions. Effective utilization of these control structures ensures the correct execution path is chosen, reflecting complex logical relationships concisely and accurately.

3.5 Loops: for, while, and do-while

Loops are fundamental constructs in programming, allowing the repeated execution of a block of code. Groovy supports three primary types of loops: for, while, and do-while. Each loop type has its own use-case scenarios and advantages. Understanding the differences and proper applications of these loops is crucial for writing efficient Groovy programs.

The for **Loop** The for loop in Groovy operates similarly to many other programming languages but offers additional features due to Groovy's expressive syntax. The traditional form of the for loop iterates over a range or collection, and its syntax is:

```
for (int i = 0; i < 10; i++) {
    println i
}
```

This loop will print the numbers from 0 to 9. Groovy also supports iterating directly over ranges:

```
for (i in 0..<10) {
    println i
}
```

The ..< operator creates an exclusive range (excluding the endpoint), whereas the .. operator creates an inclusive range:

```
for (i in 0..9) {
    println i
}
```

Groovy makes working with collections easy through the use of for loops. To iterate over a list:

```
def fruits = ["apple", "banana", "cherry"]
for (fruit in fruits) {
    println fruit
}
```

In this example, each element in the list fruits is printed.

The while **Loop** The while loop repeatedly executes a block of code as long as its condition remains true. The basic syntax for a while loop in Groovy is:

```
int i = 0
while (i < 10) {
    println i
    i++
}
```

This loop prints numbers from 0 to 9. The condition $i < 10$ is evaluated before each iteration, and the loop body is executed if the condition is true.

The do-while **Loop** The do-while loop is similar to the while loop but guarantees that the block of code is executed at least once. This is because the condition check occurs after the body of the loop. The syntax for a do-while loop in Groovy is:

```
int i = 0
do {
    println i
    i++
} while (i < 10)
```

In this loop, the numbers from 0 to 9 are printed. The key difference from the while loop is that the condition $i < 10$ is checked after the loop body is executed.

Nested Loops Groovy allows for nested loops, enabling complex iteration scenarios where multiple loop levels intersect. For example:

```
for (i in 1..3) {
    for (j in 1..3) {
        println "i: $i, j: $j"
    }
}
```

This code prints each combination of i and j from 1 to 3:

```
i: 1, j: 1
i: 1, j: 2
i: 1, j: 3
i: 2, j: 1
i: 2, j: 2
i: 2, j: 3
i: 3, j: 1
i: 3, j: 2
i: 3, j: 3
```

Loop Control Statements Groovy utilizes loop control statements to manage loop execution:

- break: Exits the loop immediately.
- continue: Skips the remaining statements in the current iteration and proceeds with the next iteration.

The break statement example:

```
for (i in 0..9) {
    if (i == 5) {
        break
    }
    println i
}
```

This loop prints numbers from 0 to 4. Upon reaching $i == 5$, the break statement terminates the loop.

The continue statement example:

```
for (i in 0..9) {
    if (i % 2 == 0) {
        continue
    }
    println i
}
```

This loop prints odd numbers from 1 to 9. The continue statement skips the current iteration whenever i is even.

Understanding and utilizing these loop constructs and control statements is essential for writing efficient and effective Groovy code. Familiarity with their syntax and behavior enables the development of robust and flexible iteration logic tailored to specific problem domains.

3.6 Defining and Using Functions

Functions, also known as methods, are a fundamental component of Groovy programming. Functions encapsulate code into reusable units, making programs more modular, readable, and maintainable. This section explores how to define and utilize functions in Groovy, elucidating their syntax, return types, arguments, closures, and the contextual nuances of 'this' and 'super'.

A function in Groovy is defined using the def keyword or with a specific return type. The function syntax is straightforward, and it closely resembles that of Java. Here is a basic example of a Groovy function which adds two numbers:

```
// Function definition with def keyword
def add(int a, int b) {
    return a + b
}
```

You can also specify the return type explicitly:

```
// Function definition with explicit return type
int add(int a, int b) {
    return a + b
}
```

Both of these functions can be called in the same manner:

```
int result = add(5, 10)
println "Result is: $result"
```

```
Result is: 15
```

In Groovy, the return statement is optional. If no return statement is used, the last evaluated expression in the function is returned by default. Here is a more concise version of the add function:

```
def add(int a, int b) {
    a + b
}
```

Functions can accept a varied number of parameters, including default parameters. Default parameters allow you to call a function without specifying arguments for all parameters, using the default values instead:

```
// Function with default parameters
def greet(String name, String greeting = "Hello") {
    "$greeting, $name!"
}

println greet("Alice")
println greet("Bob", "Hi")
```

```
Hello, Alice!
Hi, Bob!
```

A powerful feature in Groovy is the ability to pass closures as parameters to functions. A closure is akin to a block of code that can be passed around and executed:

```
// Function accepting a closure
def executeClosure(closure) {
    closure()
}

def sayHi = { println "Hi!" }

executeClosure(sayHi)
```

```
Hi!
```

Closures themselves can take parameters:

```
def greetClosure = { String name -> println "Hello, $name" }
greetClosure("Alice")
```

```
Hello, Alice
```

Given the dynamic nature of Groovy, functions can also be defined with varying numbers of arguments using varargs notation:

```
// Function with varargs
def sum(int... numbers) {
    int result = 0
    numbers.each { result += it }
```

```
    result
}
println sum(1, 2, 3, 4)
```

10

Groovy supports method overloading, allowing multiple functions with the same name but different parameter lists. The correct function is invoked based on the argument types and count:

```
def process(int a, int b) {
    a + b
}

def process(String a, String b) {
    a + b
}

println process(10, 20)
println process("Hello, ", "world!")
```

30
Hello, world!

In class contexts, Groovy methods can leverage this and super to refer to the current object and the parent class methods respectively:

```
class Parent {
    def method() {
        "Parent Method"
    }
}

class Child extends Parent {
    def method() {
        "Child Method"
    }

    def callParentMethod() {
        super.method()
    }
}

Child c = new Child()
println c.method()
println c.callParentMethod()
```

Child Method
Parent Method

Anonymous functions or methods can also be effectively utilized within Groovy. For example, an anonymous function can be implemented to sort a collection:

```
def numbers = [3, 1, 4, 1, 5, 9, 2]
numbers.sort { a, b -> a <=> b }
println numbers
```

[1, 1, 2, 3, 4, 5, 9]

In advanced scenarios, such as within domain-specific languages (DSLs) or scripting, Groovy's flexible function definitions greatly enhance its expressive power and ability to manage code succinctly.

3.7 Exception Handling

Exception handling in Groovy is a critical mechanism for managing errors and other exceptional conditions in a controlled manner. The fundamental constructs for handling exceptions in Groovy are try-catch blocks, and the language supports control structures that are modern, intuitive, and integrate seamlessly with Java's exception framework.

Groovy improves upon Java's syntax and introduces some additional capabilities while maintaining backward compatibility. This section explores the syntax and usage of exception handling constructs in Groovy.

1. The try-catch Block

In Groovy, the try-catch block encloses the code that might throw an exception. Multiple catch blocks can be defined to handle different types of exceptions. Consider the following example:

```
try {
    // Code that might throw an exception
    def result = 10 / 0
} catch (ArithmeticException e) {
    println "Caught an arithmetic exception: ${e.message}"
} catch (Exception e) {
    println "Caught a general exception: ${e.message}"
} finally {
    println "This block is always executed."
}
```

In this example: - The try block contains code that may throw an ArithmeticException due to division by zero. - The first catch block specifically catches and handles ArithmeticException. - The second catch block handles any other general exceptions. - The finally block is always executed regardless of whether an exception is thrown or not, ensuring cleanup activities such as closing resources.

2. The finally Block

The finally block is optional and can be used to execute code after the try and catch blocks have executed. This block is particularly useful for resource cleanup operations like closing a database connection or releasing file handles.

```
try {
    // Resource allocation or risky code
} catch (SomeException e) {
    // Handle exception
} finally {
    // Cleanup code
}
```

Groovy guarantees the execution of the finally block regardless of how the try block exits.

3. Exception Propagation

Exceptions can be re-thrown to propagate them to the calling code. This allows higher-level methods to handle exceptions in centralized error-handling logic.

```
void riskyMethod() throws SomeException {
    try {
        // Code that may throw SomeException
    } catch (SomeException e) {
        println "Handling SomeException in riskyMethod"
        throw e // re-throw the exception
    }
}
```

In this example, riskyMethod catches SomeException but then re-throws it to allow higher-level methods to handle it further.

4. Groovy @Catch Annotation

Groovy introduces the @Catch annotation as a shorthand for catching exceptions in closures. This concise syntax simplifies exception handling within closures:

```
def closure = {
    throw new RuntimeException("Error in closure")
} as @Catch(Exception)
closure()
```

Here, the @Catch annotation is applied to the closure, ensuring any exceptions thrown within the closure are caught and can be handled appropriately.

5. Custom Exceptions

Creating custom exceptions can provide more contextual information about errors in your application. Define a custom exception by extending the Exception class or any of its subclasses:

```
class CustomException extends Exception {
    CustomException(String message) {
        super(message)
    }
}

try {
    throw new CustomException("Custom error occurred")
} catch (CustomException e) {
    println "Caught custom exception: ${e.message}"
}
```

The CustomException class extends Exception, and when thrown, it can be caught and handled specifically.

6. Exception Handling Best Practices

- Catch specific exceptions rather than using a generic Exception class. This practice helps in identifying and resolving specific issues more efficiently.
- Always release resources in a finally block or use Groovy's automatic resource management (ARM) feature.
- Avoid using exceptions for flow control; they should only be used for exceptional conditions.
- Provide meaningful messages when throwing exceptions to make debugging easier.
- Log exceptions appropriately for audit trails and debugging without exposing sensitive information.

By leveraging these exception handling constructs and best practices, Groovy programmers can ensure robust and maintainable code that gracefully handles runtime anomalies.

3.8 Groovy Script Structure

Groovy, being both a dynamic language akin to Python and Ruby as well as being compilable to bytecode for the Java Virtual Machine (JVM), showcases a unique blend of scripting and programming capabilities. To get maximum benefit from Groovy's powerful features, understanding the script structure is paramount.

A Groovy script is essentially a program that may contain various constructs such as variable declarations, function definitions, control structures, and annotations. Scripts are generally placed in files with the .groovy extension. Below is a detailed explanation of the components and the structure of a Groovy script.

- **Package Declaration**: While not mandatory, declaring a package at the beginning of a script can help organize code, especially in larger projects. This is similar to Java and helps in avoiding class name conflicts.

```
package com.example.myproject
```

- **Import Statements**: Import statements allow the inclusion of other classes and packages. These can be from Groovy's libraries, Java's libraries, or any other third-party libraries. The import statement is similar to Java's syntax.

```
import groovy.json.JsonSlurper
import java.util.ArrayList
```

- **Variable Declarations**: Variables can be defined with or without explicit types, thanks to Groovy's type inference. Variable declaration follows the pattern def variableName or type variableName.

```
def name = "John Doe"
int age = 30
List<String> colors = ["Red", "Blue", "Green"]
```

- **Function Definitions**: Functions in Groovy are defined with the def keyword or a specific return type. Functions can return values or be void.

```
def greet(String name) {
    return "Hello, ${name}!"
}

int add(int a, int b) {
    return a + b
}
```

- **Control Structures and Loops**: Groovy supports control structures such as if-else, switch, and looping constructs like for, while, and do-while. Their syntax remains relatively close to Java, providing a smooth transition for those familiar with the latter.

```
if (age > 18) {
    println("Adult")
```

```
} else {
    println("Minor")
}

switch (age) {
    case 18:
        println("Just became an adult")
        break
    case 30:
        println("Thirty years old")
        break
    default:
        println("Age is just a number")
}

for (color in colors) {
    println(color)
}
```

- **Annotations**: Groovy allows the use of annotations to provide metadata and influence the behavior of scripts or functions. Common annotations include @Grab for dependency management and @TypeChecked for stricter type-checking.

```
@Grab(group='org.slf4j', module='slf4j-api', version='1.7.25')
import org.slf4j.LoggerFactory

@TypeChecked
def logMessage(String message) {
    def logger = LoggerFactory.getLogger(this.getClass())
    logger.info(message)
}
```

- **Exception Handling**: Groovy embraces Java's exception handling mechanism, making use of try-catch-finally blocks. Exceptions ensure robust and error-resistant codes.

```
try {
    def result = 10 / 0
} catch (ArithmeticException e) {
    println("Cannot divide by zero")
} finally {
    println("Division operation attempted")
}
```

- **Script Execution**: The entry-point for Groovy scripts is typically at the script level itself, as opposed to a main method in Java. The script is executed from the first line to the last line.

```
println(greet(name))
println("Sum of 5 and 3 is: ${add(5, 3)}")
```

Groovy's scripting capabilities simplify tight integration with Java, concatenation of different logic constructs, and ease of reading with its dynamic typing and concise syntax.

3.9 Using Annotations

Annotations in Groovy provide a powerful mechanism to add metadata to your code. This metadata can influence the way programs are compiled and executed. Annotations are typically used for various purposes such as providing information to the compiler, runtime processing of metadata, and simplifying code through automated behaviors.

In Groovy, annotations resemble those in Java and can be applied to classes, methods, fields, parameters, and local variables. Let's explore the syntax and application of annotations in Groovy through examples and detailed explanations.

Basic Annotation Syntax

Annotations are defined with the @ symbol followed by the annotation name. They can be placed before declarations of methods, classes, fields, or other elements.

```
import groovy.transform.ToString

@ToString(includeNames=true, includeFields=true)
class Person {
    String firstName
    String lastName
}
```

In this example, the @ToString annotation from the groovy.transform package is used to automatically generate the toString() method for the Person class, including the names and fields specified.

Built-in Groovy Annotations

Groovy provides several built-in annotations that facilitate common tasks:

- groovy.transform.CompileStatic: Statically compiles the annotated Groovy code to improve performance and type safety.
- groovy.transform.ToString: Auto-generates the toString() method.
- groovy.transform.EqualsAndHashCode: Generates equals() and hashCode() methods.

- groovy.transform.Immutable: Defines an immutable class.
- groovy.transform.Canonical: Auto-generates common methods like toString(), equals(), and hashCode().

Custom Annotations

Groovy also allows the creation of custom annotations. To define a custom annotation, use the @interface keyword:

```
@interface MyCustomAnnotation {
    String value() default "default"
    int number() default 0
}
```

This example defines an annotation MyCustomAnnotation with two attributes: value and number, both of which have default values.

You can use this annotation in your code as follows:

```
@MyCustomAnnotation(value="example", number=5)
class AnnotatedClass {
    void display() {
        println "AnnotatedClass method called"
    }
}

AnnotatedClass ac = new AnnotatedClass()
ac.display()
```

Retrieving Annotations at Runtime

Annotations can be retrieved at runtime using reflection. This allows the program to examine and react to the annotations present on various elements.

```
import java.lang.annotation.Annotation

AnnotatedClass ac = new AnnotatedClass()
Class clazz = ac.class

Annotation[] annotations = clazz.getAnnotations()
annotations.each { Annotation annotation ->
    println annotation
}
```

This code snippet retrieves and prints all annotations applied to the AnnotatedClass.

Meta-annotations

Meta-annotations are annotations applied to other annotation definitions to dictate their behavior. Common meta-annotations in Groovy include:

- @Retention: Specifies how long the annotation is retained (e.g., source, class, runtime).
- @Target: Specifies where the annotation can be applied (e.g., method, field, type).
- @Inherited: Indicates that an annotation type is automatically inherited.
- @Documented: Marks that the annotation should be included in the Javadoc.

Example illustrating the use of meta-annotations:

```
import java.lang.annotation.*

@Retention(RetentionPolicy.RUNTIME)
@Target(ElementType.TYPE)
@interface CustomAnnotation {
    String description()
}

@CustomAnnotation(description="Example class")
class ExampleClass {
    void exampleMethod() {
        println "ExampleMethod executed"
    }
}

ExampleClass example = new ExampleClass()
example.exampleMethod()
```

Annotations enable adding declarative information to code, enhancing readability, reducing boilerplate, and allowing introspection at compile-time and runtime. Understanding their usage equips you with a robust tool for crafting more maintainable and expressive Groovy programs.

3.10 Comments and Documentation

Comments and documentation are essential aspects of programming, helping to maintain code quality and ensuring that it is understandable for others, including your future self. Groovy, like many other programming languages, offers several ways to document code through comments. Comments in Groovy can be single-line, multi-line, or based on GroovyDoc for more formal documentation. This section will explore each type in detail and provide guidance on effective documentation practices.

The simplest form of comment in Groovy is the single-line comment. These comments begin with two forward slashes (//) and continue until the end of the line. Single-line comments are useful for short explanations or notes.

```
// This is a single-line comment
int x = 42 // Assigning 42 to variable x
```

For comments that span multiple lines, Groovy uses the multi-line comment syntax. Multi-line comments begin with /* and end with */. These comments are beneficial for more extensive descriptions or for temporarily disabling blocks of code during debugging.

```
/*
 * This is a multi-line comment
 * It can span multiple lines
 */
int y = 10 /* This is an inline multi-line comment */
```

A more structured approach to documentation in Groovy is through GroovyDoc, which is similar to Java's Javadoc. GroovyDoc comments start with /** and end with */. These comments can include annotations and are typically used to document classes, methods, and fields, providing more formal and detailed information.

```
/**
 * This is a GroovyDoc comment.
 * It provides documentation for the MyClass class.
 */
class MyClass {
    /**
     * The x field represents an integer value.
     */
    int x

    /**
     * The MyClass constructor initializes the x field.
     *
     * @param x initial value for the x field
     */
    MyClass(int x) {
        this.x = x
    }

    /**
     * This method returns the value of the x field.
     *
     * @return the current value of x
     */
    int getX() {
        return x
    }

    /**
     * This method sets a new value for the x field.
     *
```

```
     * @param x the new value to set
     */
    void setX(int x) {
        this.x = x
    }
}
```

To facilitate better understanding and maintainability of code, developers should adhere to a few best practices when adding comments and documentation:

- Use descriptive comments that explain the *why* behind code decisions, not just the *what*. This makes the reasoning behind complex logic more transparent.
- Avoid redundant comments that simply restate the code. For example, `// Increment x by 1` is redundant if the corresponding code is `x++`.
- Keep comments up to date. Outdated comments can be more misleading than helpful.
- Use GroovyDoc comments for all public classes and methods to provide clear API documentation. This practice is essential when creating libraries or APIs for use by other developers.
- Incorporate annotations like `@param`, `@return`, and `@throws` within GroovyDoc comments to specify method parameters, return types, and potential exceptions.
- Employ a consistent style and formatting for comments, making them easy to read and navigate. For example, start each comment block with a capital letter and end it with a period.

The example below demonstrates a well-documented class using all types of comments discussed.

```
/**
 * The Calculator class provides basic arithmetic operations.
 */
class Calculator {

    // The result field stores the current result of calculations.
    private double result = 0.0

    /**
     * Adds a number to the current result.
     *
     * @param number the number to be added
     */
```

```
    void add(double number) {
        result += number
    }

    /**
     * Subtracts a number from the current result.
     *
     * @param number the number to be subtracted
     */
    void subtract(double number) {
        result -= number
    }

    /**
     * Returns the current result of the calculator.
     *
     * @return the current result
     */
    double getResult() {
        return result
    }

    // Main method demonstrating the use of Calculator class
    static void main(String[] args) {
        Calculator calc = new Calculator()

        // Add 5 to the initial result
        calc.add(5.0)

        // Subtract 2 from the result
        calc.subtract(2.0)

        // Output the final result
        println("Final result: " + calc.getResult()) // Expected output: 3.0
    }
}
```

Documentation tools can further aid in generating readable and navigable documentation from GroovyDoc comments. For example, the Groovy Documentation Tool is a tool specifically designed to process GroovyDoc comments and generate HTML documentation, similar to Javadoc. By adhering to these documentation practices and utilizing such tools, developers can ensure that their codebases are well-documented and maintainable.

Chapter 4

Working with Collections

This chapter delves into Groovy's rich collections framework, focusing on lists, sets, and maps. It explores the various operators and methods for manipulating collections, as well as techniques for iterating, filtering, searching, transforming, and sorting collection data. Additionally, it covers advanced collection techniques to provide a comprehensive understanding of how to efficiently handle data within Groovy applications.

4.1 Introduction to Collections

Groovy, as a dynamically typed language that runs on the Java platform, provides an extensive and versatile framework for working with collections. At its core, Groovy simplifies handling data structures that store multiple elements, such as lists, sets, and maps, each serving unique purposes and offering various operations and methods tailored to efficiently manage and manipulate data.

Lists are ordered collections of elements, allowing duplicates and preserving the sequence of elements. They are useful when the order of elements is significant, and operations like index-based access or dynamic resizing are required.

```
def aList = [1, 2, 3, 4, 5]
println aList[0] // Output: 1
```

Sets are unordered collections that inherently prevent the duplication of elements. They are optimal for scenarios where the uniqueness of elements is critical, such as maintaining a collection of unique user IDs.

```
def aSet = [1, 2, 3, 4, 5] as Set
aSet.add(3) // No effect, 3 already exists in the set
println aSet // Output: [1, 2, 3, 4, 5]
```

```
[1, 2, 3, 4, 5]
```

Maps are collections that store key-value pairs, enabling efficient retrieval, insertion, and deletion operations based on unique keys. This collection is crucial for applications requiring quick access to values indexed by unique keys, such as configurations or user profile attributes.

```
def aMap = [name: 'John Doe', age: 35, city: 'New York']
println aMap['name'] // Output: John Doe
```

```
John Doe
```

Understanding these core types is fundamental as they provide the basis for more complex operations and tasks. Groovy enhances these standard collection types with concise syntax and powerful capabilities inherited from the Java Collection Framework, including dynamic typing, operator overloading, and native support for common operations such as filtering, transforming, and sorting.

When working with collections, we often need to perform various operations that include adding, removing, updating, and querying elements. Groovy provides a rich set of methods that make these tasks easier and more intuitive compared to traditional Java. Here are some examples of basic operations used across different collection types:

```
def list = [1, 2, 3]
// Adding an element
list << 4
// Removing an element
list.remove(0) // Removes the element at index 0
// Updating an element
list[0] = 10

def set = [1, 2, 3] as Set
// Adding an element
set.add(4)
// Removing an element
set.remove(2)

def map = [name: 'John', age: 30]
// Adding/updating an element
map['city'] = 'New York'
// Removing an element
map.remove('age')
```

Collections in Groovy also support easy iteration. There are several ways to iterate over collections, and Groovy's syntax improvements over Java make this task straightforward and expressive:

```
def list = [1, 2, 3]
list.each { println it } // Iterates over each element and prints it

def map = [name: 'John', age: 30, city: 'New York']
map.each { key, value -> println "\${key}: \${value}" }
```

```
1
2
3
name: John
age: 30
city: New York
```

Groovy also provides capabilities for creating and manipulating collections using special operators. For example, using the *. operator to apply a method to all elements of a collection or the ?[] operator for performing safe indexing.

```
def list = ['John', 'Jane', 'Doe']
def uppercasedList = list*.toUpperCase()
println uppercasedList // Output: [JOHN, JANE, DOE]

def map = [name: 'John', age: 30, city: 'New York']
def city = map?['city']
println city // Output: New York
```

```
[JOHN, JANE, DOE]
New York
```

Advanced operations like finding elements that match certain criteria, grouping elements, or even transforming collections involve more complex methods and patterns which are covered in subsequent sections of this chapter. These operations draw on functional programming paradigms, leveraging closures and higher-order functions to accomplish powerful data manipulations succinctly and efficiently.

The ability to filter collections based on specific conditions is a powerful feature in Groovy. Using the findAll method, we can extract subsets of collections that meet particular criteria:

```
def list = [1, 2, 3, 4, 5]
def evenNumbers = list.findAll { it % 2 == 0 }
println evenNumbers // Output: [2, 4]
```

```
[2, 4]
```

Similarly, the collect method allows transforming each element in a collection into a new form, producing a new collection of the transformed elements:

```
def list = [1, 2, 3, 4, 5]
def squaredNumbers = list.collect { it * it }
println squaredNumbers // Output: [1, 4, 9, 16, 25]
```

```
[1, 4, 9, 16, 25]
```

This concise introduction to collections in Groovy sets up the reader for deeper exploration of the topics mentioned earlier in this chapter, paving the way for mastering the intricacies and leveraging the full potential of Groovy collections in real-world applications.

4.2 Working with Lists

Groovy lists are versatile and provide a dynamic array that can grow or shrink as needed. They are instances of the java.util.ArrayList class and offer both the convenience of standard Java lists and additional Groovy-specific enhancements.

To create a list, we use square brackets to denote the list literal. Here is an example of creating a Groovy list containing integers:

```
def numbers = [1, 2, 3, 4, 5]
```

Lists in Groovy can contain elements of any type, thanks to Groovy's support for dynamic typing. For instance, you can create a heterogeneous list:

```
def mixedList = [1, "Groovy", true, 3.14]
```

Accessing Elements

Elements in a list can be accessed using their index. Groovy supports both positive and negative indices:

```
def thirdElement = numbers[2] // Accessing third element
def lastElement = numbers[-1] // Accessing the last element
```

If you attempt to access an index that is out of bounds, Groovy throws an IndexOutOfBoundsException.

Groovy also allows for sublist extraction using ranges:

```
def subset = numbers[1..3] // Extracting from index 1 to 3 inclusive
```

Modifying Lists

Lists in Groovy can be modified by adding or removing elements and by changing elements at specific indices. To add elements:

```
numbers << 6 // Append to the list
numbers.add(7) // Using add method
```

To insert elements at a specific index:

```
numbers.add(2, 8) // Insert 8 at index 2
```

To remove elements:

```
numbers.remove(2) // Remove element at index 2
numbers -= 4 // Remove first occurrence of element with value 4
```

Iterating Over Lists

Iterating over list elements is straightforward using Groovy's each method or traditional for loops. With each method:

```
numbers.each { number ->
    println number
}
```

Using a for loop:

```
for (number in numbers) {
    println number
}
```

Transforming Lists

Groovy's collect method is a powerful tool for transforming lists. It applies a given closure to each element of the list and collects the results into a new list:

```
def squares = numbers.collect { it * it }
println squares // Prints [1, 4, 9, 16, 25]
```

Filtering Lists

To filter lists based on a condition, use the findAll method:

```
def evenNumbers = numbers.findAll { it % 2 == 0 }
println evenNumbers // Prints [2, 4]
```

List Specific Operators

Groovy lists support various operators that simplify common list operations. For instance, the spread operator (*) can be used to flatten a list of lists:

```
def nestedList = [[1, 2], [3, 4], [5]]
def flatList = nestedList*.flatten()
```

```
println flatList // Prints [1, 2, 3, 4, 5]
```

Miscellaneous Methods

Groovy extends Java's List interface with additional methods that are especially useful. Some include:

- count: Counts the number of elements matching a condition.
- isEmpty: Checks if the list is empty.
- intersect: Finds common elements between two lists.

Example usage of isEmpty:

```
def isEmpty = numbers.isEmpty() // Returns false
```

Demonstration of intersect:

```
def list1 = [1, 2, 3]
def list2 = [2, 3, 4]
def commonElements = list1.intersect(list2)
println commonElements // Prints [2, 3]
```

Understanding and utilizing Groovy lists effectively forms the basis of data manipulation within Groovy applications. Groovy's enhancements provide robust, flexible, and expressive methods for working with collections.

4.3 Working with Sets

Groovy's Set interface inherits from the Collection interface and provides the functionality to store unique elements. Sets are advantageous when it is necessary to prevent duplicate values and when the order of elements is not important. Groovy offers multiple implementations for the Set interface, with HashSet being the most commonly used. To create and manipulate sets effectively, familiarity with the various methods and properties provided by the Set interface is crucial.

Creating a set in Groovy is straightforward. You can use the HashSet class directly or use Groovy's convenient as Set syntax:

```
def numbersSet = new HashSet()
numbersSet.add(1)
numbersSet.add(2)
numbersSet.add(3)
```

```
// or using the Groovy shorthand syntax
def lettersSet = ['a', 'b', 'c', 'd'] as Set
```

Sets automatically manage duplicates, ensuring each element is unique. Attempting to add a duplicate element results in no change to the set:

```
def uniqueSet = ['apple', 'banana', 'apple'] as Set
assert uniqueSet.size() == 2 // 'apple' appears only once
```

The Set interface supports various methods to manipulate and query set contents. Some of the most commonly used methods include:

- add(element): Adds the specified element to the set if it is not already present.
- remove(element): Removes the specified element from the set if it is present.
- contains(element): Returns true if the set contains the specified element.
- isEmpty(): Returns true if the set contains no elements.
- size(): Returns the number of elements in the set.
- clear(): Removes all elements from the set.

Groovy also supports a fluent API for manipulating sets, providing a more expressive and readable syntax. For example, chaining methods:

```
def fluentSet = new HashSet().add('Groovy').add('Java').add('Kotlin')
assert fluentSet.contains('Groovy')
```

Operations such as union, intersection, and difference between sets are integral for many applications. These operations can be performed using various Groovy operators:

- +: Union of two sets.
- -: Difference between two sets.
- intersect: Intersection of two sets.

```
def setA = [1, 2, 3, 4] as Set
def setB = [3, 4, 5, 6] as Set

def union = setA + setB // [1, 2, 3, 4, 5, 6]
def difference = setA - setB // [1, 2]
def intersection = setA.intersect(setB) // [3, 4]
```

Utilizing set operations can significantly reduce the complexity and enhance the readability of code dealing with collections of unique elements. To maximize the efficiency of these operations, it is essential to understand the underlying data structures and algorithms.

Iterating over sets is similar to other collection types, utilizing loops or Groovy's each method:

```
def colors = ['red', 'green', 'blue'] as Set

// Using the each method
colors.each { color ->
    println(color)
}

// Using a loop
for (color in colors) {
    println(color)
}
```

Filtering a set requires the findAll method, which returns a new set containing all elements that match the specified predicate. This method is particularly useful for extracting subsets based on specific criteria:

```
def numberSet = [10, 15, 20, 25, 30] as Set
def filteredSet = numberSet.findAll { it > 15 }
assert filteredSet == [20, 25, 30] as Set
```

Transforming sets involves applying a closure to each element and collecting the results. The collect method provides this functionality:

```
def originalSet = [1, 2, 3] as Set
def squaredSet = originalSet.collect { it * it }
assert squaredSet == [1, 4, 9] as Set
```

Sorting elements in a set is generally not required due to the unordered nature of sets. If sorted data is necessary, converting the set to a list before sorting is the recommended approach:

```
def unsortedSet = [5, 3, 1, 4, 2] as Set
def sortedList = unsortedSet.toList().sort()
assert sortedList == [1, 2, 3, 4, 5]
```

Groovy's support for sets is extensive, ensuring that developers can efficiently handle collections of unique elements with minimal effort.

Employing these methods and properties effectively in applications enhances code clarity, reduces errors, and improves performance.

4.4 Working with Maps

Maps in Groovy are collections of key-value pairs, allowing for efficient data retrieval by referencing unique keys. A map can be considered similar to dictionaries in Python or hash tables in Java. Groovy provides a comprehensive set of operators and methods to work with maps, making them a versatile tool for managing data.

Creating a map in Groovy is straightforward. A map can be instantiated using the [:] syntax or via the constructor HashMap(). Here's an example of both approaches:

```
def mapByLiteral = [name: 'John', age: 30, city: 'New York']
def mapByConstructor = new HashMap()
mapByConstructor.put('name', 'John')
mapByConstructor.put('age', 30)
mapByConstructor.put('city', 'New York')
```

Maps can also elegantly handle different data types for both keys and values, thanks to Groovy's dynamic typing:

```
def diverseMap = [1: 'one', 'two': 2, 3.0: true]
```

Accessing values in a map can be achieved either by using brackets or the get method:

```
def name = mapByLiteral['name']
def age = mapByConstructor.get('age')
```

Modifying map entries is equally simple:

```
mapByLiteral['age'] = 31
mapByConstructor.put('city', 'Los Angeles')
```

A noteworthy feature of Groovy maps is their ability to safely retrieve values using the ? operator to avoid null pointer exceptions. This is particularly useful when working with potentially null values:

```
def country = mapByLiteral['country'] ?: 'Unknown'
```

Iterating over maps can be done in several ways. Groovy's maps are considered collections, allowing them to be iterated with loops. Key-value pairs can be accessed using a Map.Entry object:

```
mapByLiteral.each { entry ->
    println "Key: ${entry.key}, Value: ${entry.value}"
}
```

Keys and values can also be directly retrieved using destructuring:

```
mapByLiteral.each { k, v ->
    println "Key: $k, Value: $v"
}
```

Using the collect method, we can transform maps into other collections:

```
def keyList = mapByLiteral.collect { it.key }
def valueList = mapByLiteral.collect { it.value }
```

Filtering a map based on keys or values is another powerful feature. For instance, to filter out all entries where the value is a string:

```
def filteredMap = diverseMap.findAll { k, v -> v instanceof String }
```

Removing entries from maps is facilitated by the remove method, which can remove an entry by key, or by using entries' criteria:

```
mapByLiteral.remove('age')
mapByConstructor.findAll { k, v -> v == 'Los Angeles' }.each { k, v ->
      mapByConstructor.remove(k) }
```

The plus operator can be used to merge two maps:

```
def map1 = [a: 1, b: 2]
def map2 = [b: 3, c: 4]
def mergedMap = map1 + map2 // mergedMap is [a:1, b:3, c:4]
```

For scenarios requiring unmodifiable maps, Groovy offers the Collections.unmodifiableMap method, ensuring that the internal structure cannot be altered:

```
def unmodifiable = Collections.unmodifiableMap(mapByLiteral)
```

Deep copying maps is crucial when modifications should not affect the original map. Groovy allows this using the collectEntries method:

```
def deepCopy = mapByLiteral.collectEntries { k, v -> [(k): v] }
```

Understanding maps at a deeper level entails recognizing the utility of map methods such as size, isEmpty, and clear:

```
assert mapByLiteral.size() == 2
assert mapByLiteral.isEmpty() == false
mapByLiteral.clear()
assert mapByLiteral.isEmpty() == true
```

Maps in Groovy encapsulate not only a vast range of functionalities but also integrate seamlessly into the language's dynamic nature. The ability to manipulate, transform, and interrogate map structures with minimal syntax highlights their utility in Groovy programming, extending from simple applications to complex data-handling frameworks.

4.5 Collection Operators and Methods

Collection operators and methods in Groovy provide powerful and concise tools for manipulating and querying collections. Understanding these tools enhances the capability to handle data effectively and perform complex operations with minimal code. The following section delves into essential operators and methods, showcasing their utility with practical examples.

Spread operators offer a convenient way to perform operations across all elements of a collection. The syntax involves using the *. operator. For instance, applying a method to each element of a list:

```
def list = [1, 2, 3, 4, 5]
def squaredList = list*.multiply(2)
println(squaredList)
```

```
[2, 4, 6, 8, 10]
```

This example demonstrates the multiplication of each element by 2. The *. operator simplifies the application of a common operation across all elements.

Finding elements within collections is facilitated by the find and findAll methods. The find method locates the first element that satisfies a given condition, while findAll retrieves all elements meeting the criteria:

```
def list = [1, 2, 3, 4, 5]
def firstEven = list.find { it % 2 == 0 }
def allEven = list.findAll { it % 2 == 0 }
println(firstEven)
println(allEven)
```

```
2
[2, 4]
```

Collecting elements is another common operation, achievable via the collect method. This method transforms each element of a collection through a closure, returning a new collection of the results:

```
def list = [1, 2, 3, 4, 5]
def squaredList = list.collect { it * it }
```

```
println(squaredList)
```

[1, 4, 9, 16, 25]

Grouping elements by a specific criterion can be conducted using the groupBy method. The groupBy method aggregates elements into a map based on the closure's return value:

```
def list = ['apple', 'banana', 'cherry', 'blueberry', 'avocado']
def grouped = list.groupBy { it[0] }
println(grouped)
```

[a:[apple, avocado], b:[banana, blueberry], c:[cherry]]

Aggregating data within collections often involves methods such as inject, sum, min, and max. The inject method is particularly versatile, allowing the accumulation of results through a binary operation:

```
def list = [1, 2, 3, 4, 5]
def sum = list.inject(0) { acc, val -> acc + val }
println(sum)
```

15

Similarly, the sum, min, and max methods provide straightforward aggregation:

```
def list = [1, 2, 3, 4, 5]
println(list.sum())
println(list.min())
println(list.max())
```

15
1
5

Reduction operations can be performed using the reduce method, which combines elements of a collection using a binary closure and returns a single value. An example would be finding the largest value in a list:

```
def list = [1, 2, 3, 4, 5]
def maxVal = list.reduce { a, b -> a > b ? a : b }
println(maxVal)
```

5

Transforming collections is integral to Groovy programming, with methods like collectEntries converting collections into maps based on key-value pairs defined by a closure:

```
def list = ['a', 'b', 'c']
def map = list.collectEntries { [it, it.toUpperCase()] }
```

```
println(map)
```

```
[a:A, b:B, c:C]
```

Operators for collections in Groovy include union (+), intersection (intersect), and difference (-). The union operator concatenates collections, the intersect operator finds common elements, and the difference operator computes elements in one collection not present in another:

```
def list1 = [1, 2, 3]
def list2 = [3, 4, 5]
def union = list1 + list2
def intersection = list1.intersect(list2)
def difference = list1 - list2
println(union)
println(intersection)
println(difference)
```

```
[1, 2, 3, 3, 4, 5]
[3]
[1, 2]
```

Sorting collections can be easily accomplished using the sort method. Sorting can be tailored with closures defining custom ordering criteria:

```
def list = [5, 1, 3, 4, 2]
def sortedList = list.sort { it }
println(sortedList)
```

```
[1, 2, 3, 4, 5]
```

For advanced sorting, comparison logic can be incorporated within the closure:

```
def list = ['apple', 'banana', 'cherry']
def sortedList = list.sort { a, b -> a.length() <=> b.length() }
println(sortedList)
```

```
[apple, banana, cherry]
```

Mastery of these operators and methods significantly enhances proficiency in data handling within Groovy, allowing developers to write less and achieve more with their collections.

4.6 Iterating Over Collections

Iterating over collections is a fundamental operation that enables you to process each element in a collection. Groovy provides several constructs to iterate over lists, sets, and maps efficiently. Here, we will explore different looping mechanisms Groovy offers, including traditional for loops, each method, and other advanced iteration techniques.

The traditional for loop is familiar to those with experience in other programming languages. In Groovy, the for loop can iterate over a collection in a straightforward manner.

```
def list = [1, 2, 3, 4, 5]
for (int i = 0; i < list.size(); i++) {
    println(list[i])
}
```

The output of the above code is:

```
1
2
3
4
5
```

While the traditional for loop is useful, Groovy's each method provides a more idiomatic way to iterate over collections. The each method takes a closure that operates on each element in the collection.

```
def list = [1, 2, 3, 4, 5]
list.each { element ->
    println(element)
}
```

The above code also produces the same output:

```
1
2
3
4
5
```

Using the eachWithIndex method allows you to access both the element and its index during iteration. This can be particularly useful when you need to know the position of each element.

```
def list = [1, 2, 3, 4, 5]
list.eachWithIndex { element, index ->
    println("Index $index has value $element")
}
```

The output of this snippet is:

```
Index 0 has value 1
Index 1 has value 2
Index 2 has value 3
Index 3 has value 4
Index 4 has value 5
```

Iteration over maps involves accessing both the key and the value. This can be achieved with the each method by defining a closure that takes two parameters.

```
def map = [a: 1, b: 2, c: 3]
map.each { key, value ->
    println("$key -> $value")
}
```

The output is:

```
a -> 1
b -> 2
c -> 3
```

When dealing with nested collections, the each method can be effectively used in a nested manner. Consider a list of lists scenario:

```
def nestedList = [[1, 2], [3, 4], [5, 6]]
nestedList.each { innerList ->
    innerList.each { element ->
        println(element)
    }
}
```

The output is:

```
1
2
3
4
5
6
```

For those looking for more control, Groovy's collect method can transform items in the collection during iteration. collect applies the given closure to each item and returns a new list containing the results.

```
def list = [1, 2, 3, 4, 5]
def squaredList = list.collect { it * it }
println(squaredList)
```

This produces:

```
[1, 4, 9, 16, 25]
```

Another powerful iteration method is findAll, which filters the elements based on the given closure, returning a new collection with only those elements for which the closure returns true.

```
def list = [1, 2, 3, 4, 5]
def evenList = list.findAll { it % 2 == 0 }
println(evenList)
```

The output is:

```
[2, 4]
```

Similarly, the groupBy method can categorize elements of the collection into groups based on a specified criterion.

```
def list = ['apple', 'banana', 'cherry', 'date']
def groupByLength = list.groupBy { it.length() }
println(groupByLength)
```

This will result in:

```
[5:[apple, mango], 6:[banana], 7:[cherry], 4:[date]]
```

Different iteration methods in Groovy provide flexibility and enhanced readability. Depending on the context, any of these methods can be used to iterate over collections efficiently while ensuring clean and concise code.

4.7 Filtering and Searching Collections

Groovy provides powerful mechanisms for filtering and searching through collections. Utilizing built-in methods and closures, Groovy simplifies the process of identifying and extracting elements that match specific criteria. This section highlights key techniques and examples to enhance your ability to manipulate and query collections effectively.

Filtering Collections:

Filtering involves creating a subset of a collection based on specific conditions. Groovy's findAll method is a quintessential tool for such operations. The findAll method iterates over each element of the collection and applies a closure that defines the filtering condition. Elements that satisfy the closure's boolean condition are included in the resulting collection.

Consider a list of integers:

```
def numbers = [1, 2, 3, 4, 5, 6, 7, 8, 9, 10]
```

To filter out the even numbers, use the findAll method with a closure:

```
def evenNumbers = numbers.findAll { it % 2 == 0 }
println evenNumbers
```

This will produce:

```
[2, 4, 6, 8, 10]
```

In this example, the closure it represents each element in the list, and the condition $it \% 2 == 0$ checks whether an element is even.

Searching Collections:

Searching involves locating specific elements within a collection that meet certain criteria. Groovy offers several methods for searching, including find, any, and every.

- **find**: Finds the first element in the collection that matches the condition specified in the closure. If no element matches, it returns null.

```
def firstEven = numbers.find { it % 2 == 0 }
println firstEven // Outputs: 2
```

- **any**: Returns true if any element in the collection matches the condition specified in the closure.

```
def hasEven = numbers.any { it % 2 == 0 }
println hasEven // Outputs: true
```

- **every**: Returns true if all elements in the collection match the condition specified in the closure.

```
def allEven = numbers.every { it % 2 == 0 }
println allEven // Outputs: false
```

Combining Conditions:

Groovy allows combining multiple conditions within closures for more complex filtering and searching.

Filtering a list to obtain odd numbers greater than 5:

```
def oddAndGreaterThanFive = numbers.findAll { it % 2 != 0 && it > 5 }
println oddAndGreaterThanFive
```

This will yield:

```
[7, 9]
```

Using Groovy's collect Method with Filtering:

The collect method can be combined with filtering techniques to transform elements while filtering. The collect method applies a given closure to each element and collects the results in a list.

Transforming even numbers into their squares:

```
def squaredEvenNumbers = numbers.findAll { it % 2 == 0 }.collect { it * it }
println squaredEvenNumbers
```

This generates:

[4, 16, 36, 64, 100]

Filtering and Searching in Maps:

Maps, another fundamental Groovy collection type, support filtering and searching operations through their entrySet and keySet methods.

Consider the following map of people and their ages:

```
def people = [ 'Alice': 30, 'Bob': 25, 'Charlie': 35, 'Dave': 40 ]
```

To filter out people older than 30:

```
def olderThanThirty = people.findAll { entry -> entry.value > 30 }
println olderThanThirty
```

This will present:

[Charlie:35, Dave:40]

To fetch names of people older than 30 using collect after filtering:

```
def namesOfOlderThanThirty = people.findAll { it.value > 30 }.collect { it.key }
println namesOfOlderThanThirty
```

This results in:

[Charlie, Dave]

By mastering filtering and searching in collections, you can significantly enhance your data manipulation capabilities in Groovy, allowing for cleaner, more readable, and efficient code. Understanding and effectively utilizing these tools forms an essential part of Groovy proficiency.

4.8 Transforming Collections

Transforming collections in Groovy involves modifying or converting existing collections to new collections that adhere to specific criteria or formats. This process leverages Groovy's powerful and flexible syntax, which simplifies common collection transformations. This section will explore various Groovy methods and techniques for transforming lists, sets, and maps.

The most commonly used transformation methods include collect, findAll, and the inject method, which are part of Groovy's GDK (Groovy Development Kit). We will examine each in detail through practical examples.

Collect Method:

The collect method is used to transform each element of a collection and return a new collection. The method applies a specified closure to each element, collecting the results into a new list. For example:

```
def numbers = [1, 2, 3, 4, 5]
def squaredNumbers = numbers.collect { it * it }
println squaredNumbers
```

The output of the above code will be:

```
[1, 4, 9, 16, 25]
```

In this code, the collect method applies the closure it * it to each element of the list numbers, yielding a new list squaredNumbers containing the squares of the original numbers.

FindAll Method:

The findAll method filters elements in a collection, returning a new collection containing all elements that match the specified criteria. This method can be used to selectively include certain elements based on a condition. For instance:

```
def numbers = [1, 2, 3, 4, 5]
def evenNumbers = numbers.findAll { it % 2 == 0 }
println evenNumbers
```

The output of the above code will be:

```
[2, 4]
```

Here, the findAll method filters the list numbers and collects only the even numbers into the list evenNumbers.

Inject Method:

The inject method, also known as reduce or fold, combines all elements of a collection into a single result using an initial value and a specified binary operation. This method is useful for accumulating results. For example:

```
def numbers = [1, 2, 3, 4, 5]
def sum = numbers.inject(0) { acc, element -> acc + element }
println sum
```

The output of the above code will be:

```
15
```

In this instance, the inject method starts with an initial value of 0 and iteratively adds each element in the numbers list to produce the total sum, stored in the variable sum.

Advanced Transformations:

Groovy also offers advanced transformation methods for manipulating nested collections and converting between different collection types. These include the flatten, groupBy, and collectEntries methods.

The flatten method is used to convert a nested collection into a flat list. For example:

```
def nestedList = [[1, 2], [3, 4], [5]]
def flatList = nestedList.flatten()
println flatList
```

The output of the above code will be:

```
[1, 2, 3, 4, 5]
```

In this example, flatten takes the nested list nestedList and produces a single flattened list flatList containing all the elements.

The groupBy method groups elements of a collection based on a specified criterion and returns a map. For instance:

```
def numbers = [1, 2, 3, 4, 5, 6]
def groupedByOddEven = numbers.groupBy { it % 2 == 0 ? 'even' : 'odd' }
println groupedByOddEven
```

The output of the above code will be:

```
[odd:[1, 3, 5], even:[2, 4, 6]]
```

Here, groupBy divides the numbers list into a map containing two lists: one for odd numbers and one for even numbers.

The collectEntries method transforms a collection into a map by applying a closure that returns a map entry (key-value pair) for each element. For example:

```
def numbers = [1, 2, 3, 4, 5]
def numberMap = numbers.collectEntries { [(it): it * it] }
println numberMap
```

The output of the above code will be:

```
[1:1, 2:4, 3:9, 4:16, 5:25]
```

In this instance, collectEntries transforms the numbers list into a map where each key is a number and the corresponding value is its square.

These transformation methods enable efficient and concise manipulation of collections in Groovy, facilitating the development of robust and flexible applications.

4.9 Sorting Collections

Sorting is a fundamental operation that allows collections to be ordered based on specified criteria. Groovy provides robust sorting mechanisms for lists and maps, leveraging various methods and comparator support to achieve custom ordering logic.

Groovy's List and Map classes come with built-in methods to facilitate sorting. We will explore sorting List first, followed by Map.

For List, the most commonly used methods are sort() and collectSorted(). The sort() method sorts the list in place, altering the original list, whereas collectSorted() returns a new sorted list, leaving the original list unchanged.

Consider the following example:

```
def numbers = [5, 3, 9, 1, 7]
numbers.sort()
println(numbers) // Output: [1, 3, 5, 7, 9]

def sortedNumbers = numbers.collectSorted()
println(sortedNumbers) // Output: [1, 3, 5, 7, 9]
println(numbers) // Output: [1, 3, 5, 7, 9]
```

The default sorting order is ascending and is determined by the natural ordering of the elements. For complex sorting, we use a closure that defines the sort logic. For instance:

```
def words = ['banana', 'apple', 'pear', 'kiwi']
words.sort { a, b -> a.length() <=> b.length() }
println(words) // Output: ['kiwi', 'pear', 'apple', 'banana']
```

In the above code, we sort the list of words by their lengths. The <=> (spaceship) operator is used for comparison, returning -1, 0, or 1 based on the comparison outcome.

Sorting List of complex objects requires a similar approach. Consider a Person class with properties name and age:

```
class Person {
    String name
    int age
}
```

```
def people = [new Person(name: 'Tom', age: 34),
              new Person(name: 'Anna', age: 24),
              new Person(name: 'Mike', age: 50)]

people.sort { it.age }
println(people*.name) // Output: ['Anna', 'Tom', 'Mike']
```

Here, people.sort { it.age } sorts the list by the age property of each Person object.

Sorting can also be done in descending order:

```
people.sort { -it.age }
println(people*.name) // Output: ['Mike', 'Tom', 'Anna']
```

Alternatively, use the Comparator syntax:

```
people.sort { a, b -> b.age <=> a.age }
println(people*.name) // Output: ['Mike', 'Tom', 'Anna']
```

Next, we consider sorting Map collections. Unlike List, Map sorting handles entries based on keys or values and not directly on the map itself. We often convert the map entries to a list, sort it, and reconstitute it back into a map.

Here's an example of sorting a Map by values:

```
def scores = [Alice: 42, Bob: 75, Charlie: 61]

def sortedByValue = scores.sort { a, b -> a.value <=> b.value }
println(sortedByValue) // Output: [Alice:42, Charlie:61, Bob:75]
```

Sorting by keys can be similarly achieved:

```
def sortedByKey = scores.sort { a, b -> a.key <=> b.key }
println(sortedByKey) // Output: [Alice:42, Bob:75, Charlie:61]
```

It is critical to remember that the sort method creates a new Map, leaving the original Map unaltered.

For more advanced sorting scenarios involving nested collections or multiple criteria, the method chaining and nested comparisons within closures become valuable strategies. For instance, you can sort a list of Person objects first by name and then by age:

```
people.sort { a, b ->
    a.name <=> b.name ?: a.age <=> b.age
}
println(people*.name) // Output: ['Anna', 'Mike', 'Tom']
```

Here, ?: is the Elvis operator, allowing a secondary sorting criterion if the primary one results in a tie.

As part of Groovy's seamless integration with Java, the utilization of Java's Comparator interface can be applied for sorting complex collections. The support for Lambda expressions further enriches the flexibility of sorting logic definition.

For highly specialized sorting cases, implementing the Comparator in a separate class could be beneficial. Such an approach grants reusability and clarity, especially for enterprise-grade applications where adherence to Separation of Concerns (SoC) principles is critical.

Exploring these sorting mechanisms emphasizes Groovy's sophistication in handling collections, reinforcing its capability to streamline and empower development workflows.

4.10 Advanced Collection Techniques

Groovy provides a rich set of advanced techniques for operating on and manipulating collections. This section delves into several advanced functionalities, extending the foundational knowledge covered in previous sections to empower the reader with sophisticated methods for handling complex data transformation scenarios.

Group By Method: The groupBy method is utilized to group elements of a collection based on a specified criterion. This method returns a map where the keys are the group identifiers and the values are lists of items belonging to those groups.

```
def list = [1, 2, 3, 4, 5, 6, 7, 8, 9, 10]
def evenOddGroups = list.groupBy { it % 2 == 0 ? 'Even' : 'Odd' }

println evenOddGroups
```

```
[Even:[2, 4, 6, 8, 10], Odd:[1, 3, 5, 7, 9]]
```

CollectMany Method: The collectMany method is an advanced transformation technique that applies a function to each element of a collection and flattens the result into a single collection. This method is highly useful for scenarios where you need to merge multiple collections or extract nested elements into a flat structure.

```
def nestedList = [[1, 2, 3], [4, 5], [6, 7, 8, 9]]
def flatList = nestedList.collectMany { it }

println flatList
```

```
[1, 2, 3, 4, 5, 6, 7, 8, 9]
```

Partition Method: The collate method partitions a collection into sublists of a specified size. This method is particularly useful for batching operations or processing large collections in chunks.

```
def largeList = (1..20).toList()
def partitions = largeList.collate(5)

println partitions
```

```
[[1, 2, 3, 4, 5], [6, 7, 8, 9, 10], [11, 12, 13, 14, 15], [16, 17, 18, 19, 20]]
```

Using Spread Operator for Collection Operations: The spread operator (*) is another powerful tool for working with collections. It allows for the expansion of collections in method calls and for various operations like constructing lists, maps, and executing methods on all elements.

```
def numbers = [1, 2, 3]
def result = sum(*numbers)

def sum(a, b, c) {
    a + b + c
}
println result
```

```
6
```

Combining Collections - Zip and Unzip Operations: The transpose method can zip multiple collections together, transforming them into a list of lists where each inner list groups the corresponding elements of the input lists. Conversely, it can also flatten zipped lists back into original collections.

```
def names = ["Alice", "Bob", "Charlie"]
def ages = [25, 30, 35]

def zipped = [names, ages].transpose()
println zipped

def (unzippedNames, unzippedAges) = zipped.transpose()
println unzippedNames
println unzippedAges
```

```
[[Alice, 25], [Bob, 30], [Charlie, 35]]
[Alice, Bob, Charlie]
[25, 30, 35]
```

Combining Collections - Cartesian Product: The combinations method generates the Cartesian product of two or more collections, resulting in all possible pairs of elements combined from each collection.

```
def setA = [1, 2]
def setB = ['A', 'B']
```

```
def cartesianProduct = setA.combinations(setB)

println cartesianProduct
```

[[1, A], [1, B], [2, A], [2, B]]

Unique and Distinct Elements: The unique method eliminates duplicate elements from a collection, returning only distinct elements. It's applicable to lists and sets, enabling the enforcement of element uniqueness.

```
def listWithDuplicates = [1, 2, 2, 3, 4, 4, 5]
def uniqueList = listWithDuplicates.unique()

println uniqueList
```

[1, 2, 3, 4, 5]

Sorting with Custom Comparators: The sort method, enhanced with a custom comparator or closure, allows sorting based on multiple attributes or complex criteria. Implementing custom sorting logic can optimize data organization and retrieval processes.

```
def studentList = [
    [name: 'John', grade: 88],
    [name: 'Jane', grade: 92],
    [name: 'Jim', grade: 76]
]

studentList.sort { a, b -> b.grade <=> a.grade }

println studentList
```

[[name:Jane, grade:92], [name:John, grade:88], [name:Jim, grade:76]]

These advanced collection techniques enable more efficient data handling and complex collection manipulations within Groovy applications. Fluent utilization of these methods can streamline codebases and enhance the overall performance of collection operations.

Chapter 5

Closures and Functional Programming

This chapter introduces closures in Groovy, explaining their definition, usage, and key concepts such as parameters and return values. It also covers the application of closures in collections, the roles of delegate and owner, and advanced techniques like currying. The chapter delves into Groovy's built-in higher-order functions and functional programming techniques, illustrating how to write modular and maintainable code and demonstrating practical examples of combining closures with Domain-Specific Languages (DSLs).

5.1 Introduction to Closures

Closures are one of the core features of Groovy that distinguish it from other programming languages. They encapsulate functionality in a block of code that can be referenced, passed around, and executed at a later point. This powerful concept forms the basis for many advanced programming techniques, including functional programming and Domain-Specific Languages (DSLs).

In Groovy, closures are instances of the groovy.lang.Closure class. They can be defined using curly braces {} and can enclose a set of statements. The basic syntax for a closure is illustrated below:

```
def myClosure = { println "Hello, Groovy!" }
```

To execute the closure, use the call() method or the shorthand () operator:

```
myClosure.call()
// or simply
myClosure()
```

Executing this closure will output:

```
Hello, Groovy!
```

One of the defining characteristics of closures in Groovy is their ability to capture variables from their surrounding scope. This is known as closure's lexical scope or closure scope. Consider the following example:

```
def greeting = "Hello"
def myClosure = { println "${greeting}, Groovy!" }
myClosure()
```

This closure captures the greeting variable from the surrounding scope, and its execution will produce the following output:

```
Hello, Groovy!
```

Closures can also accept parameters and return values. Parameters are defined within the vertical bar delimiters | at the beginning of the closure, and they operate much like a method. Here is an example of a closure that accepts a single parameter:

```
def greet = { name -> println "Hello, ${name}!" }
greet("Alice")
```

This closure takes a name as an argument and prints a greeting. The output is:

```
Hello, Alice!
```

Groovy also supports the declaration of closures with multiple parameters by separating them with commas:

```
def add = { a, b -> a + b }
println add(5, 3)
```

Executing this closure will result in the following output:

```
8
```

One of the powerful aspects of closures is their ability to be passed as arguments to methods and functions. This allows for highly flexible and modular programming patterns. Consider the following example where a closure is passed to a method:

```
def repeat(times, closure) {
    for (i in 1..times) {
        closure(i)
    }
}

repeat(3) { println "Iteration ${it}" }
```

In this example, the repeat method takes a closure that is executed a specified number of times. The it variable is a default parameter name used when the closure has no explicit parameter name defined. Hence, the output is:

```
Iteration 1
Iteration 2
Iteration 3
```

Closures can also be used in constructing Domain-Specific Languages (DSLs). By taking advantage of closures' flexibility, you can design more readable and expressive APIs. We will examine practical applications of closures in the context of DSLs in subsequent sections.

Closures inherently support various functional programming paradigms, including first-class functions, higher-order functions, and lazy evaluation. This enables Groovy developers to write more concise and expressive code, promoting a functional style.

Understanding the fundamental properties and use cases of closures is crucial as we delve deeper into more advanced topics, such as currying, higher-order functions, and the combination of closures with DSLs. This foundational knowledge is paramount for mastering Groovy's functional programming capabilities.

5.2 Defining and Using Closures

In Groovy, a closure is an anonymous block of code that can accept parameters, be passed as arguments, return values, and be assigned to variables. Understanding closures is fundamental to harnessing their potential in creating expressive and flexible code. Let us delve into the syntax and the essential concepts of defining and utilizing closures in Groovy.

A closure can be defined using the curly braces {} and the -> operator to separate the parameter list from the code block. The following example illustrates a basic closure definition:

```
def greet = { String name -> println "Hello, $name!" }
```

In this example, the closure greet takes a single parameter, name, which is of type String. The code block within the closure prints a greeting message. To invoke the closure, we call it like a method:

```
greet('Alice')
```

Hello, Alice!

Closures can be defined with a varying number of parameters or even no parameters at all. If no parameters are defined, the -> arrow can be omitted:

```
def sayHello = { println "Hello, world!" }
```

When invoked, sayHello will simply print the default greeting:

```
sayHello()
```

Hello, world!

Closures in Groovy also allow for more concise syntax when dealing with single-parameter closures. Specifically, the special variable it is used to refer to the implicit parameter:

```
def square = { it * it }
println square(5)
```

25

In this example, it represents the single implicit parameter passed to the closure, allowing us to define a closure that squares a given number with minimal syntax.

Closures can capture their surrounding environment, including local variables, which is a powerful feature known as lexical scoping. This capability simplifies creating functions that operate with external state. Consider the following example:

```
def factor = 3
def multiply = { num -> num * factor }
println multiply(5)
```

15

Here, the closure multiply captures the variable factor from its surrounding context and uses it inside the closure body. Changing the value of factor affects the closure's behavior:

```
factor = 4
println multiply(5)
```

```
20
```

Closures can be leveraged as arguments to methods, enabling high-order functions. Groovy provides built-in methods for collections that take closures as parameters. For example, the each method applies a closure to each element in a collection:

```
def numbers = [1, 2, 3, 4, 5]
numbers.each { println it }
```

```
1
2
3
4
5
```

Closures enhance the expressiveness of loops, transforming code into more readable and compact forms. They are also pivotal in defining custom control structures and Domain-Specific Languages (DSLs).

Closures in Groovy can explicitly return a value using the return statement. However, Groovy implicitly returns the last evaluated expression if no return statement is present:

```
def add = { a, b -> return a + b }
def addImplicit = { a, b -> a + b }
println add(10, 5)
println addImplicit(10, 5)
```

```
15
15
```

Closures enable defining and managing control flow, constructing reusable code blocks that streamline tasks. In Groovy, closures are objects of type groovy.lang.Closure, allowing them to interact seamlessly with Java code and libraries.

Understanding closures is fundamental to mastering Groovy. Their flexibility, power, and integration capabilities make them indispensable structures for writing effective Groovy programs.

5.3 Closure Parameters and Return Values

Closures in Groovy are versatile constructs that allow for encapsulating a block of code along with its environment. Understanding how to work with parameters and return values in closures is essential for writing robust and modular Groovy code. This section examines the syntax, parameter passing, and return value behavior in Groovy closures.

The signature of a closure in Groovy can include a parameter list, just like a method. Parameters passed to a closure are enclosed within vertical bars | |. Consider the following example where a closure defines two parameters:

```
def sum = { int a, int b ->
    a + b
}
```

In this closure, sum takes two integer parameters, a and b, and returns their sum. You can invoke the closure using the call method or the shorthand parentheses:

```
assert sum(3, 4) == 7
assert sum.call(5, 6) == 11
```

A key feature of Groovy closures is their flexibility in handling parameters. If no explicit parameters are defined, the closure implicitly uses a default parameter, it. This is particularly useful for concise expressions:

```
def square = { it * it }
assert square(5) == 25
```

Closures can have an arbitrary number of parameters, including optional parameters with default values:

```
def greet = { String name, String greeting = "Hello" ->
    "${greeting}, ${name}"
}
assert greet("Alice") == "Hello, Alice"
assert greet("Bob", "Hi") == "Hi, Bob"
```

In Groovy, closures always return a value. If no explicit return keyword is specified, the last evaluated expression in the closure body is returned. This behavior simplifies code and enhances readability:

```
def multiply = { int x, int y ->
    x * y // This value is implicitly returned
}
assert multiply(3, 4) == 12
```

However, the return keyword can be used explicitly for clarity or to return early from the closure:

```
def checkEvenOdd = { int number ->
    if (number % 2 == 0) return "Even"
    "Odd" // This serves as the default return value
}
assert checkEvenOdd(2) == "Even"
assert checkEvenOdd(3) == "Odd"
```

Furthermore, closures can return other closures, enabling higher-order functions and functional programming patterns. This is often useful for creating more specialized or partially applied functions:

```
def adder = { int x ->
    return { int y -> x + y }
}
def addFive = adder(5)
assert addFive(10) == 15 // 5 + 10
```

This example demonstrates a closure adder that generates another closure adding a fixed number (x) to its parameter (y).

Parameters in closures can be of any data type, including primitives, objects, and collections. The following example demonstrates a closure with a list parameter:

```
def sumList = { List<Integer> numbers ->
    int sum = 0
    numbers.each { sum += it }
    return sum
}
assert sumList([1, 2, 3, 4]) == 10
```

In this example, sumList takes a list of integers, iterates through the list, and computes their sum. The each method iterates using the implicit it parameter within the closure.

In addition to explicitly passing parameters, Groovy closures support varargs, allowing the closure to accept a variable number of arguments:

```
def concatenate = { String... words ->
    words.join(' ')
}
assert concatenate("The", "quick", "brown", "fox") == "The quick brown fox"
```

Here, the closure concatenate accepts any number of string arguments and joins them into a single string.

Correct handling of closure parameters and return values is crucial for effectively leveraging Groovy's functional programming capabilities. The ability to seamlessly pass varying numbers and types of parameters, utilize implicit return values, and compose higher-order functions showcases the flexibility and power of closures in Groovy.

Understanding closure parameters and return values fundamentally supports modular and maintainable code, enhancing not only the developer's productivity but also the overall software quality.

5.4 Closures in Collections

Groovy provides powerful means to manipulate collections using closures. Collections, such as lists, maps, and sets, are fundamental structures in any programming language. This section will delve into how closures can be used to efficiently process and manage these collections, enabling you to write more concise and expressive code.

Using Closures with Lists

Lists are ordered collections, and closures can be applied to iterate, transform, filter, and reduce these lists. The each method iterates over list elements, applying the closure to each element.

```
// Initialize a list
def numbers = [1, 2, 3, 4, 5]

// Iterate using a closure
numbers.each { number ->
    println "Number: $number"
}
```

The output of the above code will be:

```
Number: 1
Number: 2
Number: 3
Number: 4
Number: 5
```

Groovy also supports the collect method, which transforms each element of a list by applying a specified closure and collects the results into a new list.

```
// Transform list using collect
def squares = numbers.collect { number ->
    number * number
}

println squares
```

The output of the above code will be:

```
[1, 4, 9, 16, 25]
```

Filtering a list can be done using the findAll method. This method evaluates the closure for each element and returns a new list containing elements for which the closure returns true.

```
// Filter list using findAll
def evenNumbers = numbers.findAll { it % 2 == 0 }

println evenNumbers
```

The output of the above code will be:

```
[2, 4]
```

Reducing a list to a single value can be accomplished with the inject method, which is synonymous with the fold or reduce operations in other functional programming paradigms.

```
// Reduce list using inject
def sum = numbers.inject(0) { accumulator, number ->
    accumulator + number
}

println sum
```

The output of the above code will be:

```
15
```

Using Closures with Maps

Maps are key-value pairs collections. Closures in Groovy allow for efficient manipulation of these structures as well. The each method is also applicable to maps, iterating over each entry.

```
// Initialize a map
def map = [name: "Groovy", type: "Programming Language", year: 2003]

// Iterate using a closure
map.each { key, value ->
    println "$key: $value"
}
```

The output of the above code will be:

```
name: Groovy
type: Programming Language
year: 2003
```

Maps can be transformed similarly to lists using the collectEntries method. This method applies a closure to each map entry and collects the results into a new map.

```
// Transform map using collectEntries
def upperCaseKeys = map.collectEntries { key, value ->
    [(key.toUpperCase()): value]
```

```
}
println upperCaseKeys
```

The output of the above code will be:

```
[NAME:Groovy, TYPE:Programming Language, YEAR:2003]
```

Filtering maps can be achieved using the findAll method, returning a map containing only those entries for which the closure evaluates to true.

```
// Filter map using findAll
def stringKeys = map.findAll { key, value ->
    key instanceof String
}
println stringKeys
```

The output of the above code will be:

```
[name:Groovy, type:Programming Language]
```

Using Closures with Sets

Sets are unordered collections of unique elements. Closures provide similar functionalities for sets as seen with lists. The each method iterates over set elements.

```
// Initialize a set
def uniqueNumbers = [1, 2, 3, 3, 4, 5, 5] as Set

// Iterate using a closure
uniqueNumbers.each { number ->
    println "Unique Number: $number"
}
```

The output of the above code will be:

```
Unique Number: 1
Unique Number: 2
Unique Number: 3
Unique Number: 4
Unique Number: 5
```

Transformation and filtering are achieved using collect and findAll methods respectively, similar to how they are used with lists.

```
// Transform set using collect
def factorial = uniqueNumbers.collect { number ->
    (1..number).inject(1) { acc, val -> acc * val }
}
println factorial
```

The output of the above code will be:

```
[1, 2, 6, 24, 120]
```

```
// Filter set using findAll
def greaterThanTwo = uniqueNumbers.findAll { it > 2 }

println greaterThanTwo
```

The output of the above code will be:

```
[3, 4, 5]
```

Employing closures with collections in Groovy can lead to more readable, maintainable, and expressive code. By transforming, filtering, and reducing collections, closures facilitate elegant solutions to common programming tasks.

5.5 Delegate and Owner in Closures

Understanding the concepts of delegate and owner in Groovy closures is crucial for mastering more advanced programming techniques. These two properties significantly influence how closures interact with their surrounding context and parent objects.

In Groovy, every closure has three special variables: this, owner, and delegate. Each of these pointers plays a unique role in the execution context of the closure.

this always refers to the enclosing class where the closure is defined.

owner points to the object in the closest context where the closure is defined.

delegate, initially set to the same object as owner, can be reassigned to any object, allowing flexible scoping and dynamic method resolution.

To demonstrate the role of owner and delegate, consider the following example:

```
class Enclosing {
    def whatIsThis() {
        def closure = {
            println "this: ${this.getClass().name}"
            println "owner: ${owner.getClass().name}"
            println "delegate: ${delegate.getClass().name}"
        }
        closure()
    }
}

class Outer {
    def method() {
```

```
        def enclosing = new Enclosing()
        enclosing.whatIsThis()
    }
}

new Outer().method()
```

The output from this code is as follows:

```
this: Enclosing
owner: Enclosing
delegate: Enclosing
```

In this scenario, within the closure, this, owner, and delegate all refer to the Enclosing class since that is where the closure is defined and invoked.

Let's delve deeper by introducing an example where we change the delegate property of the closure:

```
class Person {
    String name
    int age
}

class Worker {
    String job
}

class Enclosing {
    def closure

    Enclosing() {
        closure = {
            "Owner: ${owner}, Delegate: ${delegate}"
        }
    }

    String executeClosure() {
        closure()
    }
}

def person = new Person(name: 'John', age: 30)
def worker = new Worker(job: 'Developer')

def enclosingInstance = new Enclosing()
enclosingInstance.closure.delegate = worker

println enclosingInstance.executeClosure()
```

The expected output is:

```
Owner: Enclosing@... , Delegate: Worker@...
```

In this code, we define a closure within the Enclosing class and assign the worker instance as the delegate. When calling executeClosure, the closure's delegate points to Worker, showcasing different object contexts.

Having the ability to change the delegate dynamically is powerful, particularly when building DSLs. This allows extending the closure's abilities to access properties and methods of other objects, enhancing the flexibility and expressiveness of code.

Another scenario where understanding this, owner, and delegate proves valuable is nested closures. Groovy uses certain resolution strategies in such cases, prioritizing delegations. Observe the below example:

```
class Layered {
    def outerClosure

    Layered() {
        outerClosure = {
            def innerClosure = {
                println "this: ${this.getClass().name}"
                println "owner: ${owner.getClass().name}"
                println "delegate: ${delegate.getClass().name}"
            }
            innerClosure.delegate = this
            innerClosure()
        }
    }

    void execute() {
        outerClosure()
    }
}

new Layered().execute()
```

Output will be:

```
this: Layered
owner: Layered$_closure1
delegate: Layered
```

In this case, this refers to the instance of the Layered class since that is the parent class of both closures. However, owner changes to the closest enclosing closure (Layered_closure1), and delegate refers to the instance of Layered because we explicitly set it.

Recognizing the distinct contexts provided by this, owner, and delegate in Groovy closures enhances the ability to write clean, dynamic, and maintainable code, particularly in the realm of DSLs and nested structures. Remaining clear on what context is referred to by each keyword allows for precise control and predictable behavior in more complex closure usages.

5.6 Using Currying in Closures

Currying is a powerful concept in functional programming that involves transforming a function with multiple arguments into a sequence of functions, each with a single argument. In Groovy, currying allows us to fix a number of arguments to a closure, producing a new closure with fewer arguments. This technique is especially useful for creating more flexible and reusable code.

In Groovy, the curry() method is used to carry out currying on closures. Let's start with an example to see how currying works:

```
def multiply = { a, b -> a * b }
def multiplyByTwo = multiply.curry(2)

assert multiplyByTwo(5) == 10
```

In this example, the multiply closure takes two arguments a and b, and returns their product. Using the curry(2) method, we create a new closure multiplyByTwo where the first argument a is fixed to 2. Now, this new closure only requires one argument, which will be assigned to the second parameter b. Consequently, calling multiplyByTwo with 5 results in 2×5, which equals 10.

It is important to note that you can curry multiple arguments at different levels. Here's an example that demonstrates currying multiple arguments:

```
def greet = { greeting, name, punctuation -> "$greeting, $name$punctuation" }
def sayHello = greet.curry('Hello')
def sayHelloToJohn = sayHello.curry('John')

assert sayHelloToJohn('!') == 'Hello, John!'
```

In this code, the greet closure takes three parameters: greeting, name, and punctuation. The sayHello closure is created by currying the first argument greeting to "Hello". Then, by currying sayHello with the name "John", we produce sayHelloToJohn, a closure that only requires the punctuation argument. Calling sayHelloToJohn with "!" correctly returns "Hello, John!".

Groovy also offers a method called rcurry() to curry arguments from the rightmost side of the closure, and ncurry() to curry arguments at specific positions. Let's see examples of these methods:

```
def calculateVolume = { length, width, height -> length * width * height }
def calculateArea = calculateVolume.rcurry(1)
```

```
assert calculateArea(3, 4) == 12
```

In this example, the calculateVolume closure computes the volume of a rectangular solid. By applying rcurry(1), we create a new closure calculateArea that fixes the height parameter to 1, effectively turning the closure into an area calculation for a rectangle.

Next, we'll demonstrate ncurry() for more complex currying scenarios:

```
def performOperation = { x, y, z -> (x + y) * z }
def addFiveThenMultiply = performOperation.ncurry(0, 5)

assert addFiveThenMultiply(3, 2) == 16
```

Here, performOperation is a closure that performs an operation on three arguments. Using ncurry(0, 5), we fix the first argument, x, to 5. The new closure, addFiveThenMultiply, requires only y and z arguments, adding 5 to y before multiplying by z. Therefore, addFiveThenMultiply(3, 2) yields $(5+3) \times 2 = 16$.

Currying is a beneficial tool when configuring specific behavior in closures, as it allows for presetting arguments, achieving better modularity and code reusability. It also works well with Groovy's closures within Domain-Specific Languages (DSLs), enhancing flexibility by breaking down operations into smaller, composable pieces.

When employing currying in Groovy, developers should be conscientious of the closure's argument structure to ensure the correct application of fixed values, guaranteeing accurate functionality of the resulting closures.

5.7 Groovy's Built-in Higher Order Functions

In Groovy, higher-order functions are a powerful feature that allows functions to be passed as parameters and returned as values, enabling a functional programming style that enhances code flexibility and reusability. Groovy provides several built-in higher-order functions that work seamlessly with closures, making the language both expressive and concise.

One of the most common use cases for higher-order functions in Groovy is within collections. Groovy's List and Map classes contain numerous methods that accept closures, providing convenient mechanisms for performing operations such as transformation, filtering, and iteration.

```
def numbers = [1, 2, 3, 4, 5]

// Using the 'each' method to iterate through the list
numbers.each { number ->
    println number
}

// Using the 'collect' method to transform the list
def squaredNumbers = numbers.collect { number ->
    number * number
}
println squaredNumbers
```

In the example above, the each method iterates through every element in the numbers list, applying the provided closure to each element, which prints each number. The collect method, on the other hand, transforms each element in the numbers list by applying the closure, resulting in a new list where each element is the square of the original element.

Another important built-in higher-order function is findAll, which filters elements based on a condition specified in a closure. This method returns a new collection containing only the elements that satisfy the condition.

```
def evenNumbers = numbers.findAll { number ->
    number % 2 == 0
}
println evenNumbers
```

Here, the findAll method filters out the even numbers from the numbers list. The closure checks if each number is divisible by 2, and only those that satisfy this condition are included in the resultant list.

Groovy also supports the find method, which is similar to findAll but returns only the first element that matches the condition.

```
def firstEvenNumber = numbers.find { number ->
    number % 2 == 0
}
println firstEvenNumber
```

The find method returns the first even number it encounters in the list, demonstrating its usefulness in scenarios where only one matching element is needed.

Another useful higher-order function is any, which checks if any elements in the collection match the given condition.

```
def hasEvenNumber = numbers.any { number ->
    number % 2 == 0
}
println "Contains even number: $hasEvenNumber"
```

The any method evaluates the closure for each element in the numbers list and returns true if at least one element satisfies the condition; otherwise, it returns false.

Similarly, the every method checks if every element in the collection matches the given condition.

```
def allEvenNumbers = numbers.every { number ->
    number % 2 == 0
}
println "All are even numbers: $allEvenNumbers"
```

In this example, the every method returns false because not all elements in the numbers list are even. This method is valuable when a collective condition needs to be verified across all elements in a collection.

Groovy's higher-order functions also extend to maps. For example, the each method can be utilized to iterate through key-value pairs in a map.

```
def userMap = [name: 'Alice', age: 25, city: 'Seattle']

userMap.each { key, value ->
    println "$key: $value"
}
```

In this snippet, the each method iterates through the userMap map, printing each key and its associated value. This provides a clear and concise way to process map entries using closures.

The collectEntries method is another higher-order function that transforms each entry in a map and constructs a new map based on the transformation.

```
def transformedMap = userMap.collectEntries { key, value ->
    [key.toUpperCase(), value]
}
println transformedMap
```

Here, the collectEntries method converts each key in the userMap to uppercase, resulting in a new map where all keys are in uppercase while preserving the original values.

Algorithm 1: Operations using Groovy's built-in higher-order functions

Data: numbers list, userMap
Result: squaredNumbers, evenNumbers, firstEvenNumber, hasEvenNumber, allEvenNumbers, transformedMap

```
each on numbers;
collect on numbers → squaredNumbers;
findAll on numbers → evenNumbers;
find on numbers → firstEvenNumber;
any on numbers → hasEvenNumber;
every on numbers → allEvenNumbers;
each on userMap;
collectEntries on userMap → transformedMap;
```

These higher-order functions, along with many others, exemplify Groovy's functional programming capabilities, providing developers with tools to write more concise, expressive, and modular code. By leveraging these functions, one can easily perform complex operations on collections and maps with minimal boilerplate code. Understanding and utilizing these built-in higher-order functions is essential for mastering Groovy's functional programming paradigm.

5.8 Functional Programming Techniques

Functional programming is a paradigm centered around the usage of functions as first-class citizens. In Groovy, closures are integral to achieving functional programming concepts. This section explores various techniques to leverage functional programming within Groovy, including pure functions, immutable data structures, higher-order functions, and the use of closures.

Pure functions are functions where the output is determined solely by the input parameters and does not cause side effects. Side effects include modifying global variables, changing input parameters, and performing I/O operations. An example of a pure function in Groovy:

```
// Pure function - no side effects and depends solely on input parameters
def add(a, b) {
    return a + b
}
assert add(2, 3) == 5
```

In contrast, impure functions have side effects, which can lead to difficult-to-track bugs and make testing harder. Consider the following impure function example:

```
def count = 0

// Impure function - modifies external state
def increment() {
    count += 1
}

increment()
assert count == 1
```

Immutability is another core concept in functional programming, promoting the idea that data structures are not to be changed after creation. In Groovy, Lists and other collections can be made immutable using the asImmutable method. This encourages safer code by preventing unintended modifications:

```
def immutableList = [1, 2, 3].asImmutable()

// Attempting to modify immutable list leads to an exception
try {
    immutableList.add(4)
} catch (UnsupportedOperationException e) {
    assert e.message.contains('Unsupported operation')
}
```

Higher-order functions are functions that take other functions as parameters or return them as results. Using closures in Groovy, we can easily create higher-order functions. Here is an example illustrating a higher-order function that applies a given closure to each element in a list:

```
def applyToEachElement(list, closure) {
    list.collect(closure)
}

def list = [1, 2, 3]
def doubleClosure = { it * 2 }
def doubledList = applyToEachElement(list, doubleClosure)

assert doubledList == [2, 4, 6]
```

Closures as first-class citizens provide the flexibility needed for functional programming. For example, you can pass a closure as a parameter to another function or assign it to a variable. Below is an example where a closure is assigned to a variable and then invoked:

```
def greeter = { name -> "Hello, $name!" }

assert greeter('World') == 'Hello, World!'
```

Currying, another functional programming technique, involves transforming a function that takes multiple arguments into a series of functions that each take a single argument. This is especially useful for creating partially applied functions with some preset arguments. Groovy supports currying using the curry method:

```
def multiply(a, b) {
    return a * b
}

def multiplyByTwo = multiply.curry(2)

assert multiplyByTwo(5) == 10
```

In addition to currying, Groovy facilitates the creation of partial functions using the ncurry method, which allows currying of parameters not just from the leftmost positions:

```
def volume(length, width, height) {
    return length * width * height
}

def fixedWidthVolume = volume.ncurry(1, 3) // fix width to 3

assert fixedWidthVolume(2, 4) == 24 // length 2, width 3 (fixed), height 4
```

Functional programming also extends to handling data transformations efficiently using map, filter, and reduce operations. These operations are intrinsic to many functional programming languages and are used for processing collections in a declarative manner:

```
def numbers = [1, 2, 3, 4, 5]

// Map operation to square each number
def squares = numbers.collect { it * 2 }
assert squares == [2, 4, 6, 8, 10]

// Filter operation to retain only even numbers
def evenNumbers = numbers.findAll { it % 2 == 0 }
assert evenNumbers == [2, 4]

// Reduce operation to sum all numbers
def sum = numbers.inject(0) { acc, num -> acc + num }
assert sum == 15
```

Groovy's syntactic flexibility and robust support for closures significantly lower the barriers to employing functional programming techniques. These techniques promote code that is modular, easier to reason about, and inherently testable, thus leading to higher quality software.

5.9 Combining Closures and DSLs

Domain-Specific Languages (DSLs) are specialized mini-languages designed to solve problems in specific domains more effectively than general-purpose languages. Groovy, with its flexible syntax and dynamic nature, is particularly well-suited to creating internal DSLs. Closures, being first-class citizens in Groovy, play a crucial role in enabling and enhancing DSL capabilities. This section explores the synergy between closures and DSLs in Groovy, demonstrating how closures can be leveraged to design intuitive and powerful DSLs.

A key advantage of using closures in DSLs is their ability to encapsulate behavior and defer execution, providing a clean and readable syntax. Closures can be passed around as arguments, returned from methods, and stored in variables, allowing DSLs to mimic natural language constructs.

To illustrate the integration of closures with DSLs, consider a simple DSL for defining configurations. This example will show how closures can be used to build a configuration block that specifies settings for a hypothetical application.

We begin by defining a configuration class that utilizes closures to set various parameters:

```
class Configuration {
    Map settings = [:]

    void setting(String key, def value) {
        settings[key] = value
    }

    void settings(Closure closure) {
        closure.delegate = this
        closure.resolveStrategy = Closure.DELEGATE_ONLY
        closure.call()
    }
}
```

Here, the Configuration class includes a map to store settings and a method to add or update a setting. The settings method accepts a closure and sets its delegate to the current instance of Configuration, ensuring that any calls within the closure are delegated to this instance.

Next, we define a DSL script using our configuration class:

```
def config = new Configuration()
config.settings {
    setting 'database', 'MySQL'
    setting 'host', 'localhost'
```

```
    setting 'port', 3306
    setting 'maxThreads', 100
}

println config.settings
```

Executing this script will produce the following output:

```
[database:MySQL, host:localhost, port:3306, maxThreads:100]
```

The example demonstrates how closures provide a domain-specific language with a clean and intuitive syntax for configuring an application. The closeness of the DSL to natural language enhances readability and maintainability.

Another powerful feature of closures in DSLs is their ability to capture contextual information through variables. Consider an example DSL for building SQL queries:

```
class SqlBuilder {
    StringBuilder query = new StringBuilder()

    void select(String columns) {
        query << "SELECT ${columns} "
    }

    void from(String table) {
        query << "FROM ${table} "
    }

    void where(Closure closure) {
        query << "WHERE "
        closure.delegate = this
        closure.resolveStrategy = Closure.DELEGATE_ONLY
        closure.call()
    }

    void eq(String column, def value) {
        query << "${column} = '${value}' "
    }

    String build() {
        return query.toString()
    }
}
```

The SqlBuilder class provides methods to construct different parts of an SQL query. The where method accepts a closure, which allows for defining complex conditions within the DSL.

Using this class, we can create a DSL script to build an SQL query:

```
def sql = new SqlBuilder()
sql.select '*'
sql.from 'users'
sql.where {
    eq 'name', 'John Doe'
```

```
    eq 'status', 'active'
}
println sql.build()
```

The execution output will be:

```
SELECT * FROM users WHERE name = 'John Doe' status = 'active'
```

This example showcases how closures enhance the expressiveness and flexibility of a DSL. The where method's closure can contain nested method calls, allowing for complex query conditions to be represented succinctly.

Groovy's closures facilitate the definition of adaptable and modular DSLs. By encapsulating behavior, capturing context, and deferring execution, closures contribute significantly to the design of intuitive and powerful domain-specific languages. This enables developers to build DSLs that are not only syntactically similar to natural language but also robust and maintainable, improving the overall efficiency and readability of the code.

5.10 Practical Examples of Functional Programming

To solidify our understanding of functional programming principles within Groovy, we will explore several practical examples that leverage closures and higher-order functions. These will illustrate how to apply functional programming techniques to real-world problems, enhancing code readability, modularity, and maintainability.

First, consider the task of filtering a list of integers to retain only the even numbers. Using Groovy's findAll method, we can elegantly achieve this with a closure. The findAll method is a higher-order function that takes a closure as its argument and returns a new list containing all elements for which the closure returns true.

```
def numbers = [1, 2, 3, 4, 5, 6, 7, 8, 9, 10]
def evenNumbers = numbers.findAll { it % 2 == 0 }
println(evenNumbers)
```

```
[2, 4, 6, 8, 10]
```

In this example, the closure { it % 2 == 0 } is passed to findAll, and evenNumbers holds the resulting list of even integers.

Another common functional programming task is transforming a list of data. Suppose we have a list of strings, and we want to convert each string to uppercase. We can use the collect method, another powerful higher-order function, along with a closure that defines the transformation logic.

```
def words = ["hello", "world", "groovy", "functional", "programming"]
def upperCaseWords = words.collect { it.toUpperCase() }
println(upperCaseWords)
```

[HELLO, WORLD, GROOVY, FUNCTIONAL, PROGRAMMING]

The closure { it.toUpperCase() } is applied to each element in the words list, producing a new list with all strings converted to uppercase.

Functional programming often involves combining multiple functions to process data in steps. Groovy's method chaining allows for fluent API design. Consider filtering a list of integers to find those divisible by 3 and then squaring these numbers. We can use the sequence of findAll and collect.

```
def numbers = [1, 2, 3, 4, 5, 6, 7, 8, 9, 10]
def results = numbers.findAll { it % 3 == 0 }.collect { it * it }
println(results)
```

[9, 36, 81]

The findAll method filters the elements divisible by 3, and the collect method squares each of these filtered elements.

Next, let us delve into a practical example involving maps (dictionaries). Suppose we have a map of student names and their corresponding scores, and we need to determine students who scored above a certain threshold.

```
def studentScores = [Alice: 85, Bob: 72, Charlie: 90, Dave: 63]
def topStudents = studentScores.findAll { name, score -> score > 75 }
println(topStudents)
```

[Alice:85, Charlie:90]

In this example, the closure { name, score -> score > 75 } filters the map entries, producing a new map containing only the students who scored above 75.

Another useful functional programming technique is the reduction of a collection to a single value. The inject method in Groovy serves this purpose. For instance, to compute the sum of a list of numbers, we can use inject with an initial accumulator value of 0.

```
def numbers = [1, 2, 3, 4, 5]
def sum = numbers.inject(0) { acc, num -> acc + num }
println(sum)
```

15

Here, the closure { acc, num -> acc + num } adds each element of the list to the accumulator acc, resulting in the total sum.

Groovy's support for currying enables partial function application. For example, consider a closure that adds two numbers. We can create a new closure that adds a fixed number to any given number using currying.

```
def add = { a, b -> a + b }
def addFive = add.curry(5)
println(addFive(10))
```

15

The addFive closure is a specialized version of add that always adds 5 to its argument.

Combining these functional techniques, we can solve more complex problems. Suppose we need to process a list of transactions to find the total value of transactions above a certain threshold. We can use findAll, collect, and inject.

```
def transactions = [120.0, 45.5, 300.0, 75.0, 200.0]
def threshold = 100.0
def totalValue = transactions.findAll { it > threshold }
                             .inject(0.0) { sum, value -> sum + value }
println(totalValue)
```

620.0

In this example, the transactions list is first filtered to retain only those above the threshold. The resulting list is then summed using the inject method.

These practical examples demonstrate the power and flexibility of functional programming in Groovy, illustrating how closures and higher-order functions can be combined to write expressive and efficient code.

Chapter 6

Object-Oriented Programming in Groovy

This chapter covers the essential principles of Object-Oriented Programming (OOP) in Groovy, including the creation and use of classes and objects, attributes, and methods. It discusses constructors, initializers, inheritance, polymorphism, encapsulation, and access modifiers. Additionally, it explores abstract classes, interfaces, traits, and mixins, as well as the use of Groovy's @CompileStatic annotation. Practical advice on best practices for OOP in Groovy ensures readers can design robust and scalable applications.

6.1 Introduction to Object-Oriented Programming (OOP)

Object-Oriented Programming (OOP) is a paradigm centered on objects and data rather than actions and logic. This paradigm facilitates the organization of code around objects rather than functions and logic, allowing us to model real-world entities more effectively. In OOP, an object can be considered a self-contained component with properties (attributes) and behaviors (methods). Using OOP principles, software development becomes more manageable, maintainable, and scalable.

OOP in Groovy, a powerful and dynamic language for the Java platform, leverages the flexibility and ease of use typical of dynamically typed languages while providing robust class and object management.

Key Concepts:

- **Classes and Objects:** A class is a blueprint for creating objects (instances). Each object created from a class can have different attribute values while sharing the same behaviors.
- **Attributes and Methods:** Attributes (or fields) represent the data stored in an object, while methods define the actions or behaviors of the object.
- **Encapsulation:** Encapsulation is the concept of bundling data and methods that operate on the data within one unit, usually a class, and restricting access to some of the object's components.
- **Inheritance:** Inheritance allows a new class to acquire the properties and methods of an existing class. This helps in reusing and organizing code effectively.
- **Polymorphism:** Polymorphism allows objects to be treated as instances of their parent class rather than their actual class. This leads to simpler code and more flexible interfaces.
- **Abstraction:** Abstraction simplifies complex reality by modeling classes appropriate to the problem, and working at the most relevant level of inheritance for a particular aspect of the problem.

Classes and Objects in Groovy:

In Groovy, defining a class is straightforward. Here is a simple example of a Groovy class definition, an instantiation of an object from that class, and invoking its methods:

```
// Define a Groovy Class
class Person {
    String name
    int age

    void displayInfo() {
        println "Name: ${name}, Age: ${age}"
    }
}

// Instantiate an Object
def person = new Person(name: 'Alice', age: 30)
person.displayInfo()
```

The above code snippet illustrates a Person class with two attributes: name and age. The displayInfo method is used to print these attributes. An instance of the Person class is created with the name 'Alice' and age 30, and the displayInfo method is called to display the information.

Encapsulation in Groovy:

Encapsulation is achieved through access modifiers in Groovy. By default, Groovy provides public visibility for class members. We can restrict access using private and protected keywords.

```
class Account {
    private String accountNumber
    private double balance

    // Constructor
    Account(String accNumber, double bal) {
        this.accountNumber = accNumber
        this.balance = bal
    }

    // 'get' and 'set' methods for balance
    double getBalance() {
        return balance
    }

    void deposit(double amount) {
        if(amount > 0) {
            balance += amount
        }
    }

    void withdraw(double amount) {
        if(amount > 0 && amount <= balance) {
            balance -= amount
        }
    }
}
```

In the Account class, the accountNumber and balance attributes are declared private, preventing direct access from outside the class. Instead, methods such as getBalance(), deposit(), and withdraw() are provided to interact with these attributes. This ensures the integrity and encapsulation of the object's state.

Inheritance in Groovy:

Inheritance promotes code reuse and logical hierarchical classifications. A subclass inherits fields and methods from its superclass, allowing enhancements or changes without modifying the superclass. Below is an example demonstrating inheritance in Groovy:

```
class Vehicle {
    String brand
    String color
```

```
    void startEngine() {
        println "${brand} engine started."
    }
}

class Car extends Vehicle {
    int doors

    void displayDetails() {
        println "Brand: ${brand}, Color: ${color}, Doors: ${doors}"
    }
}

// Instantiate the subclass
def myCar = new Car(brand: 'Toyota', color: 'red', doors: 4)
myCar.startEngine()
myCar.displayDetails()
```

In this example, the Car class extends the Vehicle class, inheriting its properties and methods. The Car class adds its own property, doors, and a method, displayDetails(). When we create an instance of Car, it possesses both the properties and methods from both Vehicle and Car.

Polymorphism in Groovy:

Polymorphism allows methods to be used generically across different objects. Here, a method call regards the object's type during runtime, enabling more versatile interfaces and recycled code.

```
class Animal {
    void sound() {
        println "Some sound..."
    }
}

class Dog extends Animal {
    void sound() {
        println "Bark"
    }
}

class Cat extends Animal {
    void sound() {
        println "Meow"
    }
}

def makeSound(Animal animal) {
    animal.sound()
}

makeSound(new Dog())
makeSound(new Cat())
```

The Animal class declares a sound() method. Dog and Cat classes override this method with their implementations. The makeSound(Animal animal) function accepts any Animal type and calls the sound() method, demonstrating polymorphism as it acts on different subclasses.

Ultimately, understanding OOP concepts is crucial for developing efficient and logical applications in Groovy. These foundational principles–classes, objects, encapsulation, inheritance, and polymorphism–form the bedrock of sophisticated and maintainable codebases. Integrating these concepts skillfully enhances a programmer's ability to leverage Groovy's capabilities fully for robust and scalable software development.

6.2 Classes and Objects in Groovy

Classes and objects are the fundamental building blocks of Object-Oriented Programming (OOP) in Groovy. A *class* is a blueprint for creating objects, providing initial values for state (member variables) and implementations of behavior (member functions or methods). An *object* is an instance of a class. Exploring the nature of classes and objects in Groovy entails understanding their syntax, properties, methods, object instantiation, and dynamic features inherent to the language.

Groovy simplifies the creation and use of classes, allowing for concise and expressive code. Let us examine the basics of defining a class and creating objects from that class.

Defining a Class
A class declaration in Groovy begins with the class keyword followed by the class name. Member variables, also known as attributes or properties, and methods are defined within the class body. Consider the following example of a simple class definition:

```
class Car {
    String brand
    String model
    int year

    void displayDetails() {
        println "Brand: ${brand}, Model: ${model}, Year: ${year}"
    }
}
```

In this example, the Car class has three properties: brand, model, and year. It also has one method, displayDetails, which outputs the details of the car.

Creating Objects

To create an instance of a class, the new keyword is used. The following line creates an instance of the Car class:

```
def myCar = new Car()
```

This statement initializes a new object, myCar, of type Car. Once instantiated, the properties of the object can be accessed and modified as follows:

```
myCar.brand = 'Toyota'
myCar.model = 'Camry'
myCar.year = 2020

myCar.displayDetails()
```

The output of the displayDetails method will be:

```
Brand: Toyota, Model: Camry, Year: 2020
```

Groovy Bean Properties

In Groovy, properties are associated with getter and setter methods implicitly. For instance, the property brand is internally managed by getter (getBrand()) and setter (setBrand(String)) methods. These methods are automatically generated, providing convenient access and modification of properties.

Constructors

Constructors are special methods invoked when an object is instantiated. Groovy provides default constructors and allows the definition of custom constructors. Here is how to define a custom constructor for the Car class:

```
class Car {
    String brand
    String model
    int year

    Car(String brand, String model, int year) {
        this.brand = brand
        this.model = model
        this.year = year
    }

    void displayDetails() {
        println "Brand: ${brand}, Model: ${model}, Year: ${year}"
    }
}
```

Using this constructor, an object can be instantiated with specific property values:

```
def myCar = new Car('Honda', 'Civic', 2018)
myCar.displayDetails()
```

The output will be:

```
Brand: Honda, Model: Civic, Year: 2018
```

Dynamic Nature of Groovy

One of the powerful features of Groovy is its dynamic nature. Properties and methods can be added to classes and objects at runtime. This adds flexibility and extends the capabilities of classes and objects beyond their static definitions.

Adding Properties at Runtime

In Groovy, it is possible to add properties to an object after it has been created:

```
myCar.color = 'Blue'
println "Color: ${myCar.color}"
```

The output will be:

```
Color: Blue
```

ExpandoMetaClass

The ExpandoMetaClass feature allows modifications to existing classes, ensuring dynamic method additions:

```
Car.metaClass.startEngine = { -> println "Engine started for ${brand} ${model}" }
myCar.startEngine()
```

The output will be:

```
Engine started for Honda Civic
```

Mixing Static and Dynamic Typing

Groovy allows for both static and dynamic typing. Static typing defines types explicitly, while dynamic typing allows type determination at runtime. While static typing provides compile-time type checking, dynamic typing provides flexibility but may introduce runtime type errors. Consider the following dynamic typing example:

```
def dynamicCar = new Car('Mazda', 'MX-5', 2021)
dynamicCar.horsepower = 181
println "Horsepower: ${dynamicCar.horsepower}"
```

The output will be:

```
Horsepower: 181
```

While Groovy's dynamic capabilities are powerful, balancing between static and dynamic typing can lead to more maintainable and error-resistant code.

Expanding Object Methods
In addition to adding properties, Groovy allows the addition of methods to objects dynamically. For instance:

```
Car.metaClass.stopEngine = { -> println "Engine stopped for ${brand} ${model}" }
myCar.stopEngine()
```

Output:

```
Engine stopped for Honda Civic
```

Understanding the interplay between classes and objects in Groovy provides a foundation for mastering more advanced OOP concepts. The dynamic capabilities of Groovy also introduce techniques to enhance the flexibility and expressiveness of class and object interactions.

6.3 Attributes and Methods

In Groovy, attributes (often referred to as fields) and methods are fundamental components of classes. Attributes represent the state or data of a class, while methods define the behavior. Understanding how to properly define and utilize attributes and methods is crucial for developing robust and maintainable Groovy applications.

Attributes in Groovy can be defined using variable declarations within a class. Groovy provides syntactic sugar that makes its class definitions cleaner and more concise than those in languages such as Java. For example, consider the following class definition:

```
class Person {
    String name
    int age
}
```

In this example, name and age are attributes of the Person class. The types of these attributes are String and int, respectively.

Groovy automatically generates getter and setter methods for these attributes, which follow JavaBean conventions. This means you can access and modify the attributes like so:

```
Person person = new Person()
person.name = 'John Doe' // Sets the name attribute
```

```
person.age = 30 // Sets the age attribute

println person.name // Retrieves the name attribute
println person.age // Retrieves the age attribute
```

```
John Doe
30
```

These getters and setters can be explicitly defined if custom behavior is needed. To manually define a getter or setter, use the following syntax:

```
class Person {
    private String name
    private int age

    String getName() {
        return name
    }

    void setName(String name) {
        this.name = name
    }

    int getAge() {
        return age
    }

    void setAge(int age) {
        this.age = age
    }
}
```

Methods in Groovy, similar to attributes, can be defined within a class to execute various operations. Here is an example that adds methods to the Person class:

```
class Person {
    String name
    int age

    void displayInfo() {
        println "Name: ${name}, Age: ${age}"
    }

    String getFullName() {
        return "Mr./Ms. ${name}"
    }
}
```

In this example, the displayInfo() method prints the information of the Person instance, while the getFullName() method returns a formatted string using the name attribute. These methods can be invoked as follows:

```
Person person = new Person(name: 'Jane Doe', age: 25)
person.displayInfo()
println person.getFullName()
```

```
Name: Jane Doe, Age: 25
Mr./Ms. Jane Doe
```

Groovy overloads methods in a streamlined manner. Method overloading allows multiple methods in the same class to have the same name but different parameters. For example:

```
class MathOperations {
    int add(int a, int b) {
        return a + b
    }

    double add(double a, double b) {
        return a + b
    }

    int add(int a, int b, int c) {
        return a + b + c
    }
}
```

The MathOperations class has three add methods, each with different parameters. The appropriate method is chosen based on the arguments passed:

```
MathOperations math = new MathOperations()
println math.add(1, 2)
println math.add(1.5, 2.5)
println math.add(1, 2, 3)
```

```
3
4.0
6
```

It is also essential to understand the concept of method overriding when dealing with inheritance in Groovy. When a subclass provides a specific implementation for a method declared in its superclass, it overrides that method. Here's an example that extends the Person class:

```
class Employee extends Person {
    String company

    void displayInfo() {
        super.displayInfo()
        println "Company: ${company}"
    }
}
```

In this Employee class, the displayInfo() method is overridden to also print the company attribute:

```
Employee employee = new Employee(name: 'John Doe', age: 30, company: 'ACME
    Corp.')
employee.displayInfo()
```

```
Name: John Doe, Age: 30
Company: ACME Corp.
```

Attributes and methods form the backbone of any Groovy class, enabling the encapsulation of data and the definition of behaviors essential for object-oriented design. Proficiency in these areas is foundational to mastering Groovy programming.

6.4 Constructors and Initializers

Understanding constructors and initializers is crucial for efficiently creating and initializing instance variables in Groovy classes. Constructors are special methods within a class that are invoked when an instance of the class is created. Initializers, on the other hand, allow for the setup of instance variables either directly at the point of declaration or using initializer blocks.

A constructor in Groovy is defined similarly to how it is in Java. The primary differences stem from Groovy's syntactic sugar and default behaviors.

Consider the following Groovy class Person with instance variables name and age:

```
class Person {
    String name
    int age

    // Constructor
    Person(String name, int age) {
        this.name = name
        this.age = age
    }
}
```

When you create an instance of Person, the constructor is called, allowing for initialization of the instance variables:

```
// Creating a new Person object
def person = new Person("John Doe", 30)
```

The person object now has its name attribute set to "John Doe" and its age attribute set to 30.

Default Constructor

In Groovy, if no constructor is provided, a default no-argument constructor is automatically generated. Thus, the class:

```
class Animal {
```

```
    String type
    int legs
}
```

Can be instantiated with:

```
def animal = new Animal()
```

Both instance variables, type and legs, are initialized to null and 0 respectively, their default values.

Constructor Overloading

Groovy supports constructor overloading, which allows multiple constructors with different parameter lists within the same class:

```
class Book {
    String title
    String author
    int pages

    // No-arg constructor
    Book() {}

    // Parameterized constructor
    Book(String title, String author, int pages) {
        this.title = title
        this.author = author
        this.pages = pages
    }
}
```

You can now create Book objects using different constructors:

```
def emptyBook = new Book()
def filledBook = new Book("Groovy Programming", "Jane Smith", 450)
```

Initializer Blocks

Initializer blocks are another powerful feature in Groovy for setting up instance variables. They allow complex initialization code that cannot be achieved via standard constructor parameters alone. Groovy supports both static and instance initializers.

An instance initializer block runs every time an instance is created, similar to instance variable declaration assignments:

```
class Car {
    String model
    int year

    // Instance Initializer Block
    {
        model = "Default Model"
        year = 2000
```

```
    }

    // Construct with parameters and override initialization
    Car(String model, int year) {
        this.model = model
        this.year = year
    }
}
```

The above class ensures that even if no parameters are supplied, model and year have default values set through the initializer block.

Combining Initializer Blocks and Constructors

Combining both initializer blocks and constructors can be beneficial as it permits assigning default values while allowing the flexibility of parameter overwriting:

```
class Laptop {
    String brand
    String processor

    // Instance Initializer Block
    {
        brand = "GenericBrand"
        processor = "Core i5"
    }

    // Parameterized constructor
    Laptop(String brand, String processor) {
        this.brand = brand
        this.processor = processor
    }
}
```

Static Initializer Blocks

Static initializers are executed once when the class is loaded. These are useful for initializing static variables:

```
class Config {
    static String configSetting

    // Static Initializer Block
    static {
        configSetting = "DefaultConfig"
    }
}
```

The configSetting variable is initialized with "DefaultConfig" the first time the Config class is loaded.

Applying constructors and initializers skillfully can lead to robust class designs in Groovy, facilitating flexible and clear object instantiation and initialization patterns.

6.5 Inheritance and Polymorphism

Inheritance and polymorphism form the backbone of Object-Oriented Programming (OOP) in Groovy, enabling the creation of reusable and scalable software components. Understanding these concepts is essential for designing systems that are both modular and maintainable.

Inheritance allows a class (referred to as the subclass or derived class) to inherit fields and methods from another class (referred to as the superclass or base class). Through inheritance, a subclass can extend the functionality of a superclass, facilitating code reuse and the creation of a class hierarchy. In Groovy, classes can inherit from one and only one superclass, following the principle of single inheritance.

Consider the following example:

```
class Animal {
    String name

    void eat() {
        println("${name} is eating.")
    }
}

class Dog extends Animal {

    void bark() {
        println("${name} is barking.")
    }
}

Dog dog = new Dog()
dog.name = "Buddy"
dog.eat() // Inherited from Animal
dog.bark() // Defined in Dog
```

In this example, the Dog class inherits the name attribute and the eat() method from the Animal class. Additionally, Dog adds a bark() method, illustrating how subclasses can extend superclasses with additional behavior.

Polymorphism, on the other hand, allows objects to be treated as instances of their parent class rather than their actual class. This enables a single interface to be used for a general class of actions. The most common use of polymorphism in Groovy is through method overriding, where a subclass provides a specific implementation of a method already defined in its superclass.

Given the previous classes, let us see how polymorphism works using method overriding:

```
class Animal {
    String name

    void makeSound() {
        println("${name} is making a sound.")
    }
}

class Dog extends Animal {

    @Override
    void makeSound() {
        println("${name} is barking.")
    }
}

class Cat extends Animal {

    @Override
    void makeSound() {
        println("${name} is meowing.")
    }
}

Animal myDog = new Dog()
myDog.name = "Buddy"
myDog.makeSound() // Outputs: Buddy is barking.

Animal myCat = new Cat()
myCat.name = "Whiskers"
myCat.makeSound() // Outputs: Whiskers is meowing.
```

In this code snippet, both Dog and Cat override the makeSound() method from the Animal class. The overridden methods provide specialized behavior for each subclass, showcasing polymorphism. Notice how the Animal reference can hold objects of both Dog and Cat types, and the correct makeSound() method is called based on the actual object type.

When designing with inheritance, it is common to define methods in the superclass that are intended to be overridden. The @Override annotation is used to indicate that a method is overriding a method from its superclass, making the code more readable and reducing errors. However, it is good practice to only use inheritance when there is a genuine is-a relationship. Misuse of inheritance can lead to fragile and hard-to-maintain codebases.

Another aspect of inheritance in Groovy is the use of the super keyword to explicitly call superclass methods or constructors. This can be crucial when a subclass needs to extend or customize the behavior of its superclass. Consider the following example:

```
class Animal {
    String name
```

```
    Animal(String name) {
        this.name = name
    }

    void eat() {
        println("${name} is eating.")
    }
}

class Dog extends Animal {

    Dog(String name) {
        super(name) // Call to the superclass constructor
    }

    @Override
    void eat() {
        super.eat() // Call to the superclass method
        println("${name} is eating dog food.")
    }
}

Dog myDog = new Dog("Buddy")
myDog.eat()
// Outputs:
// Buddy is eating.
// Buddy is eating dog food.
```

Here, the super keyword is used within the Dog constructor to invoke the constructor of the Animal class, initializing the name attribute. Additionally, the overridden eat() method in the Dog class calls the eat() method from the Animal class, illustrating how superclass functionality can be incorporated and extended within a subclass.

Understanding inheritance and polymorphism in Groovy enables developers to design more flexible and extensible systems, leveraging the hierarchy and shared behavior of classes while allowing for specific customizations in subclasses. These principles facilitate the creation of robust and scalable object-oriented designs, contributing to their widespread use in software engineering.

6.6 Encapsulation and Access Modifiers

Encapsulation is a fundamental concept in Object-Oriented Programming (OOP) that refers to the bundling of data (attributes) and methods (functions) that operate on the data into a single unit, or class. By encapsulating data, we hide the internal state of an object from the outside world and expose only those operations necessary for the object's intended use. This principle helps to maintain a clear separation between an object's internal state and its external behavior, promoting modularity and reducing complexity.

In Groovy, as in other OOP languages, encapsulation is achieved using access modifiers. These modifiers control the visibility of class members (attributes and methods) from other classes. Groovy supports the following access modifiers:

- public
- protected
- private
- package-private (default)

Each modifier specifies a different level of access control:

- public: Members declared as public are accessible from any other class. This is the highest level of visibility.
- protected: Members declared as protected are accessible within their own class, from subclasses, and within the same package.
- private: Members declared as private are accessible only within their own class. This is the most restrictive level of visibility.
- package-private: If no access modifier is specified, Groovy assumes package-private access. Members are accessible only within classes in the same package.

Consider the following example that demonstrates the use of these access modifiers in Groovy:

```
class Person {
    public String name
    protected int age
    private String socialSecurityNumber
    String email // package-private access

    public String getName() {
        return name
    }

    protected int getAge() {
        return age
    }

    private String getSocialSecurityNumber() {
        return socialSecurityNumber
```

```
    }

    String getEmail() { // package-private access
        return email
    }
}
```

In the above example, the Person class has four attributes, each with a different level of visibility:

- name: publicly accessible
- age: protected access
- socialSecurityNumber: private access
- email: package-private access

The same visibility rules apply to methods. This encapsulation of data ensures that only relevant parts of an object's internal state are exposed while the rest remains hidden and protected.

Encapsulation allows changes to be made to a class's implementation without affecting other parts of the program. For instance, if the Person class's internal logic changes, other classes that interact with it through its public interface can remain unaffected.

Consider modifying the age attribute from protected to private and providing public getters and setters to access and modify the value indirectly:

```
class Person {
    public String name
    private int age
    private String socialSecurityNumber
    String email // package-private access

    public String getName() {
        return name
    }

    public void setName(String name) {
        this.name = name
    }

    public int getAge() {
        return age
    }

    public void setAge(int age) {
        if (age > 0) {
            this.age = age
        }
    }
```

```
    private String getSocialSecurityNumber() {
        return socialSecurityNumber
    }

    String getEmail() { // package-private access
        return email
    }
}
```

In this modification, the age attribute is now private, and thus directly inaccessible from outside the Person class. Instead, it can be accessed and modified through the public getAge() and setAge(int age) methods. The setter method includes a constraint that ensures age cannot be set to a negative value, illustrating how encapsulation can be used to enforce valid states for an object's attributes.

To ensure the Person class's interface remains flexible and unrestrictive, Groovy also permits the use of property accessors. Properties in Groovy are implicitly backed by private fields, and the default getter and setter methods can be overridden as needed:

```
class Person {
    public String name
    private int age

    int getAge() {
        return age
    }

    void setAge(int age) {
        if (age > 0) {
            this.age = age
        }
    }
}
```

Thus, encapsulation combined with the appropriate use of access modifiers creates robust and maintainable code. They help prevent unintended interactions between different parts of a program and provide the means to expose only the relevant parts of a class's functionality. This approach is essential for building scalable and error-resistant applications.

6.7 Abstract Classes and Interfaces

In Groovy, abstract classes and interfaces are fundamental constructs to enable powerful Object-Oriented Programming (OOP) paradigms. They facilitate the designing of complex systems by providing structured and reusable code. Understanding how to use these constructs effectively is critical for mastering Groovy programming.

An abstract class in Groovy is a class that cannot be instantiated on its own and is meant to be subclassed. It can contain concrete methods, which have actual method implementations, as well as abstract methods, which are declared without an implementation. An abstract class is useful when creating a base class with common functionality shared across multiple subclasses, while leaving certain methods to be implemented by each subclass.

Below is an example of declaring an abstract class in Groovy:

```
abstract class Animal {
    String name

    // Abstract method with no implementation
    abstract void makeSound()

    // Concrete method
    void eat() {
        println("${name} is eating.")
    }
}
```

In this example, Animal is an abstract class with an abstract method makeSound() and a concrete method eat(). Any subclass inheriting from Animal must provide an implementation for the makeSound() method.

Groovy interfaces, similar to those in Java, are collections of method definitions (abstract methods) that a class promises to implement. Interfaces are a way to achieve multiple inheritance. A class can implement multiple interfaces, providing a mechanism to model complex inheritance structures.

An example of an interface in Groovy:

```
interface Flyable {
    void fly() // Abstract method
}

interface Swimmable {
    void swim() // Abstract method
}
```

Here, the Flyable and Swimmable interfaces declare the methods fly() and swim(), respectively. A class implementing an interface must provide concrete implementations for all the abstract methods defined in that interface.

A class can implement multiple interfaces, as shown below:

```
class Duck extends Animal implements Flyable, Swimmable {
    Duck(String name) {
        super.name = name
    }

    @Override
    void makeSound() {
        println("${name} says Quack!")
    }

    @Override
    void fly() {
        println("${name} is flying.")
    }

    @Override
    void swim() {
        println("${name} is swimming.")
    }
}
```

In this example, the Duck class extends Animal and implements both the Flyable and Swimmable interfaces. The Duck class provides concrete implementations for the makeSound(), fly(), and swim() methods.

To further implement these concepts systematically, consider the following algorithm demonstrating the steps to declare and implement abstract classes and interfaces:

Understanding the differences between abstract classes and interfaces allows developers to utilize these constructs appropriately. Abstract classes are useful when sharing common state or behavior, while interfaces are effective for defining capabilities that can be shared across different classes.

Groovy also supports the implementation of multiple interfaces, enabling robust and flexible designs. A well-structured application benefits greatly from the use of abstract classes and interfaces to maintain clean, modular, and reusable code. This approach not only enhances code readability but also provides a strong foundation for the extension and maintenance of the codebase.

6.8 Traits and Mixins

Groovy introduces a powerful feature known as traits, which provide a way to compose behavior in objects without relying on traditional inheritance hierarchies. Traits are similar to interfaces but can also contain concrete methods and state. They enable the construction of classes

Algorithm 2: Steps to Declare and Implement Abstract Classes and Interfaces

```
Result: Declaring and Implementing Abstract Classes and
        Interfaces
Function DeclareAbstractClass(()abstractClass, methods):
    Data: Define an abstract class with the name abstractClass
    foreach method in methods do
        if method is abstract then
            Declare the method without implementation
        else
            Provide implementation for the method

Function DeclareInterface(()interfaceName, methods):
    Data: Define an interface with the name interfaceName
    foreach method in methods do
        Declare the abstract method

Function CreateConcreteClass(()className, parentClass,
  interfaces, methods):
    className extends parentClass implements interfaces
    Create constructor and class attributes
    foreach method in methods do
        Provide concrete implementation for the method
```

with reusable components called *mixins*, promoting code modularity and reducing duplication.

Trait declarations resemble class declarations but employ the trait keyword. Below is an example of a simple trait in Groovy and how it can be utilized:

```
trait Greeter {
    String greet() {
        return "Hello from Greeter"
    }
}
```

In the above example, Greeter is a trait with a single method greet. To use this trait in a class, the implements keyword or trait composition can be employed:

```
class Person implements Greeter {}

Person person = new Person()
println(person.greet()) // Output: Hello from Greeter
```

Traits can also contain abstract methods, which must be implemented by the class or another trait using the trait. Here is an example that demonstrates this capability:

```
trait Speaker {
    String speak()
}

trait FormalGreeter implements Speaker {
    String greetFormally() {
        return "Good day!"
    }
}

class Diplomat implements FormalGreeter {
    String speak() {
        return "I am a diplomat."
    }
}

Diplomat diplomat = new Diplomat()
println(diplomat.greetFormally()) // Output: Good day!
println(diplomat.speak()) // Output: I am a diplomat.
```

In this case, Speaker is a trait with an abstract method speak, and FormalGreeter implements the Speaker trait while adding its own method greetFormally. The Diplomat class further implements Speaker by providing a concrete implementation of speak.

Traits can also define fields. These fields can be private, or they can be public so that they can be accessed directly by classes implementing such traits:

```
trait Identifiable {
    String id

    void identify() {
        println("ID: $id")
    }
}

class Product implements Identifiable {
    Product(String id) {
        this.id = id
    }
}

Product product = new Product("P12345")
product.identify() // Output: ID: P12345
```

The example above defines a Identifiable trait with a field id and a method identify that prints the id. The Product class implements this trait and assigns a value to id upon instantiation.

Traits in Groovy facilitate the use of multiple inheritance, a feature absent in Java due to complexity and ambiguity issues. A class can implement multiple traits, thereby inheriting behavior from several sources:

```
trait Walker {
    String walk() {
        return "Walking"
    }
}

trait Runner {
    String run() {
        return "Running"
    }
}

class Athlete implements Walker, Runner {}

Athlete athlete = new Athlete()
println(athlete.walk()) // Output: Walking
println(athlete.run()) // Output: Running
```

When a class implements multiple traits, each inherited method's accessibility and functionality can be finely controlled. This capability ensures the customization of methods, and in cases of method conflicts, further specific resolution strategies can be applied:

```
trait Flyer {
    String move() {
        return "Flying"
    }
}

trait Swimmer {
```

```
    String move() {
        return "Swimming"
    }
}

class Duck implements Flyer, Swimmer {
    // Specifying which move method to use
    String move() {
        return Swimmer.super.move()
    }
}

Duck duck = new Duck()
println(duck.move()) // Output: Swimming
```

In this scenario, the move method is defined in both Flyer and Swimmer traits. Within the Duck class, the method resolution is specified explicitly: the move method from Swimmer is selected.

Mixin annotation in Groovy offers an alternative approach to trait-based composition. Mixins dynamically add behavior to an existing class using a different syntactical structure:

```
class Dog {
    String bark() {
        return "Woof!"
    }
}

class Bird {
    String chirp() {
        return "Chirp!"
    }
}

@Mixin(Dog)
class Parrot {}

Parrot parrot = new Parrot()
println(parrot.bark()) // Output: Woof!
println(parrot.chirp()) // Exception: groovy.lang.MissingMethodException
```

In this case, Parrot inherits the bark method from Dog by using the Mixin annotation, enhancing its behavior dynamically.

Overall, traits and mixins are invaluable tools in Groovy for achieving code reusability and modularity. They enable the flexible construction of classes while avoiding the limitations of single inheritance, making software design more adaptable and maintainable.

6.9 Using Groovy's @CompileStatic

The @CompileStatic annotation in Groovy enables static compilation of code, enhancing performance and enabling stronger type checks. Static compilation contrasts with Groovy's default dynamic behavior, where types are typically resolved at runtime. This section delves into the usage, benefits, considerations, and implications of using @CompileStatic in Groovy.

The @CompileStatic annotation, when applied, instructs the Groovy compiler to perform static type checking and use static dispatch. To apply @CompileStatic, import it from the groovy.transform package. You can annotate a class, method, or even a code block.

```
import groovy.transform.CompileStatic

@CompileStatic
class StaticPerson {
    String name
    int age

    String greet() {
        return "Hello, my name is " + name + " and I am " + age + " years old."
    }
}
```

In this example, the class StaticPerson and its methods are statically compiled. This means that the method calls and type checks are resolved at compile-time, improving execution speed.

Advantages of @CompileStatic

1. **Performance**: Static compilation can significantly improve performance as method calls are resolved at compile time, eliminating runtime overhead. 2. **Type Safety**: Statically compiled code offers stronger type checking, catching type-related errors at compile time rather than runtime. 3. **Tool Support**: Enhanced support from Integrated Development Environments (IDEs) due to better type resolution and error detection during coding.

Example: Performance Improvement

Consider the following dynamically compiled Groovy class:

```
class DynamicCalculator {
    def add(a, b) {
        return a + b
    }
}

DynamicCalculator calculator = new DynamicCalculator()
```

```
println calculator.add(10, 20)
```

Translating this example to use @CompileStatic:

```
import groovy.transform.CompileStatic

@CompileStatic
class StaticCalculator {
    int add(int a, int b) {
        return a + b
    }
}

StaticCalculator calculator = new StaticCalculator()
println calculator.add(10, 20)
```

By adding the @CompileStatic annotation, the add method becomes statically compiled. This leads to method calls being resolved at compile time, reducing the overhead of dynamic dispatch and enhancing runtime performance.

Scope of @CompileStatic

The @CompileStatic annotation can be utilized at different granularities:

- **Class-Level**: Applying @CompileStatic at the class level affects all methods and fields within that class.
- **Method-Level**: Annotating specific methods with @CompileStatic ensures only those methods are statically compiled.
- **Block-Level**: Inline static compilation can be achieved using the CompileStatic annotation on code blocks.

```
@CompileStatic
class MixedClass {
    def dynamicMethod() {
        return "This method is dynamically compiled."
    }

    @CompileStatic
    int staticMethod() {
        return 42
    }

    def methodWithStaticBlock() {
        @CompileStatic
        int staticBlock() {
            return 10 + 20
        }

        return staticBlock()
    }
```

```
}

MixedClass mixed = new MixedClass()
println mixed.dynamicMethod()
println mixed.staticMethod()
println mixed.methodWithStaticBlock()
```

In this example, MixedClass has a mix of dynamic and static methods. The staticMethod and staticBlock methods are statically compiled, while dynamicMethod remains dynamically compiled.

Considerations When Using @CompileStatic

1. **Type Casts and Coercion**: Explicit casts may be required in code sections where inferred typing is ambiguous, potentially making the code less concise. 2. **Dynamic Features**: Some dynamic features of Groovy, such as metaprogramming or dynamic method invocation, may not work with @CompileStatic. 3. **Interoperability**: Ensuring compatibility with Groovy and Java libraries that are dynamically compiled might necessitate additional type-checking logic.

```
import groovy.transform.CompileStatic

@CompileStatic
class CastingExample {
    Number addNumbers(Number a, Number b) {
        // Explicit cast to Integer
        return (Integer) a + (Integer) b
    }
}
```

Here, explicit casting is necessary for addNumbers method to seamlessly add numbers under static compilation rules.

Integrating @CompileStatic in Existing Projects

To integrate @CompileStatic, refactor code incrementally. Start by applying the annotation to computationally intensive methods or performance-sensitive parts. Gradually extend its use as type-related issues are resolved.

```
import groovy.transform.CompileStatic

@CompileStatic
class SystemMonitor {
    double calculateLoad(double load1, double load2) {
        return (load1 + load2) / 2
    }

    static void main(String[] args) {
        SystemMonitor monitor = new SystemMonitor()
        println monitor.calculateLoad(1.5, 2.5)
    }
}
```

In the SystemMonitor class, the calculateLoad method employs static compilation for performance efficiency.

Effective use of @CompileStatic can lead to substantial performance gains and reduced runtime errors in Groovy applications. Analyzing and benchmarking existing code helps identify the appropriate scope for static compilation, maintaining a balance between dynamic flexibility and static efficiency.

6.10 Best Practices for OOP in Groovy

To ensure robust, maintainable, and scalable applications using Object-Oriented Programming (OOP) in Groovy, it is imperative to adhere to established best practices. This section elaborates on several key best practices that should guide your Groovy development.

1. Follow the Single Responsibility Principle (SRP)

SRP dictates that a class should have one, and only one, reason to change. In Groovy, this translates to designing classes that encapsulate a single functionality or business logic. By doing so, you make your classes more readable and easier to maintain.

```
class UserService {
    UserRepository userRepository

    boolean addUser(User user) {
        // Business logic to add a user
    }

    List<User> getUsers() {
        // Business logic to fetch users
    }
}
```

2. Use Composition over Inheritance

While inheritance is a key feature of OOP, favoring composition often leads to more flexible and less tightly coupled code. Instead of creating large hierarchies, use classes that incorporate behaviors using fields and methods.

```
class ReportGenerator {
    DataFetcher dataFetcher
    ReportFormatter reportFormatter

    String generateReport() {
        def data = dataFetcher.fetchData()
        reportFormatter.format(data)
    }
```

```
}
```

3. Encapsulate State and Use Accessors

Access to class attributes should be controlled using getters and setters. Encapsulation helps in maintaining the integrity of the internal state of an object.

```
class BankAccount {
    private BigDecimal balance = BigDecimal.ZERO

    BigDecimal getBalance() {
        balance
    }

    void deposit(BigDecimal amount) {
        if (amount > BigDecimal.ZERO) {
            balance += amount
        }
    }

    void withdraw(BigDecimal amount) {
        if (amount > BigDecimal.ZERO && amount <= balance) {
            balance -= amount
        }
    }
}
```

4. Use Groovy's @CompileStatic Annotation

For performance-critical sections of your Groovy code, use @CompileStatic to enforce static type checking at compile time. This can significantly improve the runtime performance.

```
import groovy.transform.CompileStatic

@CompileStatic
class Calculator {
    int add(int a, int b) {
        a + b
    }

    int multiply(int a, int b) {
        a * b
    }
}
```

5. Leverage Groovy's Closures and DSL Capabilities

Groovy's closures and Domain Specific Languages (DSLs) provide powerful tools for writing expressive, concise, and readable code.

```
class Task {
    String name
    int priority
}
```

```
class TaskManager {
    List<Task> tasks = []

    void addTask(Closure closure) {
        Task task = new Task()
        closure.delegate = task
        closure()
        tasks << task
    }
}

TaskManager manager = new TaskManager()
manager.addTask {
    name = 'Write report'
    priority = 1
}
assert manager.tasks.size() == 1
```

6. Avoid Overusing Groovy's Dynamic Features

While Groovy allows dynamic typing and metaprogramming, over-relying on these features can lead to hard-to-maintain code. Use dynamic features judiciously and prefer static typing where feasible.

```
class Product {
    def id
    def name
    def price

    String toString() {
        "$name, priced at \$$price"
    }
}
```

7. Emphasize Immutable Objects Where Possible

Immutability can lead to easier-to-reason and thread-safe code. Use final fields and provide no setters or only methods that return new instances.

```
@Immutable
class Point {
    int x
    int y
}
```

8. Implement Proper Exception Handling

Use exceptions to signify error states and ensure that exceptions are handled appropriately to maintain application stability.

```
class FileProcessor {
    void process(File file) {
        try {
            // File processing logic
        } catch (IOException e) {
            log.error("Error processing file ${file.name}", e)
```

```
        }
    }
}
```

9. Follow Consistent Coding Standards

Adopt a consistent coding style within your Groovy code to enhance readability. This includes naming conventions, indentation, and code documentation.

```
// Example of consistent naming and indentation
class OrderService {
    OrderRepository orderRepository

    Order createOrder(Customer customer, List<Item> items) {
        // Order creation logic
    }

    List<Order> getOrders() {
        // Business logic to get orders
    }
}
```

10. Test Thoroughly

Employ unit and integration tests to ensure your code is functioning as expected. Groovy has excellent support for testing through frameworks like Spock and JUnit.

```
import spock.lang.Specification

class UserServiceSpec extends Specification {
    def "should add user successfully"() {
        given:
        def userService = new UserService()
        def user = new User(name: "John Doe")

        when:
        boolean result = userService.addUser(user)

        then:
        result
    }
}
```

By adhering to these best practices, your Groovy OOP code becomes more reliable, maintainable, and scalable, benefitting both current and future development efforts.

Chapter 7

Groovy and Java Integration

This chapter explores the seamless integration between Groovy and Java, detailing how to call Java code from Groovy and vice versa. It covers interoperability concerning data types and collections, the use of Java libraries within Groovy, and the mixing of Groovy and Java classes. Additionally, it discusses the use of annotations and Groovy's @Grab for dependency management, compatibility with the Java Development Kit (JDK), performance considerations, and provides practical examples to illustrate the integration process.

7.1 Introduction to Groovy and Java Integration

Groovy, as a dynamic language, extends the power of Java by offering concise syntax and additional features without compromising on performance and interoperability. Integration of Groovy with Java allows developers to utilize the strengths of both languages. This section delves into the foundational aspects of integrating Groovy with Java, setting the stage for subsequent detailed discussions.

Groovy is designed to be compatible with the Java platform, which means it seamlessly interoperates with Java code. This interoperability is achieved through several mechanisms such as shared data types, collections, and the ability to call methods and instantiate objects across both languages. Groovy's dynamic nature allows it to extend Java classes and interfaces, leading to enriched functionalities.

Basic Integration Concepts

At the core of Groovy and Java integration lies the concept of calling Java classes and methods directly from Groovy code. This is possible because Groovy compiles down to bytecode that runs on the Java Virtual Machine (JVM), just like Java. Groovy classes can instantiate Java objects, call Java methods, and vice versa without requiring any special configuration. Consider the following Groovy script that interacts with a Java class:

```
// Java class
public class Greeter {
    public void greet(String name) {
        System.out.println("Hello, " + name);
    }
}

// Groovy script
def greeter = new Greeter()
greeter.greet("World")
```

In this example, the Groovy script creates an instance of the Java class Greeter and calls its greet method. The resulting output will be:

```
Hello, World
```

This basic usage illustrates the fundamental integration capability where Groovy leverages existing Java code seamlessly.

Data Types and Collections

Both Groovy and Java share common data types, such as int, float, char, boolean, and more complex types like arrays and collections. The interaction between Groovy and Java with respect to data types is straightforward as Groovy is built upon Java. However, some differences exist due to Groovy's additional dynamic features.

Groovy enhances Java's collections framework by providing additional methods and capabilities. When using collections, such as List, Set, and Map, interoperability remains intact. Consider the following code snippets demonstrating how Groovy interacts with Java collections:

```
// Java class
import java.util.*;

public class CollectionUtil {
    public List<String> getList() {
```

```
        return Arrays.asList("Apple", "Banana", "Cherry");
    }
}

// Groovy script
def collectionUtil = new CollectionUtil()
def list = collectionUtil.getList()
list.each { println it }
```

The output of the Groovy script will be:

```
Apple
Banana
Cherry
```

Groovy adds syntactic sugar that simplifies working with collections, making it easier to iterate and manipulate them. Despite these enhancements, the interoperability of collections between Groovy and Java remains robust.

Annotations and Dependency Management

Groovy fully supports Java annotations, which are a powerful feature for adding metadata to classes, methods, fields, and parameters. This support allows Groovy to participate fully in Java's ecosystem of libraries and frameworks that rely on annotations. For example, consider a Java class with annotations:

```
// Java class with annotations
import java.lang.annotation.*;

@Retention(RetentionPolicy.RUNTIME)
@Target(ElementType.METHOD)
@interface CustomAnnotation {
    String value();
}

public class AnnotatedClass {
    @CustomAnnotation(value = "Test")
    public void annotatedMethod() {
        System.out.println("This is an annotated method.");
    }
}
```

Groovy can easily access and utilize these annotations:

```
// Groovy script using reflection
def annotatedClass = new AnnotatedClass()
def method = annotatedClass.getClass().getMethod("annotatedMethod")
def annotation = method.getAnnotation(CustomAnnotation)
println annotation.value() // Outputs: Test
```

This demonstrates how Groovy can interact with annotated Java code, which is vital for leveraging Java frameworks and libraries that make extensive use of annotations.

Furthermore, Groovy's @Grab annotation simplifies dependency management by allowing developers to easily include external libraries. This ensures quick integration of Java libraries into Groovy scripts:

```
// Groovy script with @Grab for dependency management
@Grab('org.apache.commons:commons-lang3:3.12.0')
import org.apache.commons.lang3.StringUtils

println StringUtils.capitalize("groovy and java")
```

The @Grab annotation retrieves the specified library from a repository, enabling the use of Java libraries directly in Groovy scripts. This capability is instrumental in harnessing the power of Java's extensive ecosystem.

JDK Compatibility and Performance

Groovy is fully compatible with the Java Development Kit (JDK), ensuring that any Java version can serve as the runtime for Groovy applications. This compatibility ensures that developers can leverage the latest features of the JDK while adhering to their preferred development practices in Groovy. The Groovy development team maintains this compatibility, providing timely updates to align with new JDK releases.

Performance considerations are paramount when integrating Groovy and Java. Groovy, while dynamic, offers options for optimization, such as static compilation using @CompileStatic, which improves runtime performance by generating bytecode that is more optimized for the JVM. Using @CompileStatic:

```
// Groovy script with @CompileStatic for performance
import groovy.transform.CompileStatic

@CompileStatic
class PerformanceTest {
    int add(int a, int b) {
        return a + b
    }
}

def test = new PerformanceTest()
println test.add(5, 3) // Outputs: 8
```

The use of @CompileStatic minimizes runtime overhead, making the performance closer to that of pure Java code. This optimization is vital for performance-critical applications where Groovy's dynamism might otherwise introduce latency.

Groovy and Java integration harnesses the power of both languages, enabling developers to write concise, expressive code without sacrificing access to Java's robust ecosystem and tools. This synergy allows for the creation of applications that benefit from Groovy's conciseness and Java's performance, thereby enhancing productivity and efficiency.

7.2 Calling Java from Groovy

The capability to call Java code from Groovy is one of the fundamental aspects of Groovy's seamless integration with the Java ecosystem. Groovy is designed to be fully compatible with Java, allowing developers to leverage existing Java classes and libraries effortlessly. This section delves into various ways of invoking Java code from Groovy, ensuring a comprehensive understanding of this vital feature.

Java classes can be instantiated and utilized in Groovy just as they would be in Java. Consider a simple Java class defined as follows:

```
public class MathOperations {
    public static int add(int a, int b) {
        return a + b;
    }

    public int multiply(int a, int b) {
        return a * b;
    }
}
```

To use the MathOperations class in Groovy, one can directly call its methods. Static methods can be called using the class name, while instance methods require creating an object of the class:

```
def result1 = MathOperations.add(10, 5)
println("Static Method Result: " + result1)

def mathOps = new MathOperations()
def result2 = mathOps.multiply(10, 5)
println("Instance Method Result: " + result2)
```

The output of the above Groovy code will be:

```
Static Method Result: 15
Instance Method Result: 50
```

One of Groovy's strengths is its concise syntax, which simplifies Java class usage without compromising functionality. The constructor and method calls are straightforward, enhancing readability while maintaining accuracy.

Groovy also supports calling Java constructors with named parameters. This feature, known as the named arguments constructor, allows initializing objects more intuitively. Consider a Java class representing a Book:

```
public class Book {
    private String title;
    private String author;
    private int pages;

    public Book(String title, String author, int pages) {
        this.title = title;
        this.author = author;
        this.pages = pages;
    }

    // getters and setters omitted for brevity
}
```

In Groovy, you can instantiate the Book class using named arguments as shown below:

```
def book = new Book(title: "Groovy in Action", author: "Dierk König", pages: 450)
println("Title: " + book.title + ", Author: " + book.author + ", Pages: " + book.pages
    )
```

The above code demonstrates Groovy's ability to call Java constructors more flexibly. Internally, Groovy translates the named parameters to the appropriate constructor invocation.

Accessing Java Beans properties is also streamlined in Groovy. Properties with standard getter and setter methods adhere to Groovy's property access conventions, allowing straightforward field references. For instance:

```
public class Employee {
    private String name;
    private double salary;

    // getters and setters omitted for brevity
}
```

The corresponding Groovy script to manipulate Employee properties can be:

```
def emp = new Employee()
emp.name = "John Doe"
emp.salary = 60000

println("Employee Name: " + emp.name)
println("Employee Salary: " + emp.salary)
```

This code leverages Groovy's ability to seamlessly transition between field access and method calls, providing a more natural syntax without explicit calls to getter or setter methods.

Groovy also integrates smoothly with Java's collection framework. Java collections can be used in Groovy without any issues. For example, consider a Java class that returns a list of integers:

```
import java.util.List;
import java.util.Arrays;

public class NumberGenerator {
    public static List<Integer> generateNumbers() {
        return Arrays.asList(1, 2, 3, 4, 5);
    }
}
```

In Groovy, calling this method and iterating over the list is seamless:

```
def numbers = NumberGenerator.generateNumbers()
numbers.each { number ->
    println("Number: " + number)
}
```

Furthermore, Groovy supports working with Java interfaces and abstract classes. Groovy class can implement a Java interface or extend an abstract class, thus blending the two languages. Consider a Java interface:

```
public interface GreetingService {
    String greet(String name);
}
```

Implementing this interface in Groovy is straightforward:

```
class GreetingServiceImpl implements GreetingService {
    String greet(String name) {
        return "Hello, " + name
    }
}

def service = new GreetingServiceImpl()
println(service.greet("Alice"))
```

Calling Java from Groovy also includes handling checked exceptions. Groovy allows similar exception handling patterns as Java, using try-catch blocks to manage exceptions thrown by Java methods:

```
public class FileUtil {
    public static void readFile(String filePath) throws IOException {
        // Implementation omitted for brevity
    }
}
```

The corresponding Groovy code for handling the IOException is:

```
try {
    FileUtil.readFile("/path/to/file")
```

```
} catch (IOException e) {
    println("An error occurred: " + e.message)
}
```

Groovy's native support for Java's exception handling simplifies error management, ensuring robust integration practices.

Extending Groovy's seamless interoperability, it even supports Java's annotations. Java annotations retained in Groovy allow the combination of powerful features from both languages. Consider the use of a Java's @Deprecated annotation on a method:

```
public class LegacyCode {
    @Deprecated
    public void oldMethod() {
    }
}
```

Groovy recognizes the @Deprecated annotation:

```
def legacy = new LegacyCode()
legacy.oldMethod()
```

Utilizing Java classes, constructors, methods, properties, collections, interfaces, exceptions, and annotations from Groovy code encapsulates the interoperability strengths fostering productive development practices.

7.3 Calling Groovy from Java

The ability to call Groovy code from Java enables the utilization of Groovy's powerful dynamic features and succinct syntax directly within Java applications. This section details the processes involved, and explores various methods to achieve interoperability between Java and Groovy.

Groovy classes can be instantiated and methods can be invoked from Java in a manner similar to how Java interacts with other Java classes. However, certain concepts need to be fully understood for smooth interoperation. Here, we shall discuss these concepts and illustrate them with practical examples.

Creating an Instance of a Groovy Class in Java

Assume there's a Groovy class, Greeter.groovy, defined as follows:

```
class Greeter {
```

```
    String greet(String name) {
        return "Hello, ${name}!"
    }
}
```

To call this class from a Java file, say Main.java, the class path must include the compiled Groovy classes. The following Java code demonstrates creating an instance of the Greeter class and invoking its greet method.

```
public class Main {
    public static void main(String[] args) {
        Greeter greeter = new Greeter();
        String greeting = greeter.greet("World");
        System.out.println(greeting);
    }
}
```

Upon executing Main.java, the output will be:

```
Hello, World!
```

Handling Groovy Scripts in Java

Groovy scripts can also be dynamically loaded and executed within a Java application using the Groovy Shell. First, create a Groovy script named Script.groovy:

```
def message = "Hello from Groovy Script"
return message
```

The following Java code can be used to execute this Groovy script and retrieve the returned value:

```
import groovy.lang.GroovyShell;

public class Main {
    public static void main(String[] args) {
        GroovyShell shell = new GroovyShell();
        Object result = shell.evaluate(new File("Script.groovy"));
        System.out.println(result);
    }
}
```

The execution of Main.java will yield:

```
Hello from Groovy Script
```

Using GroovyShell for More Complex Interactions

The GroovyShell allows for more than just simple script evaluation. It can be used to create scripts that incorporate variables and methods to interact with Java classes. Consider the following enhanced script,

ComplexScript.groovy:

```
class Greeter {
    String greet(String name) {
        return "Hello, ${name}!"
    }
}

def greeter = new Greeter()
def message = greeter.greet("Java Developer")
return message
```

The corresponding Java code to invoke this script may look like this:

```
import groovy.lang.GroovyShell;

public class Main {
    public static void main(String[] args) {
        GroovyShell shell = new GroovyShell();
        Object result = shell.evaluate(new File("ComplexScript.groovy"));
        System.out.println(result);
    }
}
```

Running Main.java will generate the following output:

```
Hello, Java Developer!
```

Embedding Groovy within Java Applications

Groovy can be seamlessly embedded within Java using the GroovyClassLoader. This permits dynamic loading and execution of Groovy classes. Consider the following Groovy class saved as DynamicGreeter.groovy:

```
class DynamicGreeter {
    String dynamicGreet(String name) {
        return "Hi, ${name}!"
    }
}
```

To dynamically load and execute this class from a Java application, perform the following steps:

```
import groovy.lang.GroovyClassLoader;

public class Main {
    public static void main(String[] args) throws Exception {
        GroovyClassLoader classLoader = new GroovyClassLoader();
        Class groovyClass = classLoader.parseClass(new File("DynamicGreeter.groovy")
            );

        Object groovyObject = groovyClass.newInstance();
        String result = (String)groovyClass.getDeclaredMethod("dynamicGreet", String.
            class)
                                        .invoke(groovyObject, "Java Enthusiast");
        System.out.println(result);
```

```
    }
}
```

Executing Main.java yields:

```
Hi, Java Enthusiast!
```

Handling Groovy's Dynamic Nature

When invoking Groovy code from Java, it is necessary to handle potential runtime issues due to Groovy's dynamic nature. Employing appropriate exception handling ensures robustness in the Java code. For instance:

```
import groovy.lang.GroovyShell;

public class Main {
    public static void main(String[] args) {
        try {
            GroovyShell shell = new GroovyShell();
            Object result = shell.evaluate(new File("NonExistentScript.groovy"));
            System.out.println(result);
        } catch (Exception e) {
            System.err.println("Failed to execute Groovy script: " + e.getMessage());
        }
    }
}
```

This catch block will capture any script-related exceptions, thus maintaining the integrity of the Java application.

Understanding and implementing the integration techniques showcased here allows for sophisticated interaction between Java and Groovy, leveraging the strengths of each language.

7.4 Interoperability: Data Types and Collections

Interoperability between Groovy and Java is one of the key strengths of Groovy, enabling seamless integration and allowing developers to utilize the rich ecosystem of Java libraries while leveraging Groovy's expressive syntax. Central to this interoperability are data types and collections—understanding how these are handled in Groovy when interfacing with Java code is essential for effective and error-free integration.

First, let us consider the basic data types such as integers, floats, and strings. Groovy simplifies the handling of these types, automatically converting them as needed when calling or being called from Java. In Groovy, primitive types are automatically boxed and unboxed as objects, which eliminates the need for manual conversion usually required in Java.

For example, in Java, you might use the following code to demonstrate the types:

```
public class JavaClass {
    public int addIntegers(int a, int b) {
        return a + b;
    }

    public String concatenateStrings(String str1, String str2) {
        return str1 + str2;
    }
}
```

In Groovy, these methods can be called directly without any type conversion:

```
JavaClass javaClass = new JavaClass()
assert javaClass.addIntegers(5, 10) == 15
assert javaClass.concatenateStrings("Hello, ", "World!") == "Hello, World!"
```

Here, Groovy handles the interaction seamlessly, taking care of the conversion between Groovy's dynamic types and Java's static types.

Moving on to collections, Groovy offers rich and idiomatic support for Java collections, including lists, sets, and maps, and adds syntactic sugar to make them easier to use and more expressive. Java collections can be manipulated within Groovy using default Groovy mechanisms such as GDK (Groovy Development Kit) methods, thanks to the fact that Groovy is built on top of the Java platform and extends its classes.

Consider a Java class that uses collections:

```
import java.util.List;
import java.util.Map;

public class JavaCollectionClass {
    public void printList(List<String> list) {
        for (String item : list) {
            System.out.println(item);
        }
    }

    public void printMap(Map<String, Integer> map) {
        for (Map.Entry<String, Integer> entry : map.entrySet()) {
            System.out.println(entry.getKey() + ": " + entry.getValue());
        }
    }
}
```

In Groovy, you can create and manipulate these collections easily and pass them to the Java methods:

```
JavaCollectionClass javaCollectionClass = new JavaCollectionClass()

List<String> groovyList = ["alpha", "beta", "gamma"]
javaCollectionClass.printList(groovyList)

Map<String, Integer> groovyMap = ["one": 1, "two": 2, "three": 3]
javaCollectionClass.printMap(groovyMap)
```

Groovy supports literals for lists and maps, making the code concise and readable. Furthermore, Groovy collections are backed by the same Java collections framework, ensuring compatibility. Groovy's ArrayList is a direct subclass of Java's ArrayList, and the same goes for other collection types such as sets and maps.

For compatibility with Java, it is crucial to be aware of certain pitfalls. For instance, when dealing with arrays, Groovy often uses List by default. If a specific Java method requires a precise array type, you must ensure that the correct type is provided. For example:

```
public class JavaArrayClass {
    public void printArray(String[] array) {
        for (String item : array) {
            System.out.println(item);
        }
    }
}
```

In Groovy, creating and passing an array requires explicit array creation:

```
JavaArrayClass javaArrayClass = new JavaArrayClass()
String[] groovyArray = ["apple", "banana", "cherry"] as String[]
javaArrayClass.printArray(groovyArray)
```

Similarly, Groovy's use of dynamic typing can sometimes lead to unexpected issues when interacting with Java code that expects strict type definitions. Using explicit type casts or declaring types can help prevent such issues:

```
List<String> typedList = ["one", "two", "three"]
javaCollectionClass.printList(typedList as List<String>)
```

Being aware of these interoperability nuances ensures that Groovy code works predictably when calling or being called by Java methods. This robust interoperability extends not only to primitive data types and collections but also to more complex objects and generics, allowing developers to create intricate and highly functional mixed-language applications.

Understanding and correctly utilizing Groovy's dynamic nature, alongside Java's static typing, allows for code that is both flexible and robust, leveraging the best features of both languages. This interoperability is fundamental to writing efficient and maintainable code in a polyglot environment, optimizing both performance and developer productivity.

7.5 Using Java Libraries in Groovy

Leveraging Java libraries within a Groovy environment enables the combination of Java's extensive ecosystem with the dynamic features of the Groovy language. The interoperability between Java and Groovy is one of the key advantages of adopting Groovy in Java-based projects. This section details the utilization of Java libraries in Groovy through practical examples and thorough explanations of related concepts.

Groovy seamlessly interacts with any Java library, making it possible to use Java classes, methods, and framework functionalities within Groovy scripts. This can be demonstrated through several examples, from basic utility libraries to more complex frameworks.

To use a Java library in Groovy, ensure the Java library is included in your classpath. In a Gradle project, this can be achieved by declaring the dependency in the build.gradle file:

```
dependencies {
    implementation 'group:artifact:version'
}
```

Assuming the library is correctly added to the build path, a typical example would be using the Apache Commons Lang library to manipulate strings. Here, we illustrate how to use the StringUtils class from the Apache Commons Lang library in Groovy.

Add the dependency to build.gradle:

```
dependencies {
    implementation 'org.apache.commons:commons-lang3:3.12.0'
}
```

Below is a Groovy script that utilizes the StringUtils class from the Apache Commons Lang library:

```
import org.apache.commons.lang3.StringUtils

String input = "hello world"
```

```
String reversed = StringUtils.reverse(input)

println "Original Text: $input"
println "Reversed Text: $reversed"
```

Output:

```
Original Text: hello world
Reversed Text: dlrow olleh
```

Groovy supports Java's static imports, which can be utilized to import static methods or constants from Java classes. This is particularly beneficial for concise and readable scripts. For example, consider using the Math class statically:

```
import static java.lang.Math.*

double radius = 5
double area = PI * radius * radius

println "The area of the circle is $area"
```

Output:

```
The area of the circle is 78.53981633974483
```

Java libraries often include comprehensive classes and methods, like Java's Collections Framework. Groovy can instantiate and manipulate these collections seamlessly, inheriting the vast array of utility methods provided by the framework. Consider the following example where the standard Java ArrayList class is used:

```
import java.util.ArrayList

ArrayList<String> list = new ArrayList<>()
list.add("Apple")
list.add("Banana")
list.add("Cherry")

println "Fruits: $list"
```

Output:

```
Fruits: [Apple, Banana, Cherry]
```

Groovy can also work effectively with Java libraries for more complex tasks such as file operations with Java's java.nio.file package. Below demonstrates reading from a file using the Files class:

```
import java.nio.file.Files
import java.nio.file.Paths

String path = "sample.txt"
List<String> content = Files.readAllLines(Paths.get(path))
```

```
content.each { line ->
    println line
}
```

Output (assuming sample.txt contains the lines "Hello" and "World"):

```
Hello
World
```

Integrating Swing for GUI applications illustrates Groovy's fluency with Java GUI libraries. Swing components and containers can be readily used in Groovy scripts, enabling rapid development of desktop applications. Below is a simple script demonstrating a Swing JFrame:

```
import javax.swing.JFrame
import javax.swing.JLabel

JFrame frame = new JFrame("Groovy Swing Example")
frame.setSize(300, 200)
frame.setDefaultCloseOperation(JFrame.EXIT_ON_CLOSE)

JLabel label = new JLabel("Hello, Swing!")
frame.add(label)

frame.setVisible(true)
```

When using external Java libraries, Groovy's @Grab annotation simplifies dependency management within the script itself, negating the need for external build configuration. This is especially useful for scripting and rapid prototyping. For instance, to use the Gson library from Google for JSON parsing:

```
@Grab(group='com.google.code.gson', module='gson', version='2.8.8')
import com.google.gson.Gson

class Person {
    String name
    int age
}

String json = '{"name":"John", "age":30}'
Gson gson = new Gson()
Person person = gson.fromJson(json, Person)

println "Name: ${person.name}, Age: ${person.age}"
```

Output:

```
Name: John, Age: 30
```

Using Java libraries within Groovy scripts leverages the strengths of both languages, allowing developers to build robust and versatile applications efficiently. The integration facilitates the reuse of existing Java code and frameworks, enhancing the Groovy programming environment while maintaining interoperability and performance. Through practical examples, we have demonstrated the seamless cooperation between Groovy and Java, encouraging the adoption of this synergy in a variety of applications.

7.6 Mixing Groovy and Java Classes

Groovy and Java can seamlessly interoperate, which allows developers to mix and match classes written in both languages within the same project. This section presents an overview of the techniques and considerations involved in mixing Groovy and Java classes. It will cover the use cases, specific syntax differences, how to handle constructors and inheritance, and best practices for maintaining a clean codebase when using both languages together.

A common use case for mixing Groovy and Java classes is to leverage the strengths of both languages: Java's extensive ecosystem of libraries and Groovy's concise and expressive syntax. This enables you to take advantage of Java's performance and type safety while benefiting from Groovy's script-like capabilities and DSL (Domain Specific Language) features.

```
package com.example;

public class Person {
    private String name;
    private int age;

    public Person(String name, int age) {
        this.name = name;
        this.age = age;
    }

    public String getName() {
        return name;
    }

    public int getAge() {
        return age;
    }

    public void displayInfo() {
        System.out.println("Name: " + name + ", Age: " + age);
    }
}
```

The above example defines a basic Java class Person with private fields, a constructor, and methods to get the values of these fields. Let's now see how we can use this Person class in Groovy.

```
@Grab(group='com.example', module='example-module', version='1.0')

def main() {
    def person = new com.example.Person('John Doe', 30)
    println "Name: ${person.name}"
    println "Age: ${person.age}"
    person.displayInfo()
}

main()
```

In this Groovy script, we use the @Grab annotation for dependency management, ensuring the example-module containing our Person class is included. The script then creates an instance of Person and demonstrates retrieving and printing its attributes.

When mixing classes, careful attention must be paid to constructors and field access due to the differences in how both languages handle them. Groovy automatically generates getter and setter methods for class fields, offering more concise syntax, whereas Java requires explicit definition of these methods.

To override or extend Java classes in Groovy, you can simply create a Groovy class that extends or implements a Java class/interface.

```
package com.example

class Employee extends Person {
    String position

    Employee(String name, int age, String position) {
        super(name, age)
        this.position = position
    }

    void displayInfo() {
        super.displayInfo()
        println "Position: $position"
    }
}

def e = new Employee('Jane Doe', 25, 'Developer')
e.displayInfo()
```

In this example, the Groovy class Employee extends the Java class Person, with an additional field position. The constructor in Employee invokes the super constructor of Person to initialize the inherited fields. The displayInfo method is overridden to include the new field position.

Another important concept when mixing Groovy and Java classes is handling annotations. Groovy classes can use Java annotations without issues, but the reverse requires ensuring that the annotation library is available to the Java compiler.

To avoid potential pitfalls, consider the following best practices:

- **Consistent Naming Conventions:** Ensure that both Groovy and Java classes follow a unified naming convention to reduce confusion.
- **Isolate Language-Specific Logic:** Try to isolate code that is inherently dependent on the specific features of Groovy or Java to minimize inter-language complexities.
- **Leverage Groovy's Metaprogramming Sparingly:** Groovy's metaprogramming capabilities can introduce dynamic behavior that is difficult to understand and troubleshoot when mixed with statically-typed Java code.
- **Testing:** Implement thorough testing for both Groovy and Java components to ensure interoperability correctness.

Prudent use of these practices ensures that the integration remains smooth, maintainable, and leverages the strengths of both languages while mitigating potential drawbacks.

7.7 Annotations and Groovy's @Grab

Annotations play a crucial role in both Groovy and Java, providing metadata for compiler instructions, code analysis, and runtime behavior modifications. Groovy supports all Java annotations and introduces its own for enhanced functionality. Additionally, Groovy's @Grab simplifies dependency management, enabling lightweight script development akin to using a build tool like Maven or Gradle.

Java annotations are broadly categorized into three types: *Marker*, *Single-value*, and *Full* annotations. Groovy adopts these categories while adding dynamic Groovy-specific capabilities. For instance, the @Delegate annotation in Groovy offers features beyond standard Java annotations, enabling delegation of methods to an annotated field, thus promoting cleaner and more maintainable code.

```
import java.lang.annotation.*;

@Retention(RetentionPolicy.RUNTIME)
@Target(ElementType.METHOD)
public @interface CustomAnnotation {
```

```
    String value();
}
```

```
class AnnotatedClass {
    @CustomAnnotation(value="Example")
    void annotatedMethod() {
        println "Annotated Method Executed"
    }
}

def obj = new AnnotatedClass()
obj.annotatedMethod()
```

Groovy also enables the creation of custom annotations. For instance, the following example demonstrates a custom Groovy annotation used to log method execution time.

```
import groovy.transform.CompileStatic
import java.lang.annotation.*

@Retention(RetentionPolicy.RUNTIME)
@Target(ElementType.METHOD)
@interface LogExecutionTime {}

class MethodLogger {
    @LogExecutionTime
    def performTask() {
        println "Task performed"
    }
}

def measureExecution(Closure closure) {
    long start = System.nanoTime()
    closure()
    long end = System.nanoTime()
    println "Execution time: ${(end - start) / 1e6} ms"
}

MethodLogger.metaClass.invokeMethod = { String name, args ->
    def method = MethodLogger.getDeclaredMethod(name, Object[].class)
    if(method.isAnnotationPresent(LogExecutionTime)) {
        measureExecution { delegate.metaClass.getMetaMethod(name, args).invoke(
                delegate, args) }
    } else {
        delegate.metaClass.getMetaMethod(name, args).invoke(delegate, args)
    }
}

def logger = new MethodLogger()
logger.performTask()
```

The LogExecutionTime annotation aids in performance monitoring, demonstrating Groovy's ability to enhance the introspection and behavior modification capabilities of Java annotations.

Another hallmark of Groovy is the @Grab annotation, which facilitates dependency management directly within scripts. This feature leverages the Grape (Groovy Adaptable Packaging Engine) system to fetch libraries from repositories such as Maven Central. By using @Grab, developers can include dependencies in Groovy scripts without needing an external build tool.

```
@Grab(group='org.apache.commons', module='commons-lang3', version='3.12.0')
import org.apache.commons.lang3.StringUtils

println StringUtils.capitalize("hello world")
```

In the given script, @Grab fetches the commons-lang3 library if not already present in the local repository. This functionality is particularly beneficial for scripting and quick prototyping, as it removes the need for an upfront project setup.

Groovy's native integration with Grape, paired with the use of @Grab, mirrors tools like Maven and Gradle, bringing dependency management into the script itself. This approach maintains the succinct nature of Groovy while providing powerful capabilities for dependency resolution and inclusion. The seamless combination of Java and Groovy annotations alongside @Grab enhances the expressiveness and dynamism of Groovy code, bridging the flexibility of scripting languages with the robust dependency management of build tools.

7.8 Java Development Kit (JDK) Compatibility

Understanding the compatibility between Groovy and the Java Development Kit (JDK) is essential for ensuring smooth integration. Both Groovy and Java are designed to be compatible with each other, given that Groovy is built on top of the Java platform. This section provides a comprehensive look at the various aspects of JDK compatibility with Groovy, including version compatibility, JVM considerations, and the influence of JDK features on Groovy scripts and applications.

Groovy is designed to be friendly with multiple versions of the JDK. However, certain nuanced differences between JDK versions can affect Groovy's behavior. It is crucial to comprehend how to leverage these differences to maintain compatibility and performance.

Version Compatibility: Groovy supports multiple versions of the JDK, starting from JDK 1.5 up to the latest releases. Each JDK version introduces new features, enhancements, and deprecations that Groovy needs to accommodate. The Groovy development team ensures that Groovy keeps pace with these changes to maintain compatibility.

The table below illustrates support for various JDK versions across different Groovy versions:

Groovy Version	JDK Version
Groovy 1.7 - 2.4	JDK 1.5 - 1.8
Groovy 2.5 - 2.6	JDK 1.7 - 1.10
Groovy 3.0+	JDK 8+

Compiling Groovy with JDK: Groovy scripts and classes can be compiled using different versions of the JDK. The groovyc compiler, Groovy's equivalent of javac, can be instructed to use specific JDK versions. Below is an example of compiling a Groovy script with a specific JDK version using the groovyc command:

```
groovyc -target 1.8 MyScript.groovy
```

This command ensures that the compiled bytecode is compatible with JDK 1.8. The -target option specifies the target JDK version for the compiled bytecode.

Leveraging JDK Features in Groovy: With each new JDK release, additional features such as lambda expressions, the Stream API, and the var keyword are introduced. Groovy allows the use of these features within Groovy scripts and classes, thereby enhancing functionality and performance.

For example, the introduction of lambda expressions in JDK 8 can be utilized in Groovy as shown below:

```
List<Integer> numbers = [1, 2, 3, 4, 5]
numbers.each { println it }
```

JVM Considerations: Groovy, being a JVM language, inherits the advantages and constraints of the underlying JVM. The JVM version plays a crucial role in determining the performance and compatibility of Groovy applications.

Different JVM implementations such as Oracle's HotSpot, OpenJDK, and GraalVM offer various performance benefits. Using an optimized JVM implementation can enhance the performance of Groovy applications significantly.

JDK Modules System: Introduced in JDK 9, the module system (often referred to as Project Jigsaw) enables strong encapsulation and modularity at the JVM level. Groovy is compatible with the JDK module system, allowing developers to create modular Groovy applications.

To create a module, define a module descriptor file (module-info.java) and compile it along with Groovy classes. Below is an example of a simple module descriptor file:

```
module com.example.mygroovymodule {
    requires groovy;
    exports com.example.myapp;
}
```

Compile the module using:

```
javac -d out --module-path libs src/main/java/module-info.java src/main/groovy/com/
    example/myapp/*.groovy
```

This command compiles the Groovy classes and the module descriptor file into the specified output directory, ensuring proper module encapsulation and dependency management.

Compatible Libraries and Frameworks: Numerous Java libraries and frameworks can be seamlessly integrated with Groovy. Libraries such as Spring, Hibernate, and Apache Commons are commonly used within Groovy applications, leveraging their capabilities for enterprise-level applications.

For instance, integrating Spring framework components is straightforward in Groovy:

```
@Grab('org.springframework.boot:spring-boot-starter-web:2.5.4')
import org.springframework.boot.SpringApplication
import org.springframework.boot.autoconfigure.SpringBootApplication

@SpringBootApplication
class MyGroovyApp {
    static void main(String[] args) {
        SpringApplication.run(MyGroovyApp, args)
    }
}
```

Backward Compatibility: Groovy aims to maintain backward compatibility across various JDK versions. This ensures that legacy Groovy applications continue to run without modification, even with newer JDK releases. The Groovy development team places a high value on backward compatibility, ensuring that upgrading the JDK does not adversely impact existing Groovy applications.

Groovy's @Grab Annotation: The @Grab annotation simplifies the management of dependencies in Groovy scripts. It allows developers to specify external libraries directly within the script, which are then automatically downloaded and included in the classpath.

Here is an example using @Grab:

```
@Grab(group='org.apache.commons', module='commons-lang3', version='3.12.0')
import org.apache.commons.lang3.StringUtils

println StringUtils.capitalize("groovy")
```

This Groovy script demonstrates how to grab and use the Apache Commons Lang library directly.

By understanding and utilizing these aspects of JDK compatibility, developers can better integrate Groovy with existing Java projects, harness JDK features for enhanced functionality, and ensure that their Groovy applications remain robust and performant across different JDK versions.

7.9 Performance Considerations

Evaluating and optimizing the performance of applications that integrate Groovy and Java is paramount to ensuring efficiency and responsiveness. Groovy, being a dynamic language that runs on the Java Virtual Machine (JVM), inherently introduces certain performance overheads compared to static languages like Java. This section delves into multiple facets of performance considerations, providing guidelines and insights for developers to maintain optimal performance while leveraging the flexibility of Groovy along with the robustness of Java.

The primary areas of focus in performance considerations include reflection handling, dynamic typing, method dispatch, memory usage, startup time, and optimization techniques specific to the Groovy language.

- **Reflection Handling**: Groovy relies heavily on reflection for many of its dynamic features. While reflection provides a powerful mechanism for introspection and interoperation, it can also result in slower performance due to the additional computational overhead. When possible, avoid reflection-heavy operations in performance-critical sections of code.
- **Dynamic Typing**: One of Groovy's greatest strengths is its dynamic nature, which allows developers to write more concise and

flexible code. However, this dynamism comes at a cost. Dynamic typing involves runtime resolution of types, which can be slower than static type resolution. To mitigate this, consider using explicit type declarations for critical performance paths. This can be achieved by specifying variable types, method return types, and parameter types, as shown below:

```
// Dynamic typing
def sum(a, b) {
    a + b
}

// Static typing
int sum(int a, int b) {
    return a + b
}
```

- **Method Dispatch**: Groovy supports multiple method dispatch mechanisms, including normal method calls, dynamic method calls using the invokeMethod() method, and the Meta-Object Protocol (MOP). Dynamic method dispatch can be significantly slower than static method calls. Where performance is a concern, prefer using static method dispatch:

```
// Static method call
targetObject.staticMethod()

// Dynamic method call
targetObject.invokeMethod('dynamicMethod', null)
```

- **Memory Usage**: Groovy scripts tend to use more memory due to additional Groovy-related structures around objects and classes. One strategy to manage this is to use Groovy's compilation to bytecode feature. By compiling Groovy scripts into Java bytecode, it is possible to achieve performance closer to that of Java. Use the groovyc compiler for this purpose.

```
groovyc MyGroovyScript.groovy
java MyGroovyScript
```

- **Startup Time**: Groovy scripts experience longer startup times compared to pure Java applications due to the dynamic compilation and runtime nature of Groovy. For long-running applications, this overhead is generally acceptable. However, for short-lived applications or scripts, it may be beneficial to precompile Groovy scripts to reduce the startup delay.

- **Optimization Techniques**: Employing optimization techniques specific to Groovy can yield performance benefits without sacrificing the language's expressive power. Some of these techniques include:

1. **CompileStatic Annotation**: Use the @CompileStatic annotation to guide the Groovy compiler to generate static type-checking and optimized bytecode. This can result in substantial performance gains by eliminating the overhead of dynamic dispatching.

```
@groovy.transform.CompileStatic
class StaticExample {
    String greet(String name) {
        "Hello, $name"
    }
}
```

2. **Using Primitives**: Prefer using primitive data types (e.g., int, boolean) instead of their object counterparts (e.g., Integer, Boolean). This reduces memory consumption and enhances performance due to direct addressing.

```
// Use primitive types
int x = 10
boolean flag = true
```

3. **Avoiding Groovy Truth**: Although Groovy's truth evaluation is convenient, it is less efficient. In performance-critical sections, prefer explicit boolean evaluations.

```
// Groovy truth
if (myList) { ... }

// Explicit boolean check
if (myList != null && myList.size() > 0) { ... }
```

4. **Efficient String Handling**: Use Groovy's StringBuilder or Java's StringBuilder for concatenating strings in loops to enhance performance.

```
// Inefficient string concatenation
def result = ""
for (int i = 0; i < 10; i++) {
    result += "$i "
}

// Efficient string concatenation
def sb = new StringBuilder()
for (int i = 0; i < 10; i++) {
    sb.append("$i ")
}
```

Considering these performance aspects and applying the discussed optimizations enables developers to create Groovy-Java integrated applications that are both robust and efficient, leveraging the strengths of both languages.

7.10 Practical Examples of Groovy-Java Integration

Example 1: Calling a Java Method from Groovy

Consider a Java class defining a simple arithmetic operation. The task is to access this Java class and its methods from Groovy code.

Java class definition:

```
public class ArithmeticOperations {
    public int add(int a, int b) {
        return a + b;
    }
}
```

Groovy code to call the above Java method:

```
def arithmetic = new ArithmeticOperations()
def sum = arithmetic.add(5, 10)
println("Sum: $sum")
```

Expected Output:

```
Sum: 15
```

In this example, the Groovy code instantiates the Java class ArithmeticOperations and calls its add method, passing integer arguments and printing the result.

Example 2: Using Java Collections in Groovy

To demonstrate the interoperability between Groovy and Java collections, consider the following example where a Java-based ArrayList is manipulated within Groovy.

Java class definition setting up the list:

```
import java.util.ArrayList;
import java.util.Arrays;

public class CollectionExample {
    public static ArrayList<String> getList() {
        return new ArrayList<>(Arrays.asList("apple", "banana", "cherry"));
    }
```

```
}
```

Groovy code to interact with the above Java Collection:

```
def list = CollectionExample.getList()
list.each { item -> println(item.capitalize()) }
list.add("date")
println("Updated List: $list")
```

Expected Output:

```
Apple
Banana
Cherry
Updated List: [apple, banana, cherry, date]
```

Here, the Groovy code retrieves the ArrayList from the Java class CollectionExample, iterates through its elements to print each capitalized item, adds a new fruit, and then prints the updated list.

Example 3: Implementing a Groovy Interface in Java

In this example, a Groovy interface is implemented by a Java class. The Groovy interface defines a method to be implemented.

Groovy interface definition:

```
interface GreetingService {
    String greet(String name)
}
```

Implementation in Java:

```
public class GreetingServiceImpl implements GreetingService {
    @Override
    public String greet(String name) {
        return "Hello, " + name;
    }
}
```

Groovy code to utilize the Java implementation:

```
def greetingService = new GreetingServiceImpl()
def message = greetingService.greet("John")
println(message)
```

Expected Output:

```
Hello, John
```

The Groovy script creates an instance of the Java class GreetingServiceImpl, invokes the greet method, and prints the returned greeting message.

Example 4: Utilizing Java Annotations in Groovy Classes

This example demonstrates the use of Java annotations in Groovy classes. The Java annotation is defined to provide metadata for methods.

Java annotation definition:

```
import java.lang.annotation.*;

@Retention(RetentionPolicy.RUNTIME)
@Target(ElementType.METHOD)
public @interface RunMe { }
```

Groovy class using the Java annotation:

```
class AnnotatedClass {
    @RunMe
    def annotatedMethod() {
        println("This method is annotated with @RunMe")
    }
}
```

Java code to reflectively invoke the annotated method:

```
import java.lang.reflect.Method;

public class AnnotationProcessor {
    public static void main(String[] args) throws Exception {
        AnnotatedClass obj = new AnnotatedClass();
        for (Method method : obj.getClass().getDeclaredMethods()) {
            if (method.isAnnotationPresent(RunMe.class)) {
                method.invoke(obj);
            }
        }
    }
}
```

Expected Output:

```
This method is annotated with @RunMe
```

In this scenario, a Groovy class AnnotatedClass defines a method annotated with the Java annotation @RunMe. The Java code reflectively looks for methods annotated with @RunMe and invokes them dynamically.

Example 5: Handling Java Exceptions in Groovy

Groovy can handle exceptions thrown by Java methods using familiar Groovy syntax for exception handling. Consider the following Java class that throws an exception.

Java class throwing an exception:

```
public class ExceptionThrower {
    public void throwException() throws Exception {
        throw new Exception("An error occurred");
```

```
    }
}
```

Groovy code handling the Java exception:

```
def exceptionThrower = new ExceptionThrower()
try {
    exceptionThrower.throwException()
} catch (Exception e) {
    println("Caught exception: ${e.message}")
}
```

Expected Output:

```
Caught exception: An error occurred
```

This example showcases Groovy's capability to utilize try-catch blocks to manage exceptions thrown by Java methods effectively.

These examples highlight practical scenarios where Groovy and Java integration can ease the development process by leveraging the strengths of both languages in a single application, encouraging concise, readable, and maintainable code.

Chapter 8

Metaprogramming in Groovy

This chapter delves into metaprogramming in Groovy, including dynamic method invocation and the use of ExpandoMetaClass and MetaClass. It covers method missing and property missing mechanisms, the application of categories, and Abstract Syntax Tree (AST) transformations. Both compile-time and runtime metaprogramming techniques are discussed, along with the MetaObject Protocol (MOP) and methods for intercepting method calls. Practical examples illustrate the powerful and dynamic capabilities provided by metaprogramming in Groovy.

8.1 Introduction to Metaprogramming

Metaprogramming refers to the practice of writing programs that have the ability to treat other programs as their data. In essence, a metaprogram can read, generate, analyze, or transform other programs, and even modify itself while running. Groovy, being a dynamic language, offers abundant tools for effective metaprogramming, providing flexibility and power beyond standard programming paradigms.

To understand metaprogramming's utility, one must appreciate how it allows the program structure to be altered in ways that traditional runtime utilities cannot achieve. Through Spock tests, Gradle build scripts, and Grails applications, Groovy's metaprogramming capabilities shine in scenarios demanding high flexibility and dynamic adaptation.

Aspect-Oriented Programming: In Groovy, metaprogramming enables aspects such as cross-cutting concerns, like logging and transaction handling, to be isolated from the main business logic. This separation of concerns is a cornerstone of Aspect-Oriented Programming (AOP), and Groovy's support for metaprogramming facilitates this paradigm efficiently.

Dynamic Method Invocation: Central to metaprogramming in Groovy is the ability to define new methods dynamically. When the program encounters a call to a method that does not exist, Groovy allows developers to provide the method implementation dynamically during runtime.

```
class DynamicMethods {
    def propertyMissing(String name) {
        println "Property '$name' is missing."
    }
}

def dm = new DynamicMethods()
dm.someProperty // Prints: Property 'someProperty' is missing.
```

The above example illustrates dynamic handling of missing properties, one of the many metaprogramming utilities Groovy offers.

Method Missing and Property Missing: Apart from method invocation, Groovy facilitates handling unavailable properties and methods through custom-defined hooks. The propertyMissing and methodMissing techniques allow developers to intercept and handle cases where properties or methods of an instance are accessed but not present.

```
class MissingMethods {
    def methodMissing(String name, def args) {
        println "Method '$name' with arguments ${args} is missing."
    }
}

def mm = new MissingMethods()
mm.someMethod(10, 20) // Prints: Method 'someMethod' with arguments [10, 20] is
    missing.
```

Through these capabilities, Groovy surpasses traditional lookup mechanisms, empowering developers with potent tools to dynamically manipulate class and object behavior.

ExpandoMetaClass and MetaClass: The metaclass system in Groovy, particularly the ExpandoMetaClass and MetaClass, is pivotal for advanced metaprogramming. It allows modification of classes at runtime, retrofitting new methods, properties, or even modifying existing ones without altering the source code.

```
class Example { }

Example.metaClass.addedMethod = { -> "Added method execution." }

println new Example().addedMethod() // Prints: Added method execution.
```

The above code adds a new method to the Example class dynamically, showcasing the power and flexibility of ExpandoMetaClass.

Using Categories: Groovy's Category feature enables temporary modification of classes within a given scope, thus adding new methods or altering existing methods during the category's active period. This modification scope is useful for adding class enhancements that should only be accessible within a specific block of code.

```
class TargetClass {
    String originalMethod() { "Original method" }
}

class Enhancements {
    static String enhancedMethod(TargetClass self) { "Enhanced method" }
}

use(Enhancements) {
    println new TargetClass().enhancedMethod() // Prints: Enhanced method
}
```

This example demonstrates the temporary enhancement of TargetClass with a method enhancedMethod using a Category.

AST Transformations: Abstract Syntax Tree transformations allow manipulation of code structure at compilation time, enabling compile-time metaprogramming which impacts coding patterns and behaviors predefined through annotations and transformations.

```
import groovy.transform.Immutable

@Immutable
class ImmutablePoint {
    int x, y
}
```

By using the Immutable AST transformation, the ImmutablePoint class gains immutability traits enforced during the compilation, showcasing how AST transformations can seamlessly integrate advanced metaprogramming techniques.

Compile-time and Runtime Metaprogramming: Metaprogramming distinguishes itself with two primary phases: compile-time and runtime. Compile-time metaprogramming, as observed with AST transformations, manipulates the code structure before runtime execution. Runtime metaprogramming, on the other hand, deals with in-memory code manipulation, beneficial for dynamic scripting and adjustable execution behaviors.

Finally, the MetaObject Protocol (MOP) and dynamic interceptions allow granular control of method invocation and property access, further extending the dynamic capabilities of Groovy's metaprogramming arsenal. Understanding and leveraging these principles and techniques equip developers to craft more flexible, modular, and dynamic applications, thus fully utilizing Groovy's metaprogramming prowess.

8.2 Dynamic Method Invocation

Dynamic method invocation is a pivotal concept in Groovy metaprogramming, allowing methods to be called at runtime that may not necessarily be defined at compile time. This capability is one of the primary features promoting Groovy's flexibility and dynamism.

In Groovy, the resolution of method calls can be deferred until runtime through a technique known as dynamic method invocation. This aspect significantly enhances the language's versatility, particularly in scenarios where the method names might not be known until the execution of the program. The dynamic capabilities of Groovy also allow for easier integration with dynamically typed languages and APIs.

Consider the following example where a method is invoked dynamically:

```
class DynamicInvoker {
    def dynamicMethod(String methodName, args) {
        this.metaClass."$methodName".invoke(this, args)
    }
}

def invoker = new DynamicInvoker()
invoker.metaClass.dynamicHello = { String name ->
    return "Hello, ${name}!"
}

assert invoker.dynamicMethod("dynamicHello", ["Groovy"]) == "Hello, Groovy!"
```

In this snippet, DynamicInvoker dynamically calls any method defined at runtime. The method dynamicMethod() uses Groovy's metaClass to invoke a method whose name is stored in the methodName variable. The specific implementation of the dynamicHello method is provided later, and it can be changed or augmented at runtime.

Dynamic method invocation also plays an essential role in domain-specific languages (DSLs) and frameworks like Grails. When using frameworks, the ability to dynamically create and invoke methods as needed can significantly simplify the application logic.

The following example demonstrates implementing a mock dynamic method invocation:

```
class MockService {
    def invokeMethod(String name, args) {
        println "Called $name with arguments $args"
    }
}

def service = new MockService()
service.someMethod("arg1", 2, 3.0)
```

The output from executing the above example is:

```
Called someMethod with arguments [arg1, 2, 3.0]
```

In the MockService class, the invokeMethod is automatically called whenever any method that's not explicitly defined in the class is invoked. This feature effectively captures all undefined method calls and processes them through invokeMethod. This can be instrumental for constructing mock objects in test-driven development (TDD) or creating dynamic proxies.

The robustness of dynamic method invocation lies within the MetaClass mechanism Groovy provides. Taking advantage of MetaClass' interception capabilities, the method resolution can be controlled or altered at runtime. This control allows for a powerful means of extending or modifying class behaviors dynamically.

MetaClass can be modified for an individual instance or for the entire class. Here is an illustration:

```
class Person {
    String name
}

def person = new Person(name: 'John Doe')

person.metaClass.sayName = { -> "My name is ${delegate.name}" }

assert person.sayName() == "My name is John Doe"

// Global modification
Person.metaClass.greet = { -> "Hello from ${delegate.name}" }

def person2 = new Person(name: 'Jane Doe')
```

```
assert person2.greet() == "Hello from Jane Doe"
```

This example shows that the sayName method is dynamically attached to a specific instance of Person. Meanwhile, the greet method is attached to the entire Person class, affecting all its instances.

Dynamic method invocation is not only limited to adding new methods but also encompasses modifying existing methods and handling method missing scenarios. This flexibility enables developers to create highly adaptable and responsive applications, able to meet changing requirements efficiently and effectively.

8.3 ExpandoMetaClass and MetaClass

In Groovy, the *ExpandoMetaClass* and *MetaClass* provide powerful mechanisms to dynamically alter the behavior of classes at runtime. These features enable developers to add, override, or modify methods and properties of existing classes, thus leveraging dynamic capabilities. Understanding these concepts is crucial for effective metaprogramming.

The MetaClass in Groovy is an abstraction that encapsulates the meta-information of a class, including its methods and properties. This meta-level architecture allows for the dynamic alteration of a class's behavior. The ExpandoMetaClass extends this concept, providing more flexibility and enabling the developer to make changes dynamically during runtime.

Basic MetaClass Usage

Consider a simple usage of MetaClass to dynamically add a method to an existing class. The following Groovy code demonstrates how to add a new method greet to the String class:

```
String.metaClass.greet = { ->
  return "Hello, ${delegate}!"
}
```

In this example, metaClass is accessed on the String class to define a greet method that returns a custom greeting message. The delegate keyword refers to the instance of the String class upon which the method is invoked.

To verify the addition of the greet method, execute the following:

```
def name = "Groovy"
println name.greet()
```

The output would be:

```
Hello, Groovy!
```

Using ExpandoMetaClass

The ExpandoMetaClass takes this flexibility a step further. By default, Groovy's metaclass system is read-only for Java classes, but enabling the ExpandoMetaClass allows modifications. Enable ExpandoMetaClass by configuring Groovy as follows:

```
GroovySystem.metaClassRegistry.metaClassCreationHandle = new
    ExpandoMetaClassCreationHandle()
```

Once enabled, the ExpandoMetaClass allows adding methods and properties dynamically. Here is an example demonstrating the dynamic addition of methods and properties:

```
Integer.metaClass.square = { ->
  return delegate * delegate
}

Integer.metaClass.myProperty = "Metadata"
```

With this code, the Integer class is extended to include a new method square, which calculates the square of the integer, and a new property myProperty that returns a string. Test these additions with:

```
def num = 5
println num.square() // Output: 25
println num.myProperty // Output: Metadata
```

The output of this code would be:

```
25
Metadata
```

MetaClass Method Interception

Another powerful feature of MetaClass is the ability to intercept method calls. This allows developers to add pre-processing or post-processing logic around existing methods. Consider the following example where the toString method of the Object class is intercepted:

```
Object.metaClass.toString = { ->
  return "Intercepted: " + delegate.metaClass.invokeMethod(delegate, 'toString', null)
}
```

In this example, the toString method is overridden to prepend "Intercepted: " to the original output. Verify this implementation as follows:

```
def obj = new Object()
println obj.toString()
```

The expected output would be:

```
Intercepted: java.lang.Object@1b6d3586
```

This demonstrates how method call interception can be utilized to introduce additional logic seamlessly.

ExpandoMetaClass Static Method Addition

The ExpandoMetaClass also supports the addition of static methods. Static methods are methods that belong to the class rather than any particular instance. Here's an example showing how to add a static method:

```
Integer.metaClass.'static'.isEven = { int number ->
  return number % 2 == 0
}
```

In this snippet, isEven is a static method that checks if a number is even. To invoke this static method:

```
println Integer.isEven(4) // Output: true
println Integer.isEven(5) // Output: false
```

As demonstrated, static methods added via ExpandoMetaClass can be called without creating an instance of the Integer class, showcasing the dynamic and flexible capabilities of Groovy's metaprogramming features.

Both MetaClass and ExpandoMetaClass significantly enhance the flexibility and dynamism of Groovy applications. By using these powerful tools, you can tailor existing classes to suit specific needs at runtime, thereby increasing the adaptability and functionality of your Groovy programs.

8.4 Method Missing and Property Missing

In Groovy, two critical methods, methodMissing and propertyMissing, provide powerful mechanisms for handling undefined methods and properties dynamically. These mechanisms enhance the flexibility of Groovy metaprogramming, enabling developers to create highly adaptable and resilient code. Let's delve into the intricacies of these features and understand their applications, utilization, and potential pitfalls.

methodMissing

The methodMissing is a method invoked by the Groovy runtime when an undefined method is called on an object. This dynamic handling allows the creation of handlers that can process calls to non-existent methods, which can be particularly useful for implementing proxies, delegating calls, or creating dynamic interfaces.

```
// Define a class with a methodMissing implementation
class DynamicHandler {
    def methodMissing(String name, def args) {
        println "Called method: $name with arguments: $args"
    }
}

def handler = new DynamicHandler()
handler.someUndefinedMethod('arg1', 'arg2') // This will call methodMissing
```

In the example above, the DynamicHandler class does not define a method named someUndefinedMethod. When this method is invoked, Groovy triggers the methodMissing method, passing the method name and arguments as parameters. The specified methodMissing implementation then handles this call, providing a dynamic response or behavior.

propertyMissing

Similarly, Groovy provides the propertyMissing method to handle accesses to undefined properties. This mechanism can be used to dynamically manage property access, enable lazy initialization, or integrate with external data sources seamlessly.

```
// Define a class with a propertyMissing implementation
class DynamicPropertiesHandler {
    def properties = [:]

    def propertyMissing(String name) {
        println "Getting missing property: $name"
        return properties[name]
    }

    void propertyMissing(String name, def value) {
        println "Setting missing property: $name to value: $value"
        properties[name] = value
    }
}

def handler = new DynamicPropertiesHandler()
handler.someUndefinedProperty = 'initial value' // This will call propertyMissing(
      String, def)
println handler.someUndefinedProperty // This will call propertyMissing(String)
```

The DynamicPropertiesHandler class in the example handles undefined property accesses using the overloaded propertyMissing method. It manages a map of properties, dynamically responding to get and set operations on properties that have not been explicitly defined in the class.

Applications of Method and Property Missing

methodMissing and propertyMissing are commonly employed in various sophisticated applications such as:

- **Domain-Specific Languages (DSLs)**: These mechanisms are instrumental in creating internal DSLs, allowing for flexible handling of methods and properties that conform to the DSL's syntax and semantics.
- **Proxies and Delegates**: They facilitate the creation of proxy objects that forward method calls or property accesses to other objects, enabling features like lazy initialization, logging, and access control.
- **Database Entities**: In frameworks like Grails, propertyMissing is used to dynamically manage database entity properties, enabling seamless interaction with underlying data stores.

Practical Considerations

While methodMissing and propertyMissing offer significant dynamism, their use requires careful consideration to avoid common pitfalls:

- **Performance**: Dynamic method and property handling introduce a level of indirection that can impact performance. Ensure that the benefits outweigh the potential overhead in performance-critical applications.
- **Debugging**: Debugging issues in code utilizing these features can be challenging due to the non-explicit nature of method and property definitions. Proper logging and comprehensive test coverage are essential.
- **Readability**: Code relying extensively on these mechanisms can be harder to understand and maintain. Strive for a balance between dynamism and clarity.

Consider the following example, where methodMissing is used to create a dynamic implementation of a mathematical function evaluator:

```
class DynamicMathEvaluator {
    def methodMissing(String name, def args) {
        if (name.startsWith('calculate')) {
            def functionName = name - 'calculate'
            return evaluateFunction(functionName, args)
        } else {
            throw new MissingMethodException(name, this.class, args)
        }
    }

    private def evaluateFunction(String functionName, def args) {
        switch (functionName) {
            case 'Square':
                return args[0] * args[0]
            case 'Cube':
                return args[0] * args[0] * args[0]
            default:
                throw new MissingMethodException(functionName, this.class, args)
        }
    }
}

def evaluator = new DynamicMathEvaluator()
println evaluator.calculateSquare(3) // Outputs: 9
println evaluator.calculateCube(2) // Outputs: 8
```

In this example, methodMissing intercepts calls to methods prefixed with calculate and dynamically evaluates their functionality based on the method name suffix (e.g., Square, Cube). This approach showcases the potential of methodMissing to implement flexible and extensible computational logic.

The ability to handle undefined methods and properties dynamically using methodMissing and propertyMissing provides significant leverage in crafting adaptable and robust Groovy applications. By harnessing these tools with appropriate design considerations, developers can effectively enhance their code's dynamism and functionality while maintaining readability and performance.

8.5 Using Categories

Categories in Groovy provide a means to add methods to existing classes dynamically. This mechanism allows for modifications to the behavior of classes without altering their source code. By utilizing the @Category annotation, developers can inject new methods into classes, thus temporarily extending their functionality within a certain scope. This technique is especially useful for tasks that require specific behavior enhancements without the need to subclass or modify the original class directly.

To demonstrate this concept, consider a simple example where additional methods are added to the String class using a category.

```
class StringUtilCategory {
    static String shout(String self) {
        self.toUpperCase() + "!"
    }

    static String whisper(String self) {
        self.toLowerCase() + "..."
    }
}

use(StringUtilCategory) {
    assert "hello".shout() == "HELLO!"
    assert "HELLO".whisper() == "hello..."
}
```

In this code snippet, the StringUtilCategory defines two new methods: shout and whisper. These methods are added to the String class within the scope of the use block. The @Category annotation is implicitly understood here, and it directs Groovy to enhance the String class dynamically with these methods.

The scope of these enhancements is strictly limited to the use block. Outside this block, the String class does not have the shout and whisper methods.

Another powerful capability of categories is to override existing methods of a class temporarily. For instance, consider tweaking the List class's max method to find the maximum by absolute value.

```
class ListUtilCategory {
    static Number max(List self, boolean byAbsoluteValue = false) {
        if (byAbsoluteValue) {
            return self.max { Math.abs(it) }
        }
        return self.max()
    }
}

use(ListUtilCategory) {
    def numbers = [-10, -20, 15, 5]
    assert numbers.max() == 15
    assert numbers.max(true) == -20
}
```

Here, the ListUtilCategory defines a new max method for lists, with an optional parameter byAbsoluteValue. Inside the use block, this method temporarily supersedes the original max method of the List class. The numbers.max() invocation behaves as expected, returning the maximum element according to the default behavior. However, numbers.max(true) uses the overridden method, returning the maximum by absolute value.

Categories also support method enhancements in more complex structures, such as adding factory methods. For example, adding a timesTwo method to integers that returns a list with each element being twice the original value.

```
class IntegerUtilCategory {
    static List<Integer> timesTwo(Integer self) {
        return (1..self).collect { it * 2 }
    }
}

use(IntegerUtilCategory) {
    assert 3.timesTwo() == [2, 4, 6]
    assert 5.timesTwo() == [2, 4, 6, 8, 10]
}
```

This example demonstrates how the timesTwo method is seamlessly integrated into the Integer class within the use block. The new method converts a range from 1 to the integer value into a list of elements each multiplied by two.

A crucial aspect to consider while using categories is ensuring that the enhancements do not lead to ambiguous method calls, especially when multiple categories are in use. The order of precedence and method resolution might produce unexpected results if not managed properly.

The enhancement of existing classes through categories signifies a flexible yet controlled method of extending or altering class capabilities. This approach proves its merit in scenarios where code modification or subclassing is impractical or undesirable.

8.6 AST Transformations

Abstract Syntax Tree (AST) transformations provide a powerful way to manipulate and extend Groovy's code during the compilation process. The primary focus of AST transformations is to modify the program's structure, analyzing and altering the code before it is converted into bytecode. This section covers the various facets of AST transformations, including the types, practical applications, and implementation details.

Groovy offers two types of AST transformations: global and local. Global transformations are applied to the entire codebase and are typically used for cross-cutting concerns, while local transformations are limited to specific elements such as classes or methods.

Local AST Transformations: Local transformations are implemented using annotations. The groovy.transform package provides several built-in transformations, such as @Immutable, @Delegate, and @TupleConstructor. These annotations modify the class at compile-time, injecting additional methods or altering the class's structure.

```
import groovy.transform.Immutable
import groovy.transform.Delegate

@Immutable
class Point {
    int x
    int y
}

class Rectangle {
    @Delegate Point topLeft
    @Delegate Point bottomRight
}

def rect = new Rectangle(topLeft: new Point(x: 0, y: 0), bottomRight: new Point(x: 10,
     y: 10))
println rect.x // Prints 0
println rect.y // Prints 0
```

In this example, the @Immutable annotation ensures that the Point class's instances are immutable, automatically generating constructors, equals, hashCode, and toString methods. The @Delegate annotation in the Rectangle class delegates access to the methods of the Point class, allowing seamless interaction with the topLeft and bottomRight properties.

Global AST Transformations: Global transformations require more complex setups and are implemented by creating classes that extend AbstractASTTransformation. These classes are then registered in the META-INF/services/org.codehaus.groovy.transform.ASTTransformation file. This allows the transformation to process the entire code, enabling significant structural changes.

```
package com.example

import org.codehaus.groovy.control.CompilePhase
import org.codehaus.groovy.transform.GroovyASTTransformation
import org.codehaus.groovy.ast.ASTNode
import org.codehaus.groovy.ast.builder.AstBuilder
import org.codehaus.groovy.ast.expr.MethodCallExpression
import org.codehaus.groovy.control.SourceUnit
import org.codehaus.groovy.ast.ClassNode
```

```
@GroovyASTTransformation(phase = CompilePhase.SEMANTIC_ANALYSIS)
class CustomTransformation extends AbstractASTTransformation {
    void visit(ASTNode[] nodes, SourceUnit source) {
        def classes = source.AST.classes
        classes.each { ClassNode classNode ->
            classNode.methods.each { methodNode ->
                methodNode.code = new AstBuilder().buildFromString("println 'Method
                        executed'") + methodNode.code
            }
        }
    }
}
```

The above transformation inserts a println statement into each method of the classes being compiled, adding a logging mechanism to signal method execution.

Practical Applications of AST Transformations: One of the most common use cases of AST transformations is code injection for logging, instrumentation, and enforcing coding standards.

```
package com.example

import org.codehaus.groovy.ast.ClassNode
import org.codehaus.groovy.ast.MethodNode
import org.codehaus.groovy.ast.stmt.ExpressionStatement
import org.codehaus.groovy.ast.expr.MethodCallExpression
import org.codehaus.groovy.control.CompilePhase
import org.codehaus.groovy.transform.GroovyASTTransformation
import org.codehaus.groovy.ast.AbstractASTTransformation

@GroovyASTTransformation(phase = CompilePhase.CANONICALIZATION)
class LoggingTransformation extends AbstractASTTransformation {
    @Override
    void visit(ASTNode[] nodes, SourceUnit source) {
        source.AST.classes.each { ClassNode classNode ->
            classNode.methods.each { MethodNode methodNode ->
                if(!methodNode.isAbstract() && !methodNode.isStatic() &&
                        methodNode.instructions) {
                    MethodCallExpression logCall = new MethodCallExpression(
                        null, "println", new ConstantExpression("Entering method: ${
                                methodNode.name}")
                    )
                    methodNode.instructions.add(0, new ExpressionStatement(logCall))
                }
            }
        }
    }
}
```

This transformation automatically inserts logging statements at the beginning of each non-static, non-abstract method, helping developers trace method executions during runtime.

Both local and global AST transformations offer extensive customization capabilities, allowing developers to automate repetitive coding tasks, enhance code uniformity, and implement features that would be otherwise verbose and error-prone if done manually. Through careful application of AST transformations, significant improvements in code maintainability and readability can be achieved.

8.7 Compile-time Metaprogramming

Compile-time metaprogramming in Groovy allows for more efficient and optimized manipulation of code by transforming it at compile time rather than at runtime. This approach can lead to significant performance improvements and can enforce additional compile-time checks, which enhance the robustness of the code. In Groovy, compile-time metaprogramming is primarily facilitated via Abstract Syntax Tree (AST) transformations. This section discusses the principles of AST transformations, their implementation, customization, and illustrates their practical uses.

Abstract Syntax Trees (AST) represent the structure of the source code in a tree form where each node corresponds to a construct occurring in the source code. Groovy provides a comprehensive set of tools to manipulate this tree during the compilation process. By using AST transformations, developers can inject additional behavior, validate structure, or even generate new code before the program is run.

The following example demonstrates a simple AST transformation in Groovy. We will create a custom annotation @ToUpperCase that transforms string fields to upper case.

```
import org.codehaus.groovy.ast.*
import org.codehaus.groovy.ast.builder.AstBuilder
import org.codehaus.groovy.ast.expr.*
import org.codehaus.groovy.ast.stmt.*
import org.codehaus.groovy.control.*
import org.codehaus.groovy.transform.*
import org.codehaus.groovy.transform.GroovyASTTransformationClass

@Retention(RetentionPolicy.SOURCE)
@Target([ElementType.FIELD])
@GroovyASTTransformationClass(["ToUpperCaseASTTransformation"])
@interface ToUpperCase {}
```

The @Retention and @Target annotations define that our custom annotation @ToUpperCase is applicable at the field level and the transformation should be retained only at the source level.

Next, we implement the AST transformation logic:

```
@GroovyASTTransformation(phase = CompilePhase.CANONICALIZATION)
class ToUpperCaseASTTransformation implements ASTTransformation {
    void visit(ASTNode[] nodes, SourceUnit source) {
        AnnotationNode annotationNode = (AnnotationNode) nodes[0]
        AnnotatedNode annotatedNode = (AnnotatedNode) nodes[1]

        if (annotatedNode instanceof FieldNode) {
            FieldNode fieldNode = (FieldNode) annotatedNode

            fieldNode.getDeclaringClass().methods*.code.each {
                BlockStatement block = it.getCode()
                List<Statement> statements = block.statements
                List<Statement> newStatements = statements.collect { Statement
                      statement ->
                    statement instanceof ExpressionStatement && statement.expression
                          instanceof MethodCallExpression && statement.expression.
                          methodAsString == "set${fieldNode.name.capitalize()}"
                      ? replaceWithUpperCase(statement, fieldNode.name)
                      : statement
                }
                block.statements = newStatements
            }
        }
    }

    private Statement replaceWithUpperCase(Statement statement, String fieldName) {
        ExpressionStatement exprStmt = (ExpressionStatement) statement
        MethodCallExpression methodCall = (MethodCallExpression) exprStmt.
              expression
        ArgumentListExpression args = (ArgumentListExpression) methodCall.
              arguments

        MethodCallExpression newMethodCall = new MethodCallExpression(
            new VariableExpression("this"),
            methodCall.methodAsString,
            new ArgumentListExpression(new MethodCallExpression(args[0], "
                  toUpperCase", ArgumentListExpression.EMPTY_ARRAY))
        )

        return new ExpressionStatement(newMethodCall)
    }
}
```

ToUpperCaseASTTransformation is implemented to manipulate the source code during the CANONICALIZATION phase of the Groovy compiler's lifecycle. It inspects each field annotated with @ToUpperCase and modifies setter methods to convert their input to uppercase.

A practical demonstration involves applying this transformation to a Groovy class:

```
class Example {
    @ToUpperCase
    String name

    void setName(String name) {
        this.name = name
    }
```

```
    String getName() {
        return name
    }
}

def example = new Example()
example.name = "hello"
assert example.name == "HELLO"
```

The Groovy compiler, during the compilation of the Example class, transforms the setName method to invoke the toUpperCase() method on its argument, thus automatically converting the input to uppercase.

In practice, compile-time transformations enforce stricter validation rules and inject optimized code before runtime, providing a robust, efficient, and secure method to enhance Groovy applications. They are extensively used in frameworks and libraries where automated query conditions, security checks, or logging logic can be added seamlessly. For developers, these transformations hold the key to writing cleaner, more maintainable, and higher-performing Groovy programs.

8.8 MetaObject Protocol (MOP)

MetaObject Protocol (MOP) is a fundamental part of Groovy's metaprogramming capabilities that provides an interface to alter the runtime behavior of an object. It offers a standardized way to interact with the meta-level architecture of objects, thus enabling both dynamic and static modifications of behaviors. Understanding MOP is critical for leveraging the full power of Groovy in manipulating classes, methods, and properties dynamically.

At its core, MOP enables the developer to override method calls, property access, and provide custom behavior by using meta-level operations. These operations involve the manipulation of the MetaClass, which acts as the repository of meta-level information for every Groovy object.

```
class Person {
    String name
    int age
}
```

For the class Person defined above, here is how we can interact with the MOP:

```
// Get the MetaClass of Person
MetaClass metaClass = Person.metaClass
```

```
// Add a new method dynamically
metaClass.getFullName = { -> "$name, Age: $age" }
```

In the example above, we add a new method getFullName to the Person class dynamically by accessing its MetaClass. This method concatenates the name and age properties.

```
def person = new Person(name: "John Doe", age: 30)
println person.getFullName() // Outputs: John Doe, Age: 30
```

Method and Property Interception

One of the significant features of MOP is method interception through overriding the invokeMethod and getProperty/setProperty methods. This allows for custom mechanisms when methods are invoked or when properties are accessed or modified.

```
class CustomHandler {
    def invokeMethod(String name, Object args) {
        return "Calling method $name with arguments $args"
    }

    def getProperty(String name) {
        return "Getting property $name"
    }

    def setProperty(String name, value) {
        println "Setting property $name to $value"
    }
}
```

By creating the class CustomHandler, we explicitly override the invokeMethod and getProperty/setProperty methods to intercept dynamic method calls and property accesses.

```
def handler = new CustomHandler()
println handler.someMethod("arg1", "arg2") // Outputs: Calling method someMethod with arguments [arg1, arg2]
println handler.someProperty              // Outputs: Getting property someProperty
handler.someProperty = "New value"         // Outputs: Setting property someProperty to New value
```

ExpandoMetaClass

Groovy's ExpandoMetaClass extends the MetaClass functionality by allowing more flexible and dynamic modifications. It is enabled by default and can be utilized to add methods, properties, or even constructors at runtime.

```
ExpandoMetaClass.enableGlobally()

Person.metaClass.sayHello = { -> "Hello, my name is $name" }
```

In this snippet, we enable ExpandoMetaClass globally and add a method sayHello to the Person class, which returns a personalized greeting.

```
def person = new Person(name: "Jane")
println person.sayHello() // Outputs: Hello, my name is Jane
```

Overriding Constructors

The MetaClass can also be employed to override existing constructors or add new ones dynamically. This can be particularly useful for customizing the instantiation process of classes.

```
Person.metaClass.constructor = { String defaultName ->
    new Person(name: defaultName, age: 0)
}
```

Here, we override the constructor of the Person class to accept a string argument for name and default the age to zero.

```
def person = new Person("Default Name")
println person.name // Outputs: Default Name
println person.age  // Outputs: 0
```

Performance Considerations

While MOP provides extensive flexibility, it is paramount to consider the performance implications of frequent MetaClass manipulations, especially in performance-critical applications. Utilizing MOP improperly can lead to increased memory consumption and slower method invocations. However, with judicious use, MOP allows for highly dynamic and flexible applications.

Understanding and mastering the MetaObject Protocol is a crucial aspect of Groovy metaprogramming. Through the intricate manipulation of MetaClasses, developers can unlock dynamic modifications and custom behaviors in their Groovy applications, effectively harnessing the language's full potential.

8.9 Intercepting Method Calls

Intercepting method calls is a fundamental aspect of metaprogramming that enables developers to intercept, modify, or augment the behavior of method invocations dynamically. In Groovy, this can be achieved through the MetaObject Protocol (MOP), which provides a structured way to define how method calls are handled. This section explores various techniques for intercepting method calls in Groovy, including the use of invokeMethod, metaClass, and Groovy categories.

invokeMethod is a special method in Groovy that allows the interception and handling of method calls that are not explicitly defined in a class. When an undefined method is called on an object, Groovy will delegate the call to the invokeMethod if it is defined. This can be used to add custom behavior or handle dynamic method calls as shown in the following example:

```
class DynamicMethodInterceptor {
    def invokeMethod(String name, args) {
        return "Intercepted method: ${name} with arguments: ${args.join(', ')}"
    }
}

// Using the interceptor
def interceptor = new DynamicMethodInterceptor()
println interceptor.someUndefinedMethod('arg1', 'arg2')
```

The output for the above code will be:

```
Intercepted method: someUndefinedMethod with arguments: arg1, arg2
```

Here, when someUndefinedMethod is called, it is intercepted by the invokeMethod defined in DynamicMethodInterceptor, which provides a custom response.

Adding Custom Behavior with metaClass —————————————— metaClass is another powerful feature in Groovy that facilitates the modification and extension of existing classes at runtime. By using metaClass, developers can intercept method calls, add new methods, or override existing ones. Below is an example demonstrating how to use metaClass to intercept method calls and add custom behavior:

```
class Person {
    String name
    int age
}

def person = new Person(name: 'John', age: 30)
person.metaClass.invokeMethod = { String name, args ->
    if (name == 'greet') {
        return "Hello, ${person.name}"
    }
    // delegate to the default invokeMethod
    return delegate.metaClass.getMetaMethod(name, args).invoke(delegate, args)
}

println person.greet()
println person.toString()
```

The output will be:

```
Hello, John
Person(name:John, age:30)
```

In this example, the invokeMethod of the metaClass is overridden to intercept calls to the greet method, providing a custom implementation. All other method calls are delegated to the default invokeMethod implementation.

Combining invokeMethod and metaClass ——————————— Combining invokeMethod with metaClass adds another level of flexibility. By dynamically creating or modifying methods, developers can intercept specific method calls and handle them in a customized manner. Consider the following example:

```
class Calculator {
    double add(double a, double b) {
        return a + b
    }
}

def calculator = new Calculator()
calculator.metaClass.invokeMethod = { String name, args ->
    if (name.startsWith('multiply')) {
        double result = args[0] * args[1]
        return "Intercepted multiplication: ${args[0]} * ${args[1]} = $result"
    }
    return delegate.metaClass.getMetaMethod(name, args).invoke(delegate, args)
}
println calculator.add(2, 3) // Original method call
println calculator.multiply(4, 5) // Intercepted method call
```

The result will be:

```
5.0
Intercepted multiplication: 4.0 * 5.0 = 20.0
```

In this example, calls to the multiply method are intercepted and handled with a custom implementation. Calls to the add method remain unaffected.

Interception via Groovy Categories ——————————— Groovy categories provide a way to augment existing classes with new methods through the use of static methods and method categories. This can also be used for the interception of method calls by wrapping existing methods with custom logic. The following example demonstrates the use of Groovy categories to intercept and modify the behavior of method calls:

```
class StringCategory {
    static String shout(String self) {
        return self.toUpperCase() + "!!!"
    }
}

use (StringCategory) {
    println "hello world".shout()
}
```

Producing the output:

```
HELLO WORLD!!!
```

Here, the method shout is dynamically added to the String class for the duration of the use block, effectively intercepting any calls to shout.

The combination of Groovy's dynamic capabilities through invokeMethod, metaClass, and categories empowers developers to build robust, flexible, and dynamic applications. Understanding and leveraging these techniques is crucial for mastering metaprogramming in Groovy.

8.10 Practical Examples of Metaprogramming

In this section, we explore practical examples of metaprogramming in Groovy to illustrate the principles discussed in previous sections. These examples demonstrate the power and flexibility of metaprogramming, showcasing scenarios where dynamic behavior provides substantial benefits.

Example 1: Dynamic Method Invocation

Dynamic method invocation allows dynamically constructed method names to be called at runtime. In this example, we create a class Calculator that dynamically constructs and invokes methods:

```
class Calculator {
    def invokeMethod(String name, Object args) {
        if (name.startsWith("calculate")) {
            def operation = name.substring(9).toLowerCase()
            switch (operation) {
                case "add":
                    return args[0] + args[1]
                case "subtract":
                    return args[0] - args[1]
                case "multiply":
                    return args[0] * args[1]
                case "divide":
                    return args[0] / args[1]
                default:
                    throw new MissingMethodException(name, this.class, args)
            }
        } else {
            throw new MissingMethodException(name, this.class, args)
        }
    }
}

def calculator = new Calculator()
println(calculator.calculateAdd(5, 3)) // Prints 8
println(calculator.calculateSubtract(5, 3)) // Prints 2
println(calculator.calculateMultiply(5, 3)) // Prints 15
println(calculator.calculateDivide(6, 3)) // Prints 2
```

This example demonstrates how dynamic method names can be interpreted and executed based on custom logic.

Example 2: Using ExpandoMetaClass for Dynamic Properties

The ExpandoMetaClass allows runtime modifications of classes to add methods and properties dynamically. Here we demonstrate the addition of a dynamic property:

```
class Person {
    String name
}

Person.metaClass.setAge = { int age ->
    delegate.metaClass.age = age
}

Person.metaClass.getAge = {
    return delegate.metaClass.hasProperty(delegate, 'age')?.get(delegate)
}

def person = new Person(name: 'John')
person.age = 30

println("${person.name} is ${person.age} years old.") // Prints "John is 30 years old."
```

In this example, the Person class is dynamically enhanced with a new property age, and getter and setter methods are added.

Example 3: Method Missing for Dynamic Behavior

The methodMissing mechanism is useful for catching calls to methods that are not explicitly defined. Below, a class implements a methodMissing handler to provide dynamic behavior:

```
class DynamicGreeter {
    def methodMissing(String name, def args) {
        if (name.startsWith("greet")) {
            def lang = name.substring(5).toLowerCase()
            switch (lang) {
                case "english":
                    return "Hello, ${args[0]}!"
                case "spanish":
                    return "Hola, ${args[0]}!"
                case "french":
                    return "Bonjour, ${args[0]}!"
                default:
                    throw new MissingMethodException(name, this.class, args)
            }
        } else {
            throw new MissingMethodException(name, this.class, args)
        }
    }
}

def greeter = new DynamicGreeter()
println(greeter.greetEnglish('John')) // Prints "Hello, John!"
println(greeter.greetSpanish('Maria')) // Prints "Hola, Maria!"
```

```
println(greeter.greetFrench('Marie')) // Prints "Bonjour, Marie!"
```

By employing methodMissing, the DynamicGreeter class can respond to a variety of greet methods without explicitly defining each method, providing flexible multilingual greetings.

Example 4: AST Transformations for Compile-Time Metaprogramming

Abstract Syntax Tree (AST) transformations allow for compile-time modifications of the code. Here we use an AST transformation to automatically log method entry and exit points:

```
import org.codehaus.groovy.transform.GroovyASTTransformationClass
import org.codehaus.groovy.ast.ClassNode
import org.codehaus.groovy.ast.MethodNode
import org.codehaus.groovy.ast.expr.ClosureExpression
import org.codehaus.groovy.ast.stmt.BlockStatement
import org.codehaus.groovy.ast.stmt.ExpressionStatement
import org.codehaus.groovy.ast.expr.MethodCallExpression
import org.codehaus.groovy.control.CompilePhase
import org.codehaus.groovy.transform.ASTTransformation

@GroovyASTTransformation(phase = CompilePhase.SEMANTIC_ANALYSIS)
class LogASTTransformation implements ASTTransformation {
    void visit(ASTNode[] nodes, SourceUnit source) {
        source.ast.classes.each { ClassNode classNode ->
            classNode.methods.each { MethodNode methodNode ->
                def startLog = new ExpressionStatement(new MethodCallExpression(
                    new VariableExpression('this'),
                    'println',
                    new ArgumentListExpression(new ConstantExpression("Entering ${
                        methodNode.name}"))
                ))
                def endLog = new ExpressionStatement(new MethodCallExpression(
                    new VariableExpression('this'),
                    'println',
                    new ArgumentListExpression(new ConstantExpression("Exiting ${
                        methodNode.name}"))
                ))

                def methodBlock = (BlockStatement) methodNode.code
                methodBlock.statements.add(0, startLog)
                methodBlock.statements.add(endLog)
            }
        }
    }
}

@GroovyASTTransformationClass(["example.LogASTTransformation"])
class MyService {
    void serve() {
        println("Serving...")
    }
}

new MyService().serve()
```

Output:

```
Entering serve
Serving...
Exiting serve
```

This example shows an AST transformation that adds logging around all methods of the MyService class. The transformation is applied at compile time, ensuring that all method entries and exits are logged without modifying the original source code.

Metaprogramming in Groovy provides powerful tools to dynamically modify and enhance code behavior. By leveraging dynamic method invocation, ExpandoMetaClass, methodMissing, and AST Transformations, developers can write more flexible, concise, and maintainable code.

Chapter 9

Working with XML and JSON

This chapter discusses handling XML and JSON data in Groovy, including reading XML using XmlSlurper and XmlParser, and writing XML with MarkupBuilder. It covers reading and writing JSON with JsonSlurper and JsonBuilder, navigating and querying XML, and manipulating JSON data. Additionally, it explores transforming between XML and JSON and provides real-world examples to demonstrate the practical applications of these techniques for structured data handling in Groovy.

9.1 Introduction to XML and JSON in Groovy

Groovy provides robust and convenient support for handling XML and JSON, making it an excellent choice for developers working with these popular data formats. Understanding how to manipulate XML and JSON efficiently is crucial for modern applications that often use these formats for configuration, data interchange, or storage.

XML (eXtensible Markup Language) is a versatile, widely-used markup language that defines rules for encoding documents in a format that is both human-readable and machine-readable. It allows users to create custom tags and nested structures, making it suitable for representing complex data hierarchies.

JSON (JavaScript Object Notation) is a lightweight data interchange format that is easy for humans to read and write, and easy for machines to parse and generate. JSON's syntax comprises key/value pairs and ordered lists of values, which makes it particularly useful for representing structured data in web applications.

Groovy simplifies working with XML and JSON through built-in libraries and DSLs (Domain Specific Languages). This section delves into these capabilities, providing you with the necessary tools to effectively manage XML and JSON data.

To begin, let's briefly explore Groovy's core libraries for handling XML and JSON:

- XmlSlurper and XmlParser for reading XML documents.
- MarkupBuilder for creating XML documents.
- JsonSlurper for reading JSON data.
- JsonBuilder for creating JSON data.

XmlSlurper and XmlParser are both Groovy classes used for parsing XML. The choice between them depends on the use case: XmlSlurper works best when you want to traverse the XML structure in a read-only manner, while XmlParser is more powerful for scenarios that require manipulation of XML elements.

Here is an example of parsing XML using XmlSlurper:

```
def xmlText = '''
<book>
  <title>Mastering Groovy Programming</title>
  <author>John Doe</author>
</book>
'''

def xmlSlurper = new XmlSlurper()
def book = xmlSlurper.parseText(xmlText)

println book.title.text()
println book.author.text()
```

The output of the above code:

```
Mastering Groovy Programming
John Doe
```

XmlSlurper parses the provided XML text into a tree structure of GPathResult instances, enabling easy and intuitive navigation of the XML content.

For creating XML documents, MarkupBuilder is an indispensable tool. It allows developers to build XML structures programmatically in a highly readable manner. Here is a simple usage example:

```
def writer = new StringWriter()
def xml = new MarkupBuilder(writer)

xml.book {
  title 'Mastering Groovy Programming'
  author 'John Doe'
}

println writer.toString()
```

The resulting XML:

```
<book>
  <title>Mastering Groovy Programming</title>
  <author>John Doe</author>
</book>
```

On the JSON side, JsonSlurper and JsonBuilder complement each other similarly to how XmlSlurper and MarkupBuilder complement each other for XML. JsonSlurper parses JSON text into Groovy data structures, which are easy to use in Groovy scripts:

```
def jsonText = '''
{
  "title": "Mastering Groovy Programming",
  "author": "John Doe"
}
'''

def jsonSlurper = new JsonSlurper()
def book = jsonSlurper.parseText(jsonText)

println book.title
println book.author
```

The output of the above code:

```
Mastering Groovy Programming
John Doe
```

JsonBuilder helps generate JSON text from Groovy objects, enabling the seamless creation of JSON data structures:

```
def json = new JsonBuilder()
json.book {
  title 'Mastering Groovy Programming'
  author 'John Doe'
}

println json.toPrettyString()
```

The resulting JSON:

```
{
  "book": {
    "title": "Mastering Groovy Programming",
    "author": "John Doe"
  }
}
```

Understanding these tools and their applications forms the foundation for more complex tasks involving XML and JSON in Groovy. The following sections will build upon this foundation, demonstrating advanced techniques for reading, writing, navigating, and manipulating XML and JSON data, and transforming between these formats in Groovy.

9.2 Reading XML with XmlSlurper

To handle the reading and parsing of XML data in Groovy, the XmlSlurper class provides a robust and efficient method. The XmlSlurper makes it convenient to parse XML content, allowing for easy navigation and manipulation of the XML structure. This section delves into the usage of XmlSlurper, demonstrating its capabilities through clear examples and detailed explanations.

The XmlSlurper class is part of Groovy's standard library. It is designed to work in a manner similar to the XmlParser, but with a more lenient and user-friendly approach. While XmlParser builds a Document Object Model (DOM), XmlSlurper creates a lazily-evaluated tree of GPathResult objects. This feature allows XmlSlurper to handle large XML files more efficiently.

```
import groovy.util.XmlSlurper

def xmlContent = '''
<library>
    <book id="1">
        <title>The Catcher in the Rye</title>
        <author>J.D. Salinger</author>
        <year>1951</year>
    </book>
    <book id="2">
        <title>To Kill a Mockingbird</title>
        <author>Harper Lee</author>
        <year>1960</year>
    </book>
</library>
'''

def xmlSlurper = new XmlSlurper()
def library = xmlSlurper.parseText(xmlContent)

library.book.each { book ->
    println "Title: ${book.title}, Author: ${book.author}, Year: ${book.year}"
}
```

In this example, we define a string containing XML content and parse it using XmlSlurper. The parseText method is convenient when working with XML stored as a string. It returns a GPathResult object, which enables the simple navigation of the XML structure using Groovy's GPath expressions.

The parsed XML is then traversed with library.book.each, iterating over each <book> element. The println statement displays the title, author, and year of each book using the dot notation to access the XML elements.

To demonstrate the power and flexibility of XmlSlurper, consider the following example, where we parse XML from an external file:

```
import groovy.util.XmlSlurper
import java.io.File

def xmlFile = new File('library.xml')
def xmlSlurper = new XmlSlurper()
def library = xmlSlurper.parse(xmlFile)

library.book.each { book ->
    println "Book ID: ${book.@id}"
    println "Title: ${book.title}"
    println "Author: ${book.author}"
    println "Year: ${book.year}"
}
```

Here, the parse method is used to read XML from an external file, library.xml. The XmlSlurper efficiently processes the file, and the resulting GPathResult object, library, is iterated similarly to the previous example. Note the usage of the attribute id accessed with book.@id, which demonstrates XmlSlurper's support for reading XML attributes seamlessly.

```
Book ID: 1
Title: The Catcher in the Rye
Author: J.D. Salinger
Year: 1951
Book ID: 2
Title: To Kill a Mockingbird
Author: Harper Lee
Year: 1960
```

Moreover, XmlSlurper allows for complex queries using GPath expressions. These expressions enable sophisticated navigation and filtering of XML data. The following example showcases querying specific elements:

```
import groovy.util.XmlSlurper
```

```
def xmlContent = '''
<library>
    <book id="1">
        <title>The Catcher in the Rye</title>
        <author>J.D. Salinger</author>
        <year>1951</year>
    </book>
    <book id="2">
        <title>To Kill a Mockingbird</title>
        <author>Harper Lee</author>
        <year>1960</year>
    </book>
    <book id="3">
        <title>1984</title>
        <author>George Orwell</author>
        <year>1949</year>
    </book>
</library>
'''

def xmlSlurper = new XmlSlurper()
def library = xmlSlurper.parseText(xmlContent)

def booksAfter1950 = library.book.findAll { it.year.toInteger() > 1950 }

booksAfter1950.each { book ->
    println "Title: ${book.title}, Year: ${book.year}"
}
```

In this scenario, the GPath expression library.book.findAll { it.year.toInteger() > 1950 } filters the books published after 1950. The findAll method returns a list of books matching the criteria, which is then iterated to print the titles and respective years.

```
Title: The Catcher in the Rye, Year: 1951
Title: To Kill a Mockingbird, Year: 1960
```

XmlSlurper's versatility extends further, allowing for the easy manipulation and inspection of XML data while maintaining performance and readability. Its lazy evaluation and dynamic nature make it ideal for a wide range of applications, from simple XML parsing to complex XML handling in Groovy.

9.3 Reading XML with XmlParser

The XmlParser class in Groovy provides a versatile and convenient means of parsing XML documents. Unlike XmlSlurper, which treats XML as a series of lazy-evaluated objects, XmlParser constructs a fully parsed XML tree, which allows for more powerful and flexible manipulations. This section will cover the use of XmlParser for reading XML documents, demonstrating its capabilities through a series of practical examples.

To begin using XmlParser, first ensure that you have imported the necessary class:

```
import groovy.xml.XmlParser
```

Consider the following XML document, which will be used in subsequent examples:

```
<library>
    <book>
        <title>Groovy in Action</title>
        <author>Dierk Koenig</author>
        <year>2007</year>
    </book>
    <book>
        <title>Making Java Groovy</title>
        <author>Ken Kousen</author>
        <year>2013</year>
    </book>
</library>
```

To parse this XML document using XmlParser, you can use the following code:

```
def xmlContent = """
<library>
    <book>
        <title>Groovy in Action</title>
        <author>Dierk Koenig</author>
        <year>2007</year>
    </book>
    <book>
        <title>Making Java Groovy</title>
        <author>Ken Kousen</author>
        <year>2013</year>
    </book>
</library>
"""

def parser = new XmlParser()
def library = parser.parseText(xmlContent)
```

The parseText method of XmlParser takes a String containing the XML content and returns a parsed XML tree. In this case, the library variable contains the root node of the parsed XML tree.

To access elements within the parsed XML tree, you can utilize Groovy's powerful GPath notation. For example, to retrieve a list of all book titles, you can use the following code:

```
library.book.title.each { title ->
    println title.text()
}
```

```
Groovy in Action
Making Java Groovy
```

In the example above, library.book retrieves all book nodes within the library node, and title.each iterates over each title node, printing its text content.

To access specific attributes or nested elements within the XML, you can use similar GPath expressions. For example, to extract the author and publication year of each book, you can write:

```
library.book.each { book ->
    println "Title: ${book.title.text()}"
    println "Author: ${book.author.text()}"
    println "Year: ${book.year.text()}"
}
```

```
Title: Groovy in Action
Author: Dierk Koenig
Year: 2007
Title: Making Java Groovy
Author: Ken Kousen
Year: 2013
```

Using XmlParser, it is also possible to manipulate the XML tree in memory. For instance, to add a new book to the library, you can directly modify the parsed XML tree and write it back to a string or a file:

```
def newBook = new groovy.util.Node(library, 'book')
newBook.appendNode('title', 'Programming Groovy 2')
newBook.appendNode('author', 'Venkat Subramaniam')
newBook.appendNode('year', '2013')

// Convert the modified XML back to a string
def writer = new StringWriter()
def nodePrinter = new XmlNodePrinter(new PrintWriter(writer))
nodePrinter.print(library)
println writer.toString()
```

The output will display the updated XML structure, including the new book entry:

```
<library>
  <book>
    <title>Groovy in Action</title>
    <author>Dierk Koenig</author>
    <year>2007</year>
  </book>
  <book>
    <title>Making Java Groovy</title>
    <author>Ken Kousen</author>
    <year>2013</year>
  </book>
  <book>
    <title>Programming Groovy 2</title>
    <author>Venkat Subramaniam</author>
    <year>2013</year>
  </book>
</library>
```

The above example demonstrates how to not only read but also modify an XML document using XmlParser. This ability to parse, navigate, and update XML documents highlights the flexibility and power of XmlParser in Groovy for XML processing tasks.

In cases where the XML document is stored in an external file rather than a string, XmlParser offers several methods to parse the XML directly from files or streams:

```
def parser = new XmlParser()
def library = parser.parse(new File('path/to/library.xml'))
```

This approach is useful for large XML documents or when reading from network streams or other data sources.

The XmlParser class provides the developer with the capability to handle XML documents comprehensively, enabling not only the extraction of information but also the manipulation and transformation of the XML structure to meet various application requirements.

9.4 Writing XML with MarkupBuilder

Groovy provides the MarkupBuilder class, an essential tool for generating XML documents programmatically. MarkupBuilder facilitates the creation of XML in a succinct and readable manner by leveraging a builder pattern. Let's explore the process of constructing XML documents using MarkupBuilder, investigating its capabilities to produce structured XML output with precision.

To employ MarkupBuilder, begin by importing the necessary classes. Here's a simple example illustrating how to create an XML document:

```
import groovy.xml.MarkupBuilder

def writer = new StringWriter()
def xml = new MarkupBuilder(writer)

xml.groovyProject {
    name 'Mastering Groovy Programming'
    chapters {
        chapter(id: 1, title: 'Introduction to XML and JSON in Groovy')
        chapter(id: 2, title: 'Reading XML with XmlSlurper')
        chapter(id: 3, title: 'Reading XML with XmlParser')
        chapter(id: 4, title: 'Writing XML with MarkupBuilder')
        // Additional chapers can be added similarly
    }
}

println writer.toString()
```

In this example, the MarkupBuilder object xml constructs an XML document. The document starts with the root element groovyProject, followed by child elements including nested elements and attributes.

The output of the above code is as follows:

```
<groovyProject>
  <name>Mastering Groovy Programming</name>
  <chapters>
    <chapter id='1' title='Introduction to XML and JSON in Groovy'/>
    <chapter id='2' title='Reading XML with XmlSlurper'/>
    <chapter id='3' title='Reading XML with XmlParser'/>
    <chapter id='4' title='Writing XML with MarkupBuilder'/>
  </chapters>
</groovyProject>
```

Element Creation and Attributes

The MarkupBuilder allows the seamless addition of elements and attributes. Elements can contain nested elements or text. Attributes are added using a key-value map within the element methods. For example, in the above code, chapters are created with an id and title as attributes.

Namespaces and Custom XML Markup

When creating XML documents that require namespaces, MarkupBuilder provides an easy way to incorporate them. Specify namespaces as part of the attribute map. Here is an example demonstrating namespace usage:

```
def writer = new StringWriter()
def xml = new MarkupBuilder(writer)
def ns1 = 'http://www.example.com/ns1'
def ns2 = 'http://www.example.com/ns2'

xml.setDoubleQuotes true
xml.rootTag(xmlns:ns1) {
    'ns1:child'(name: 'FirstChild')
```

```
    'ns2:child'(xmlns:ns2, name: 'SecondChild')
}

println writer.toString()
```

This code produces output with namespaces:

```
<rootTag xmlns="http://www.example.com/ns1">
  <child name="FirstChild" xmlns="http://www.example.com/ns1"/>
  <child name="SecondChild" xmlns="http://www.example.com/ns2"/>
</rootTag>
```

Special Characters and Entities

When working with XML, it is crucial to handle special characters properly. MarkupBuilder ensures special characters are correctly escaped. For example:

```
def writer = new StringWriter()
def xml = new MarkupBuilder(writer)

xml.example {
    data 'This & That'
}

println writer.toString()
```

The output shows that the ampersand is escaped:

```
<example>
  <data>This &amp; That</data>
</example>
```

Handling Complex Structures

MarkupBuilder is adept at handling complex XML structures. Consider the generation of an XML document for a detailed book catalog:

```
def writer = new StringWriter()
def xml = new MarkupBuilder(writer)

xml.catalog {
    book(id: 'bk101') {
        author 'Gambardella, Matthew'
        title 'XML Developer\'s Guide'
        genre 'Computer'
        price 44.95
        publish_date '2000-10-01'
        description 'An in-depth look at creating applications with XML.'
    }
    book(id: 'bk102') {
        author 'Ralls, Kim'
        title 'Midnight Rain'
        genre 'Fantasy'
        price 5.95
        publish_date '2000-12-16'
        description 'A former architect battles corporate zombies, an evil sorceress, and
                her own childhood to become queen of the world.'
    }
```

```
}
println writer.toString()
```

The resulting XML document is:

```
<catalog>
  <book id='bk101'>
    <author>Gambardella, Matthew</author>
    <title>XML Developer's Guide</title>
    <genre>Computer</genre>
    <price>44.95</price>
    <publish_date>2000-10-01</publish_date>
    <description>An in-depth look at creating applications with XML.</description>
  </book>
  <book id='bk102'>
    <author>Ralls, Kim</author>
    <title>Midnight Rain</title>
    <genre>Fantasy</genre>
    <price>5.95</price>
    <publish_date>2000-12-16</publish_date>
    <description>A former architect battles corporate zombies, an evil sorceress, and her own childhood to become queen of the world.</description>
  </book>
</catalog>
```

Precision is paramount when constructing XML. MarkupBuilder ensures that each element, attribute, and text node is accurately represented, maintaining the desired structure and escaping special characters as needed. The fluency of MarkupBuilder's DSL allows for intricate document creation while preserving readability and manageability, making it a valuable tool for XML generation in Groovy applications.

9.5 Reading JSON with JsonSlurper

JsonSlurper is a key class in Groovy when it comes to parsing JSON data. This powerful tool enables developers to efficiently convert JSON (JavaScript Object Notation) content into Java or Groovy data structures, such as maps, lists, and objects. JsonSlurper simplifies the process by offering an intuitive interface to digest complex JSON data easily.

To use JsonSlurper, you need to import the class from the Groovy libraries:

```
import groovy.json.JsonSlurper
```

The fundamental method provided by JsonSlurper is parse, which takes various forms such as a String, Reader, InputStream, File, or URL. Each of these forms allows JsonSlurper to adapt to different sources of JSON content.

Basic Parsing Example

Below is a simple example demonstrating how to parse a JSON string. Consider the JSON string representing a user profile:

```
def jsonStr = '''
{
    "name": "John Doe",
    "age": 30,
    "email": "john.doe@example.com",
    "address": {
        "street": "123 Main St",
        "city": "Anytown",
        "zipcode": "12345"
    }
}
'''
```

Using JsonSlurper, we can parse this JSON string as follows:

```
def jsonSlurper = new JsonSlurper()
def jsonObject = jsonSlurper.parseText(jsonStr)

println jsonObject.name // John Doe
println jsonObject.age // 30
println jsonObject.email // john.doe@example.com
println jsonObject.address.street // 123 Main St
```

In this example, the parseText method is used to parse JSON from a String. The result is a nested data structure converted into Groovy maps and lists, which makes accessing fields straightforward using dot notation.

Parsing JSON from a File

JsonSlurper can also parse JSON directly from files. For instance, given a JSON file user_profile.json, structured similarly to the previous example, you can parse it as follows:

```
// Assuming the file path is "user_profile.json"
def jsonFile = new File('user_profile.json')
def jsonObject = jsonSlurper.parse(jsonFile)

println jsonObject.name // John Doe
println jsonObject.age // 30
println jsonObject.email // john.doe@example.com
println jsonObject.address.street // 123 Main St
```

The parse method, in this case, accepts a File object, enabling seamless parsing of JSON content from a file.

Parsing JSON from a URL

JsonSlurper is versatile enough to handle JSON content loaded from a URL. For example, consider a URL that returns JSON data:

```
def url = new URL('http://example.com/api/user_profile')
def jsonObject = jsonSlurper.parse(url)

println jsonObject.name // Outputs the name retrieved from the URL
```

Handling Complex JSON Structures

JSON data is often more complex, containing arrays and nested objects. Look at the following JSON string that includes an array of user profiles:

```
def jsonStr = '''
{
    "users": [
        {
            "name": "John Doe",
            "age": 30,
            "email": "john.doe@example.com"
        },
        {
            "name": "Jane Smith",
            "age": 25,
            "email": "jane.smith@example.com"
        }
    ]
}
'''
```

Here's how to parse and access the data within it:

```
def jsonObject = jsonSlurper.parseText(jsonStr)
// Iterate through the array of users
jsonObject.users.each { user ->
    println "Name: ${user.name}, Age: ${user.age}, Email: ${user.email}"
}
```

The each method is used here to iterate over the list of users, making it easy to access individual user data.

Error Handling

When dealing with JSON data, it is essential to handle possible parsing errors gracefully. JsonSlurper does not provide built-in error handling, so you should wrap your parsing logic within a try-catch block:

```
try {
    def jsonObject = jsonSlurper.parseText(invalidJsonStr)
} catch (Exception e) {
    println "Failed to parse JSON: ${e.message}"
}
```

This ensures that any syntax errors or other issues within the JSON data do not cause the program to crash.

JsonSlurper's flexibility and ease of use make it an indispensable tool for parsing JSON in Groovy. It supports various sources and gracefully handles different JSON structures, enhancing data manipulation and retrieval efficiency.

9.6 Writing JSON with JsonBuilder

JsonBuilder in Groovy provides a flexible and powerful way to generate JSON structures, making it easier to create and manage JSON data in applications. JsonBuilder is part of the groovy.json.JsonBuilder class in Groovy and allows programmers to construct JSON objects using a straightforward and expressive syntax.

Creating a Basic JSON Object

To create a JSON object using JsonBuilder, initialize an instance of JsonBuilder and define the JSON structure within the builder's constructor. The example below demonstrates how to create a simple JSON object representing a person with attributes such as name and age:

```
import groovy.json.JsonBuilder

def jsonBuilder = new JsonBuilder()
jsonBuilder.person {
    name 'John Doe'
    age 30
}

println(jsonBuilder.toPrettyString())
```

The output of this code snippet will be:

```
{
    "person": {
        "name": "John Doe",
        "age": 30
    }
}
```

Nesting JSON Objects and Arrays

JsonBuilder allows nesting of JSON objects and arrays. Creating a more complex JSON structure involves defining objects within objects and arrays within objects. Below is an example that demonstrates nesting of JSON objects and inclusion of arrays:

```
def jsonBuilder = new JsonBuilder()
jsonBuilder.person {
    name 'Jane Doe'
    age 25
    address {
        street '123 Main St'
        city 'Anytown'
        postalCode '12345'
    }
```

```
    phones ['123-456-7890', '987-654-3210']
}

println(jsonBuilder.toPrettyString())
```

The resulting JSON object will look like:

```
{
  "person": {
    "name": "Jane Doe",
    "age": 25,
    "address": {
      "street": "123 Main St",
      "city": "Anytown",
      "postalCode": "12345"
    },
    "phones": [
      "123-456-7890",
      "987-654-3210"
    ]
  }
}
```

Dynamic Key-Value Pairs

JsonBuilder supports dynamic creation of key-value pairs. This feature is particularly useful when the keys of the JSON object need to be determined at runtime. The following example demonstrates how to use Groovy's map and list features for dynamic content creation:

```
def personData = [
    name: 'Alice Smith',
    age: 28,
    address: [
        street: '456 Elm St',
        city: 'Othertown',
        postalCode: '67890'
    ],
    phones: ['555-1234', '555-5678']
]

def jsonBuilder = new JsonBuilder(personData)
println(jsonBuilder.toPrettyString())
```

This code will generate the following JSON structure:

```
{
  "name": "Alice Smith",
  "age": 28,
  "address": {
    "street": "456 Elm St",
    "city": "Othertown",
    "postalCode": "67890"
  },
  "phones": [
    "555-1234",
    "555-5678"
  ]
}
```

JsonBuilder and GPathResult

For scenarios where you need to transform or serialize XML data into JSON, JsonBuilder can work in conjunction with GPathResult, the object model used by Groovy's XmlSlurper. Below is an example where an XML document is parsed and converted to JSON using JsonBuilder:

```
import groovy.json.JsonBuilder
import groovy.util.XmlSlurper

def xmlData = '''
<person>
    <name>David Brown</name>
    <age>45</age>
    <address>
        <street>789 Oak St</street>
        <city>Sometown</city>
        <postalCode>11223</postalCode>
    </address>
    <phones>
        <phone>555-9101</phone>
        <phone>555-1122</phone>
    </phones>
</person>
'''

def xmlSlurper = new XmlSlurper().parseText(xmlData)
def jsonBuilder = new JsonBuilder()

jsonBuilder.person {
    name xmlSlurper.name.text()
    age xmlSlurper.age.text().toInteger()
    address {
        street xmlSlurper.address.street.text()
        city xmlSlurper.address.city.text()
        postalCode xmlSlurper.address.postalCode.text()
    }
    phones xmlSlurper.phones.phone*.text()
}

println(jsonBuilder.toPrettyString())
```

The aforementioned code will generate the following JSON representation:

```
{
  "person": {
    "name": "David Brown",
    "age": 45,
    "address": {
      "street": "789 Oak St",
      "city": "Sometown",
      "postalCode": "11223"
    },
    "phones": [
      "555-9101",
      "555-1122"
    ]
  }
}
```

Customizing Output Format

JsonBuilder also provides options to customize the output format of the generated JSON string. For example, the prettyPrint method can be used to ensure the JSON output is well-formatted and easy to read:

```
def jsonBuilder = new JsonBuilder()
jsonBuilder.person {
    name 'Martin Green'
    age 35
}

def jsonOutput = jsonBuilder.toPrettyString()
println(jsonOutput)
```

Alternatively, if a compact JSON representation without whitespace and indentation is desired, the toString method can be used instead:

```
def compactJsonOutput = jsonBuilder.toString()
println(compactJsonOutput)
```

This will yield:

```
{"person":{"name":"Martin Green","age":35}}
```

JsonBuilder offers substantial flexibility and power in creating and manipulating JSON structures, making it an essential tool for developers working with JSON data in Groovy. By understanding the proper usage and various functionalities of JsonBuilder, one can efficiently generate robust and intricate JSON representations as required by their applications.

9.7 Navigating and Querying XML

Navigating and querying XML in Groovy involves leveraging the capabilities of the XmlSlurper and XmlParser classes to extract and manipulate data. These classes provide a straightforward, intuitive approach to work with XML, making Groovy an excellent choice for processing XML content. This section delves into methods for traversing XML structures and filtering nodes to retrieve desired information efficiently.

The XmlSlurper class is designed for parsing XML in a manner that supports GPath expressions, Groovy's standard way of navigating object graphs. Consider the following XML document representing a bookstore inventory:

```
<bookstore>
    <book id="1" category="fiction">
        <title lang="en">The Great Gatsby</title>
        <author>F. Scott Fitzgerald</author>
        <year>1925</year>
        <price>10.99</price>
    </book>
    <book id="2" category="non-fiction">
        <title lang="en">Sapiens</title>
        <author>Yuval Noah Harari</author>
        <year>2011</year>
        <price>19.99</price>
    </book>
</bookstore>
```

To parse and navigate this XML using XmlSlurper, initiate by creating an instance of XmlSlurper and parsing the XML content:

```
def xmlContent = '''<bookstore>
    <book id="1" category="fiction">
        <title lang="en">The Great Gatsby</title>
        <author>F. Scott Fitzgerald</author>
        <year>1925</year>
        <price>10.99</price>
    </book>
    <book id="2" category="non-fiction">
        <title lang="en">Sapiens</title>
        <author>Yuval Noah Harari</author>
        <year>2011</year>
        <price>19.99</price>
    </book>
</bookstore>'''

def bookstore = new XmlSlurper().parseText(xmlContent)
```

With the XML parsed, you can navigate the tree using GPath expressions. For example, to retrieve all book titles, the following script suffices:

```
bookstore.book.title.each { println it.text() }
```

The output from this script would be:

```
The Great Gatsby
Sapiens
```

To query specific attributes, such as retrieving the titles of all fiction books, use the attribute syntax in GPath expressions:

```
bookstore.book.findAll { it.@category == 'fiction' }.title.each { println it.text() }
```

This script first filters books by their category attribute and then prints the titles of the matching nodes.

Groovy's XmlParser class provides a more classical approach to XML processing with a similar interface. Here is how to navigate the same XML document with XmlParser:

```
def bookstore = new XmlParser().parseText(xmlContent)
bookstore.book.each { book ->
    println book.title.text()
}
```

This would produce the same output as XmlSlurper. To query attributes using XmlParser, you can filter the nodes in a similar manner:

```
bookstore.book.findAll { it.@category == 'fiction' }.each { book ->
    println book.title.text()
}
```

For advanced querying, Groovy supports a variety of techniques including XSLT transformations and XPath expressions. However, GPath provides an inherently Groovy way of querying XML data effortlessly.

GPath's expressiveness shines through in more complex queries, such as finding all book titles published after 2000:

```
bookstore.book.findAll { it.year.toInteger() > 2000 }.title.each { println it.text() }
```

This script leverages Groovy's concise syntax to filter books by year before extracting the titles.

In automated data extraction tasks, these querying capabilities simplify the code significantly. For instance, imagine needing an average price of all books. The calculation is straightforward:

```
def prices = bookstore.book.price.collect { it.toBigDecimal() }
def averagePrice = prices.sum() / prices.size()
println "Average Price: \$${averagePrice}"
```

Groovy's operator overloading and collection methods offer a powerful toolkit for succinctly performing such operations. The above script collects the prices into a list, converts them to BigDecimal for precision, and computes the average.

Navigating and querying XML with Groovy encapsulates a blend of simplicity and power, streamlining tasks that might require far more boilerplate in other languages. The integration of these features into Groovy's syntax enhances productivity and code readability, fostering efficient XML data handling.

9.8 Manipulating JSON Data

JSON (JavaScript Object Notation) is a lightweight data-interchange format that is easy for humans to read and write, and easy for machines to parse and generate. In Groovy, manipulation of JSON data is facilitated through the use of JsonSlurper and JsonBuilder classes. This section will provide a thorough examination of how to manipulate JSON data using these tools.

Creating and Modifying JSON with JsonBuilder

To begin with, let's create a sample JSON object using JsonBuilder. The JsonBuilder class in Groovy allows for the creation of a nested JSON object through a fluent API.

```
import groovy.json.JsonBuilder

def builder = new JsonBuilder()
builder.person {
    name "John Doe"
    age 40
    address {
        street "123 Main St"
        city "Anytown"
        zip "12345"
    }
    phones ["123-456-7890", "987-654-3210"]
}

println builder.toPrettyString()
```

This code snippet constructs a JSON object representing a person with various attributes. The toPrettyString method outputs the JSON in a human-readable format:

```
{
  "person": {
    "name": "John Doe",
    "age": 40,
    "address": {
      "street": "123 Main St",
      "city": "Anytown",
      "zip": "12345"
    },
    "phones": [
      "123-456-7890",
      "987-654-3210"
    ]
  }
}
```

Parsing and Modifying Existing JSON with JsonSlurper

The JsonSlurper class is used to parse JSON input into Groovy data structures (maps and lists) that can be manipulated easily. Let's start with a sample JSON string and parse it.

```
import groovy.json.JsonSlurper

def jsonString = '''
{
  "name": "Jane Smith",
  "email": "jane.smith@example.com",
  "roles": ["admin", "user"]
}
'''

def jsonSlurper = new JsonSlurper()
def jsonObject = jsonSlurper.parseText(jsonString)

assert jsonObject.name == "Jane Smith"
assert jsonObject.email == "jane.smith@example.com"
assert jsonObject.roles == ["admin", "user"]
```

This code converts the JSON string into a Groovy map. You can access individual elements using dot notation.

Adding and Removing Data

Adding new key-value pairs to the parsed JSON object is straightforward. Similarly, removing key-value pairs can be done using the remove method.

```
jsonObject.phone = "555-1234"
assert jsonObject.phone == "555-1234"

jsonObject.remove("roles")
assert jsonObject.roles == null
```

Modifying Nested Structures

Modifying nested structures requires direct access to the nested elements. Suppose we have a more complex structure:

```
def complexJson = '''
{
    "user": {
        "id": 1,
        "details": {
            "name": "Alice",
            "location": "Wonderland"
        }
    }
}
'''

def parsedJson = jsonSlurper.parseText(complexJson)

parsedJson.user.details.name = "Alice Wonderland"
parsedJson.user.details.country = "FantasyLand"

assert parsedJson.user.details.name == "Alice Wonderland"
assert parsedJson.user.details.country == "FantasyLand"
```

This example demonstrates changing a nested value and adding a new key-value pair to a nested object.

Iterating Over Elements

When working with large and complex JSON data, iteration is essential. Groovy provides convenient methods to iterate over collections:

```
def jsonArray = '''
[
    {"id": 1, "name": "Alice"},
    {"id": 2, "name": "Bob"},
    {"id": 3, "name": "Charlie"}
]
'''

def jsonList = jsonSlurper.parseText(jsonArray)

jsonList.each { item ->
    println "User ID: ${item.id}, Name: ${item.name}"
}
```

```
User ID: 1, Name: Alice
User ID: 2, Name: Bob
User ID: 3, Name: Charlie
```

The each method iterates over the list of JSON objects, allowing access to each item's properties.

Merging JSON Structures

Merging multiple JSON objects can be achieved by leveraging Groovy's map operations. Let's consider two JSON objects and merge them:

```
def json1 = '''
{
    "id": 1,
    "name": "Alice",
```

```
    "email": "alice@example.com"
}
'''

def json2 = '''
{
    "id": 1,
    "address": "Wonderland",
    "phone": "555-1234"
}
'''

def parsedJson1 = jsonSlurper.parseText(json1)
def parsedJson2 = jsonSlurper.parseText(json2)

parsedJson1.putAll(parsedJson2)

assert parsedJson1.address == "Wonderland"
assert parsedJson1.phone == "555-1234"
```

The putAll method in the map interface is used here to merge json2 into json1. This results in a combined JSON structure containing fields from both input objects.

Understanding and applying these techniques will enhance the ability to handle various JSON manipulation tasks efficiently in Groovy.

9.9 Transforming XML and JSON

Transforming data between XML and JSON formats is a common requirement in many applications. Groovy simplifies this process using its robust support for both XML and JSON paradigms. This section elaborates on the methods and techniques utilized for transforming XML data into JSON format and vice versa.

To illustrate this transformation, we will first read XML data and convert it to JSON. Subsequently, we will take JSON data and convert it back to XML. This bidirectional transformation is efficient in Groovy and leverages the language's powerful parsing and building capabilities.

Transforming XML to JSON

We begin by reading an XML document using XmlSlurper and converting it into a JSON structure using JsonBuilder. Consider the following XML data representing a catalog of books:

```
<catalog>
    <book id="bk101">
        <author>Gambardella, Matthew</author>
        <title>XML Developer's Guide</title>
        <genre>Computer</genre>
```

```
        <price>44.95</price>
        <publish_date>2000-10-01</publish_date>
        <description>An in-depth look at creating applications
        with XML.</description>
    </book>
    <book id="bk102">
        <author>Ralls, Kim</author>
        <title>Midnight Rain</title>
        <genre>Fantasy</genre>
        <price>5.95</price>
        <publish_date>2000-12-16</publish_date>
        <description>A former architect battles corporate zombies,
        an evil sorceress, and her own childhood to become queen
        of the world.</description>
    </book>
</catalog>
```

The Groovy script to transform this XML into JSON is as follows:

```
import groovy.json.JsonBuilder
import groovy.util.XmlSlurper

def xmlContent = '''
<catalog>
    <book id="bk101">
        <author>Gambardella, Matthew</author>
        <title>XML Developer's Guide</title>
        <genre>Computer</genre>
        <price>44.95</price>
        <publish_date>2000-10-01</publish_date>
        <description>An in-depth look at creating applications with XML.</
            description>
    </book>
    <book id="bk102">
        <author>Ralls, Kim</author>
        <title>Midnight Rain</title>
        <genre>Fantasy</genre>
        <price>5.95</price>
        <publish_date>2000-12-16</publish_date>
        <description>A former architect battles corporate zombies, an evil sorceress,
            and her own childhood to become queen of the world.</description>
    </book>
</catalog>
'''

def xml = new XmlSlurper().parseText(xmlContent)
def jsonBuilder = new JsonBuilder()

jsonBuilder {
    catalog {
        books xml.book.collect { book ->
            [
                id: book.@id,
                author: book.author.text(),
                title: book.title.text(),
                genre: book.genre.text(),
                price: book.price.text(),
                publish_date: book.publish_date.text(),
                description: book.description.text()
            ]
        }
    }
```

```
}
println jsonBuilder.toPrettyString()
```

Executing this script will produce the following JSON output:

```
{
  "catalog": {
    "books": [
      {
        "id": "bk101",
        "author": "Gambardella, Matthew",
        "title": "XML Developer's Guide",
        "genre": "Computer",
        "price": "44.95",
        "publish_date": "2000-10-01",
        "description": "An in-depth look at creating applications with XML."
      },
      {
        "id": "bk102",
        "author": "Ralls, Kim",
        "title": "Midnight Rain",
        "genre": "Fantasy",
        "price": "5.95",
        "publish_date": "2000-12-16",
        "description": "A former architect battles corporate zombies, an evil sorceress, and her own childhood to become queen of the world."
      }
    ]
  }
}
```

The key steps in the script above are the parsing of XML content using XmlSlurper, and constructing a JSON object using JsonBuilder. The collect method is used to iterate over each book node in the XML, extracting necessary values and formatting them into JSON.

Transforming JSON to XML

Now, we will perform the reverse transformation, converting JSON data back into an XML structure. Consider a JSON object representing a similar catalog of books:

```
{
  "catalog": {
    "books": [
      {
        "id": "bk101",
        "author": "Gambardella, Matthew",
        "title": "XML Developer's Guide",
        "genre": "Computer",
        "price": "44.95",
        "publish_date": "2000-10-01",
        "description": "An in-depth look at creating applications with XML."
      },
      {
        "id": "bk102",
        "author": "Ralls, Kim",
        "title": "Midnight Rain",
        "genre": "Fantasy",
        "price": "5.95",
        "publish_date": "2000-12-16",
        "description": "A former architect battles corporate zombies, an evil
            sorceress, and her own childhood to become queen of the world."
      }
    ]
  }
}
```

The Groovy script to convert this JSON into XML is as follows:

```
import groovy.json.JsonSlurper
import groovy.xml.MarkupBuilder

def jsonContent = '''
{
    "catalog": {
        "books": [
            {
                "id": "bk101",
                "author": "Gambardella, Matthew",
                "title": "XML Developer's Guide",
                "genre": "Computer",
                "price": "44.95",
                "publish_date": "2000-10-01",
                "description": "An in-depth look at creating applications with XML."
            },
            {
                "id": "bk102",
                "author": "Ralls, Kim",
                "title": "Midnight Rain",
                "genre": "Fantasy",
                "price": "5.95",
                "publish_date": "2000-12-16",
                "description": "A former architect battles corporate zombies, an evil
                    sorceress, and her own childhood to become queen of the world."
            }
        ]
    }
}
'''

def json = new JsonSlurper().parseText(jsonContent)
def writer = new StringWriter()
def xml = new MarkupBuilder(writer)

xml.catalog {
    json.catalog.books.each { book ->
        book(id: book.id) {
            author book.author
            title book.title
            genre book.genre
            price book.price
            publish_date book.publish_date
            description book.description
        }
    }
}

println writer.toString()
```

Executing this script will generate the following XML output:

```xml
<catalog>
  <book id="bk101">
    <author>Gambardella, Matthew</author>
    <title>XML Developer's Guide</title>
    <genre>Computer</genre>
    <price>44.95</price>
    <publish_date>2000-10-01</publish_date>
    <description>An in-depth look at creating applications with XML.</description>
  </book>
  <book id="bk102">
    <author>Ralls, Kim</author>
    <title>Midnight Rain</title>
    <genre>Fantasy</genre>
    <price>5.95</price>
    <publish_date>2000-12-16</publish_date>
    <description>A former architect battles corporate zombies, an evil sorceress, and her own childhood to become queen of the world.</description>
  </book>
</catalog>
```

In this script, we first parse the JSON content using JsonSlurper and subsequently build the XML content with MarkupBuilder. The each method iterates over each book object, appending the necessary elements to the XML structure. This process highlights Groovy's capability to seamlessly interconvert between these popular data formats.

9.10 Real-world Examples

Real-world applications often demand efficient and effective data handling, particularly with XML and JSON formats. Here, we demonstrate practical implementations within Groovy to solidify your understanding by addressing typical problems encountered in software development.

Example 1: Managing Configuration Files

Configuration files are critical for applications, often stored in either XML or JSON. Here, we illustrate loading, modifying, and saving a configuration file.

config.xml:

```xml
<config>
  <database>
    <host>localhost</host>
    <port>3306</port>
    <username>user</username>
    <password>pass</password>
  </database>
  <appSettings>
    <logLevel>DEBUG</logLevel>
    <maxConnections>100</maxConnections>
  </appSettings>
</config>
```

Loading and modifying with XmlSlurper:

```groovy
import groovy.xml.XmlSlurper
import groovy.xml.XmlUtil

def configFile = new File('config.xml')
def config = new XmlSlurper().parse(configFile)

// Modify values
```

```
config.database.host = '192.168.1.1'
config.appSettings.logLevel = 'INFO'

def writer = new StringWriter()
XmlUtil.serialize(config, writer)
println writer.toString()
```

Output:

```
<?xml version="1.0" encoding="UTF-8"?>
<config>
  <database>
    <host>192.168.1.1</host>
    <port>3306</port>
    <username>user</username>
    <password>pass</password>
  </database>
  <appSettings>
    <logLevel>INFO</logLevel>
    <maxConnections>100</maxConnections>
  </appSettings>
</config>
```

Example 2: Calling a Web Service

Interacting with web services is common. The following example demonstrates fetching data from a RESTful service that returns JSON.

Fetching and processing JSON data:

```
import groovy.json.JsonSlurper

def url = 'https://api.example.com/data'
def jsonText = url.toURL().text
def jsonData = new JsonSlurper().parseText(jsonText)

// Extracting specific data
def items = jsonData.items.collect { it.name }
println items
```

Output:

```
[Item1, Item2, Item3, ...]
```

Example 3: Generating Reports

Generating reports by transforming data from JSON to XML format can be highly beneficial. This example shows converting JSON received from an API to XML and vice versa.

Assuming apiData.json contains:

```
{
  "report": {
    "title": "Sales Report",
    "date": "2023-01-01",
    "sales": [
      {"item": "ItemA", "quantity": 10, "price": 100.0},
      {"item": "ItemB", "quantity": 5, "price": 200.0}
    ]
  }
}
```

Reading JSON and converting to XML:

```
import groovy.json.JsonSlurper
import groovy.xml.MarkupBuilder

def jsonFile = new File('apiData.json')
def jsonContent = jsonFile.text
def json = new JsonSlurper().parseText(jsonContent)

def writer = new StringWriter()
new MarkupBuilder(writer).report {
    title json.report.title
    date(json.report.date)
    sales {
        json.report.sales.each { sale ->
            sale {
                item(sale.item)
                quantity(sale.quantity)
                price(sale.price)
            }
        }
    }
}
println writer.toString()
```

Output:

```
<report>
  <title>Sales Report</title>
  <date>2023-01-01</date>
  <sales>
    <sale>
      <item>ItemA</item>
      <quantity>10</quantity>
      <price>100.0</price>
    </sale>
    <sale>
      <item>ItemB</item>
      <quantity>5</quantity>
      <price>200.0</price>
    </sale>
  </sales>
</report>
```

Example 4: Logging and Monitoring System

A practical real-world example includes integrating XML and JSON for logging and monitoring purposes.

logSettings.xml:

```
<settings>
  <logDirectory>/var/logs</logDirectory>
  <retentionDays>30</retentionDays>
  <logLevel>INFO</logLevel>
</settings>
```

Loading settings and simulate logging:

```
import groovy.xml.XmlSlurper
import groovy.json.JsonBuilder

def logFile = new File('logSettings.xml')
def settings = new XmlSlurper().parse(logFile)

// Simulate logging data
def logData = [
    timestamp: new Date(),
    level: settings.logLevel.text(),
    message: 'Application started successfully.'
]

def logJson = new JsonBuilder(logData)
println logJson.toPrettyString()
```

Output:

```
{
  "timestamp": "2023-10-25T14:45:00.000",
  "level": "INFO",
  "message": "Application started successfully."
}
```

Example 5: Handling User Data

Managing user data efficiently is vital. This example demonstrates reading a list of users from an XML file, manipulating the data, and writing it to a JSON format.

users.xml:

```
<users>
  <user>
    <name>John Doe</name>
    <email>john.doe@example.com</email>
  </user>
  <user>
    <name>Jane Smith</name>
    <email>jane.smith@example.com</email>
  </user>
</users>
```

Processing and converting to JSON:

```
import groovy.xml.XmlParser
import groovy.json.JsonBuilder

def userFile = new File('users.xml')
def xml = new XmlParser().parse(userFile)

def userList = xml.user.collect {
    [name: it.name.text(), email: it.email.text()]
}
```

```
def jsonBuilder = new JsonBuilder(userList)
println jsonBuilder.toPrettyString()
```

Output:

```
[
  {
    "name": "John Doe",
    "email": "john.doe@example.com"
  },
  {
    "name": "Jane Smith",
    "email": "jane.smith@example.com"
  }
]
```

These examples illustrate how Groovy's XML and JSON handling capabilities enable practical data manipulation and provide solid solutions to common real-world problems. This section bridges theoretical learning and practical application, providing a deeper grasp of employing Groovy for structured data handling in varied scenarios.

Chapter 10

Groovy Testing and Debugging

This chapter addresses testing and debugging in Groovy, focusing on unit testing with JUnit and Behavior-Driven Development (BDD) using Spock. It covers techniques for mocking and stubbing, integration testing, and utilizing test coverage tools. Additionally, it delves into test automation strategies, effective debugging methods, and the use of the Groovy Console for debugging. Best practices for ensuring reliable and maintainable code are also discussed.

10.1 Introduction to Testing in Groovy

Testing is an essential component in the software development lifecycle. It ensures that the code behaves as expected and that any deviations are identified early. In Groovy, testing is streamlined through integration with multiple frameworks such as JUnit and Spock, providing developers with tools to create comprehensive test suites efficiently.

Testing in Groovy can be classified into various categories, each serving a unique purpose:

- **Unit Testing:** Focuses on individual components or units of the codebase to ensure that each part functions correctly in isolation.

JUnit is a popular framework for unit testing in Groovy.

- **Behavior-Driven Development (BDD):** Aims to increase collaboration and understanding between technical and non-technical stakeholders by emphasizing specifications written in a natural language. Spock is a common BDD framework used in Groovy.

- **Integration Testing:** Examines the interaction between different modules or services to ensure that they function together correctly.

- **Test Coverage Tools:** Measures how much of the codebase is exercised by tests, helping to identify untested code.

- **Automated Testing:** Involves tools and practices that enable continuous testing and integration within the build pipeline.

JUnit is a widely adopted framework for unit testing and can be seamlessly integrated with Groovy. It allows developers to annotate test methods with @Test and provides various assertions to validate test outcomes.

```
import static org.junit.Assert.*
import org.junit.Test

class CalculatorTest {
    Calculator calc = new Calculator()

    @Test
    void additionTest() {
        assertEquals(5, calc.add(2, 3))
    }

    @Test
    void subtractionTest() {
        assertEquals(2, calc.subtract(5, 3))
    }
}
```

When executed, the test methods will confirm the functionality of the add and subtract methods in the Calculator class. The assertEquals method checks if the actual result matches the expected result.

```
$ gradle test


> Task :test
CalculatorTest > additionTest PASSED
CalculatorTest > subtractionTest PASSED
BUILD SUCCESSFUL in 1s
2 actionable tasks: 2 executed
```

Behavior-Driven Development (BDD) with Spock enhances readability and collaboration by structuring tests in a narrative style, emphasizing specifications over implementation details. Spock integrates smoothly with Groovy, leveraging its dynamic and expressive syntax.

```
import spock.lang.Specification

class CalculatorSpec extends Specification {
    def calc = new Calculator()

    def "adding two numbers"() {
        expect:
        calc.add(1, 2) == 3
    }

    def "subtracting two numbers"() {
        expect:
        calc.subtract(5, 3) == 2
    }
}
```

Spock tests are highly readable, thanks to its descriptive style. Each test case is framed within blocks like expect, when, then, and where, allowing conditions, actions, and assertions to be explicitly stated.

Executing the Spock tests provides similar feedback as JUnit but offers additional capabilities such as parameterized tests and data tables, which enhance the efficiency and readability of tests.

```
$ gradle test

> Task :test
CalculatorSpec > adding two numbers PASSED
CalculatorSpec > subtracting two numbers PASSED
BUILD SUCCESSFUL in 1s
2 actionable tasks: 2 executed
```

Mocking and stubbing are indispensable for isolating the code under test from its dependencies. They help simulate responses and behaviors, ensuring that tests remain focused and reliable. Groovy supports these techniques through libraries like Mockito and Spock.

```
import spock.lang.Specification

class UserServiceSpec extends Specification {
    def userRepository = Mock(UserRepository)
    def userService = new UserService(userRepository)

    def "find user by id"() {
        given:
        userRepository.findById(1) >> new User(id: 1, name: "John Doe")

        when:
        def user = userService.findUserById(1)

        then:
        user.name == "John Doe"
```

```
    }
}
```

The test defines a UserServiceSpec where the UserService relies on a mocked UserRepository. The given block sets up the mock behavior, when performs the action, and then asserts the expected outcome.

Each of these testing techniques contributes to a robust testing ecosystem, enabling developers to maintain high code quality, increase confidence in their software, and facilitate smoother development cycles.

Test coverage tools such as JaCoCo can be integrated within the build process to provide metrics on how much code is exercised by tests. Automated reports help identify untested or poorly tested areas, promoting better testing practices.

Ultimately, a comprehensive testing setup in Groovy involves using the right tools and practices to ensure code reliability and maintainability throughout the software development lifecycle. Whether unit testing with JUnit, adopting BDD with Spock, mocking and stubbing dependencies, or leveraging integration testing and test coverage tools, each approach plays a pivotal role in creating high-quality software.

10.2 Unit Testing with JUnit

Unit testing is a fundamental practice in software development that ensures the individual components of a program function as expected. In Groovy, JUnit is a powerful tool for writing and running these tests. JUnit provides a framework to define and execute tests and includes features for assertions, setup and teardown procedures, and test runners.

Creating a Basic JUnit Test

To begin writing a unit test with JUnit in Groovy, one first needs to create a test class. Typically, this class would reside in a separate directory designated for tests, often named src/test/groovy.

```
import org.junit.Test
import static org.junit.Assert.*

class CalculatorTest {

    @Test
    void testAddition() {
        Calculator calc = new Calculator()
        assertEquals(5, calc.add(2, 3))
```

```
    }

    @Test
    void testSubtraction() {
        Calculator calc = new Calculator()
        assertEquals(1, calc.subtract(3, 2))
    }
}
```

In the example above, CalculatorTest is the test class, and it includes two test methods annotated with @Test. These methods are executed by JUnit when the test suite runs. The assertEquals method from org.junit.Assert is used to verify that the method under test returns the expected result.

Assertion Methods

JUnit provides a robust set of assertion methods to facilitate various checks. Some commonly used assertions include:

- assertEquals(expected, actual): Verifies that two values are equal.
- assertTrue(condition): Verifies that a condition is true.
- assertFalse(condition): Verifies that a condition is false.
- assertNotNull(object): Verifies that an object is not null.
- assertNull(object): Verifies that an object is null.
- assertSame(expected, actual): Verifies that two references point to the same object.
- assertNotSame(expected, actual): Verifies that two references do not point to the same object.

These assertions can be leveraged to write comprehensive tests that validate different aspects of the code.

Setup and Teardown

In many cases, common setup or teardown procedures need to be performed for multiple tests. JUnit provides annotations @Before, @After, @BeforeClass, and @AfterClass to handle such scenarios.

```
import org.junit.Before
import org.junit.After

class CalculatorTest {

    Calculator calc
```

```
    @Before
    void setup() {
        calc = new Calculator()
    }

    @After
    void teardown() {
        calc = null
    }

    @Test
    void testAddition() {
        assertEquals(5, calc.add(2, 3))
    }

    @Test
    void testSubtraction() {
        assertEquals(1, calc.subtract(3, 2))
    }
}
```

The @Before annotated method, setup, runs before each test method, ensuring a new instance of Calculator is available for every test. The @After annotated method, teardown, runs after each test method, performing cleanup if necessary.

Parameterized Tests

Parameterized tests in JUnit allow running the same test with different inputs. This can be particularly useful for testing boundary conditions or a range of values.

```
import org.junit.runner.RunWith
import org.junit.runners.Parameterized
import org.junit.Test
import static org.junit.Assert.*

@RunWith(Parameterized)
class CalculatorParameterizedTest {

    int a
    int b
    int expected

    Calculator calc

    @Parameterized.Parameters
    static Collection<Object[]> data() {
        return [
            [1, 1, 2],
            [2, 3, 5],
            [3, 7, 10],
            [5, 6, 11]
        ];
    }

    CalculatorParameterizedTest(int a, int b, int expected) {
        this.a = a
```

```
        this.b = b
        this.expected = expected
        this.calc = new Calculator()
    }

    @Test
    void testAddition() {
        assertEquals(expected, calc.add(a, b))
    }
}
```

The @RunWith(Parameterized.class) annotation specifies that the test class should be run with the Parameterized runner. The data method provides a list of parameter sets. Each set is passed to the test class constructor, allowing the testAddition method to run various combinations of inputs.

Exception Testing

JUnit also supports testing for expected exceptions using the @Test(expected = Exception.class) annotation.

```
import org.junit.Test
import static org.junit.Assert.*

class CalculatorTest {

    @Test(expected = IllegalArgumentException.class)
    void testDivisionByZero() {
        Calculator calc = new Calculator()
        calc.divide(10, 0)
    }
}
```

The above test verifies that Calculator.divide raises an IllegalArgumentException when dividing by zero, ensuring the method handles this case correctly.

Test Runners and Suites

JUnit tests can be organized into suites, allowing for the grouping of multiple test classes to run together.

```
import org.junit.runner.RunWith
import org.junit.runners.Suite

@RunWith(Suite.class)
@Suite.SuiteClasses([CalculatorTest, AnotherTestClass])
class AllTests {
}
```

The @RunWith(Suite.class) and @Suite.SuiteClasses annotations specify that CalculatorTest and AnotherTestClass should be run as part of the AllTests suite. This approach is beneficial for large test suites requiring organization and modularity.

Using JUnit for unit testing in Groovy provides a structured and efficient way for developers to ensure their code functions correctly. Through the use of annotations for setup, teardown, and assertions, alongside the flexibility of parameterized and exception testing, a comprehensive suite of tests can be constructed to maintain robust software.

10.3 Behavior-Driven Development (BDD) with Spock

Behavior-Driven Development (BDD) is a software development methodology that emphasizes collaboration between developers, testers, and domain experts. It extends Test-Driven Development (TDD) by incorporating ideas from domain-driven design and object-oriented analysis into the testing process. BDD focuses on creating a shared understanding of the desired behavior of the application through examples described in natural language. In Groovy, one of the most powerful frameworks for implementing BDD is Spock.

Spock is a testing and specification framework for Java and Groovy applications. It tops JUnit by providing a more expressive and readable syntax, making tests easier to write and understand. Spock also includes powerful mocking and stubbing capabilities which we will explore in a later section.

Spock Specification

A Spock specification (often referred to as a Spock spec) is a class that extends spock.lang.Specification. This class contains methods annotated with @Test or Groovy's def, which define the behavior that needs to be verified. Each method typically contains one or more of the following sections: given, when, and, then.

Here is a fundamental example of a Spock specification:

```
import spock.lang.Specification

class SimpleMathSpec extends Specification {
    def "addition of two numbers"() {
        given: "two numbers"
        int a = 5
        int b = 3

        when: "they are added"
        int result = a + b
```

```
        then: "the result should be their sum"
        result == 8
    }
}
```

Sections of a Spock Specification

The structure of Spock specifications enhances readability and maintains consistency in test cases. Here is a detailed breakdown:

- given: This section initializes the context or setup for the test. It describes the initial state required to perform the test.
- when: This section shows the action or event that triggers the behavior being tested.
- then: This section contains assertions that verify the behavior and outcomes of the action triggered in the when block.
- expect: Combines when and then blocks for simple one-line tests.
- and: Enhances readability when multiple conditions or actions need to be specified in any section.

Each section signifies a vital part of a test's logic, making test cases self-explanatory.

Mocking and Stubbing in Spock

Mocking and stubbing are important capabilities in Spock. They allow developers to simulate and verify interactions between the system under test and its dependencies.

```
import spock.lang.Specification

class ServiceSpec extends Specification {

    def "service calls repository method"() {
        given: "a mocked repository"
        def repository = Mock(Repository)
        def service = new Service(repository)

        when: "service method is called"
        service.doSomething()

        then: "repository method is called once"
        1 * repository.someMethod()
    }
}
```

In the example above, Mock(Repository) creates a mock instance of Repository. The then block uses Spock's interaction language, 1 * repository.someMethod(), to specify that the someMethod should be called exactly once.

Parameterized Tests

Spock supports parameterized tests, which allow for running the same test logic over multiple sets of data.

```
class MathSpec extends Specification {

    def "maximum of two numbers"() {
        expect:
        Math.max(a, b) == result

        where:
        a | b || result
        1 | 3 || 3
        7 | 4 || 7
        0 | 0 || 0
    }
}
```

In this example, the where block specifies the different sets of inputs and expected results for the test, effectively running the expect block multiple times with each set of parameters.

Data Table Syntax

The where block uses data tables to provide multiple sets of input data, which improves readability and maintenance. The vertical bars separate the parameters, while the double vertical bars separate input from output.

For more complex scenarios, you can use multiple given-when-then blocks within a single test, or leverage Spock's powerful templating features for repeated tasks. These attributes make Spock versatile for both simple and complex testing scenarios.

10.4 Mocking and Stubbing

Mocking and stubbing are techniques used to isolate and control the behavior of dependencies in unit testing. These techniques are essential in creating repeatable and reliable tests by simulating the interactions between the system under test and its dependencies. In Groovy, there are several libraries and frameworks available for mocking and stubbing, with Spock being one of the most popular due to its expressive and concise syntax.

Mocking is the process of creating a mock object to mimic the behavior of a real object. A mock object can be programmed with predefined responses to method calls, allowing testers to verify that the system under test interacts correctly with its dependencies. Mocking is particularly useful in scenarios where the real object is unavailable, expensive to create, or has side effects that are undesirable in a testing environment.

Stubbing involves providing implementation-specific behavior for certain methods of a mock or real object. Unlike mocking, which focuses on the interactions between objects, stubbing is primarily concerned with the outputs of methods. Stubs return predefined, usually static, responses to method calls and do not keep track of the interactions.

To illustrate the concepts of mocking and stubbing in Groovy, we will use the Spock framework. Spock provides straightforward support for creating both mocks and stubs, enhancing the expressiveness and readability of tests.

```
import spock.lang.*

class PaymentServiceSpec extends Specification {

    def "processPayment should call validatePayment and sendNotification"() {
        given:
        def paymentProcessor = Mock(PaymentProcessor)
        def notificationService = Mock(NotificationService)
        def paymentService = new PaymentService(paymentProcessor,
            notificationService)

        when:
        paymentService.processPayment(100)

        then:
        1 * paymentProcessor.validatePayment(100)
        1 * notificationService.sendNotification('Payment of 100 processed')
    }

    def "calculateDiscount should return 20% discount for VIP customers"() {
        given:
        def customer = Stub(Customer) {
            isVIP() >> true
        }
        def billingService = new BillingService()

        when:
        def discount = billingService.calculateDiscount(customer)

        then:
        discount == 20
    }
}
```

In the first test, we create mock objects for PaymentProcessor and NotificationService. The processPayment method of the PaymentService class, which is under test, is called with an argument of 100. We then verify that the validatePayment method of the PaymentProcessor mock is called exactly once with the correct argument, and similarly, the sendNotification method of the NotificationService mock is called exactly once with the expected message.

In the second test, we create a stub for the Customer class. The method isVIP() of this stubbed customer is programmed to always return true. The calculateDiscount method of the BillingService class under test is expected to return a discount of 20 when provided with a VIP customer.

Both mocking and stubbing are declared using a concise and clear syntax that specifies behavior directly within the given block using the Mock and Stub methods provided by Spock. When defining behavior for mocks and stubs, the arrow operator (») is used to define the return value for method calls, enhancing readability.

There are key distinctions to keep in mind between mocks and stubs:

- **Mocks** are used when the goal is to test the interaction between the system under test and its dependencies. They can verify method calls and their parameters.

- **Stubs** are used primarily to provide preset responses to method calls. They simplify testing by eliminating external dependencies and returning consistent results.

Spock encourages the use of clear and expressive DSL to specify the behavior of mocks and stubs. For example, the expectation blocks (then:) can specify the number of times a method call is expected using cardinality specifiers like $1*$ for once and $0*$ for never. Additionally, Spock supports matchers that can be used within the expectation blocks to specify conditional behavior and parameter matching.

To fully leverage mocking and stubbing, it is best practice to maintain clarity in interactions being tested. Overusing mocks can lead to tightly coupled tests that are brittle and difficult to maintain. Conversely, stubs should return meaningful data that closely approximates the behavior of real dependencies to ensure the tests are valuable and realistic.

A thorough understanding of mocking and stubbing, as demonstrated here with Spock, is foundational for developing robust, isolated, and reliable unit tests in Groovy.

10.5 Integration Testing

Integration testing focuses on the interactions between components or systems to ensure they function together as expected. This type of testing is crucial for identifying interface defects between integrated components. In Groovy, integration testing can be accomplished using several tools and frameworks that offer robust capabilities for verifying the cohesion of various parts of the system.

Spring Boot Integration Testing

Spring Boot is a common framework used in Groovy-based applications. To facilitate integration testing with Spring Boot, the @SpringBootTest annotation is frequently employed. This annotation enables the loading of the full application context, ensuring that all components within the Spring framework are instantiated and injected correctly. To define a basic Spring Boot integration test, follow the structure below:

```
@RunWith(SpringRunner.class)
@SpringBootTest
public class ApplicationIntegrationTest {

    @Autowired
    private SomeService someService;

    @Test
    public void testServiceMethod() {
        boolean result = someService.performAction();
        assertTrue(result);
    }
}
```

In this example, SpringRunner is used to bootstrap the test with the Spring context, enabling dependency injection into test classes. The SomeService is automatically injected and its performAction method is tested within a fully instantiated Spring context.

Using Spock for Integration Testing

The Spock framework is versatile and can be used for both unit and integration testing. To conduct an integration test using Spock, you can annotate a specification with @SpringBootTest and leverage Spock's expressive syntax to write the test cases:

```
@SpringBootTest
class ApplicationIntegrationSpec extends Specification {

    @Autowired
    SomeService someService

    def "test service method"() {
```

```
        when:
        boolean result = someService.performAction()

        then:
        result == true
    }
}
```

The Specification class provides a clear and readable structure for defining the setup, execution, and assertion phases of a test. Integration testing with Spock enhances readability and maintenance of tests due to its BDD-like syntax.

Database Integration Testing

For applications that interact with databases, verifying database interactions through integration tests is essential. Groovy and the Grails framework offer GORM (Grails Object Relational Mapping) for ORM (Object-Relational Mapping) which simplifies database testing. An example of a Grails-based database integration test is shown below:

```
@TestFor(SomeDomainClass)
@Mock(SomeDomainClass)
class SomeDomainIntegrationSpec extends Specification {

    def "save and retrieve domain object"() {
        given:
        def domainInstance = new SomeDomainClass(name: "Test Name")

        when:
        domainInstance.save(flush: true)

        then:
        SomeDomainClass.findByName("Test Name") != null
    }
}
```

In this test, @TestFor and @Mock are used to configure the test environment, while GORM methods such as save and findByName are utilized to perform and verify database operations.

Interaction Between Microservices

Integration testing is also critical when dealing with microservice architectures, where multiple services interact over HTTP or other protocols. Testing these interactions often involves launching multiple services and verifying their communication. Testcontainers can be used to manage the lifecycle of containerized services during testing:

```
@Testcontainers
@SpringBootTest
public class MicroserviceInteractionTest {

    @Container
```

```
    public static GenericContainer<?> service1 = new GenericContainer<>("service1:
        latest").withExposedPorts(8080);

    @Container
    public static GenericContainer<?> service2 = new GenericContainer<>("service2:
        latest").withExposedPorts(8081);

    @Autowired
    private RestTemplate restTemplate;

    @Test
    public void testMicroserviceInteraction() {
        String service1Url = "http://localhost:" + service1.getFirstMappedPort();
        String service2Url = "http://localhost:" + service2.getFirstMappedPort();

        ResponseEntity<String> response = restTemplate.getForEntity(service1Url + "
            /endpoint", String.class);
        assertEquals(HttpStatus.OK, response.getStatusCode());

        response = restTemplate.getForEntity(service2Url + "/endpoint", String.class);
        assertEquals(HttpStatus.OK, response.getStatusCode());
    }
}
```

By harnessing Testcontainers, temporary test environments that closely mimic production can be set up to validate the interactions between microservices without the need for deploying them manually.

Test Data Management

Managing test data is an integral part of robust integration testing. Utilizing frameworks that automatically reset the state between tests ensures reliable and repeatable tests. For example, using Flyway or Liquibase for database migrations allows for consistent setup and teardown of database schema and data:

```
@Configuration
public class TestDatabaseConfig {

    @Bean
    public Flyway flyway(DataSource dataSource) {
        Flyway flyway = Flyway.configure().dataSource(dataSource).locations("
            classpath:db/migration").load();
        flyway.migrate();
        return flyway;
    }
}
```

With the integration of Flyway into the test configuration, the database schema can be managed consistently, enabling deterministic test outcomes.

Ensure the comprehensive testing of integration points between services and components, and maintain consistency in the environment setup to avoid flaky tests. The application of frameworks and tools appropriate to the context of integration testing significantly enhances the reliability and maintainability of software systems.

10.6 Test Coverage Tools

Test coverage tools are integral to the development process, providing metrics that help evaluate the extent to which the source code of a program is tested. These tools identify the portions of the codebase that are covered by tests, offering insights into areas that might require additional testing. In Groovy, several tools can be utilized to measure test coverage, with JaCoCo (Java Code Coverage) being one of the most popular choices.

To begin using JaCoCo with Groovy, it is necessary to integrate JaCoCo with the build system. Since Gradle is a widely-used build automation tool compatible with Groovy, we will demonstrate the integration using a Gradle build script. Assuming the reader is familiar with Gradle's build configuration file 'build.gradle', the following steps outline the process required to configure JaCoCo:

```
plugins {
    id 'java'
    id 'jacoco'
}

repositories {
    mavenCentral()
}

dependencies {
    testImplementation 'org.spockframework:spock-core:2.0-groovy-3.0'
    testImplementation 'junit:junit:4.13.2'
}

test {
    useJUnitPlatform()
    finalizedBy jacocoTestReport // Generate report after tests
}

jacocoTestReport {
    reports {
        xml.required = true
        csv.required = false
        html.outputLocation = layout.buildDirectory.dir('jacocoHtml')
    }
}
```

In the above configuration, the 'jacoco' plugin is applied to the project. It instructs Gradle to use the JaCoCo tool to measure code coverage. The 'dependencies' block includes the necessary testing frameworks, in this case, Spock and JUnit. The 'test' task is configured to use the JUnit platform, ensuring compatibility with Spock. Notice the 'finalizedBy jacocoTestReport' directive, which ensures that the JaCoCo report is generated after running the tests.

The 'jacocoTestReport' block configures the report generation. The configuration specifies that the XML report is required ('xml.required = true'), while the CSV report is optional ('csv.required = false'). The HTML report's output directory is set to 'build/jacocoHtml'.

To execute the tests and generate the coverage report, run the following command in the terminal:

```
./gradlew test jacocoTestReport
```

Upon successful execution, navigate to the 'build/jacocoHtml' directory and open the 'index.html' file in a web browser to view the coverage report. The report provides detailed insights into coverage metrics, such as the percentage of lines and branches covered.

Aside from JaCoCo, Groovy developers might also consider other tools such as Cobertura or SonarQube for more comprehensive analysis. These tools offer additional functionalities like tracking historical coverage data and integrating with Continuous Integration (CI) pipelines.

```
plugins {
    id 'java'
    id 'net.saliman.cobertura' version '2.6.1'
}

repositories {
    mavenCentral()
}

dependencies {
    testImplementation 'org.spockframework:spock-core:2.0-groovy-3.0'
    testImplementation 'junit:junit:4.13.2'
}

cobertura {
    coverageIncludes = ['**/com/example/project/**']
}

tasks.withType(Test) {
    finalizedBy coberturaReport // Generate report after tests
}
```

In the Cobertura example above, the 'net.saliman.cobertura' plugin is used. The 'cobertura' block allows for specifying packages or classes to include in the coverage analysis. Like JaCoCo, Cobertura will generate reports which can then be reviewed in an HTML format.

Using SonarQube involves setting up a SonarQube server and integrating the SonarQube plugin with the project. It provides not only test coverage metrics but also code quality analysis and technical debt estimation. Configuration is typically done in the 'build.gradle' as follows:

```
plugins {
    id "org.sonarqube" version "3.3"
}

sonarqube {
    properties {
        property "sonar.projectKey", "com.example.project"
        property "sonar.host.url", "http://localhost:9000"
        property "sonar.login", "your_token"
    }
}

test {
    useJUnitPlatform()
}
```

The 'sonarqube' block sets up the required properties for connecting to the SonarQube server. Running the analysis is straightforward:

```
./gradlew sonarqube
```

Upon execution, the analysis results, including coverage reports, are sent to the SonarQube server, allowing for in-depth review via the SonarQube web interface.

Adopting these tools and incorporating them into the development workflow enhances test coverage visibility, leading to better-tested and more reliable code. Adhering to these practices aligns with the chapter's emphasis on ensuring reliable and maintainable Groovy applications through robust testing and debugging strategies.

10.7 Test Automation Techniques

Test automation is a crucial aspect of a robust software development lifecycle, enabling consistent, repeatable, and efficient testing processes. Within the Groovy ecosystem, various tools and methodologies facilitate the automation of tests. This section explores these tools and methodologies, providing detailed insights into their implementation and usage.

Continuous Integration (CI): Continuous Integration is a development practice where developers frequently integrate code into a shared repository, often multiple times a day. Each integration can then be verified by an automated build and automated tests. This helps detect errors quickly and locate them more easily.

- Jenkins: Jenkins is an open-source automation server written in Java. It helps automate the parts of software development related to building, testing, and deploying, facilitating continuous integration and continuous delivery (CI/CD).

```
// Jenkinsfile
pipeline {
    agent any

    stages {
        stage('Build') {
            steps {
                sh 'groovy build.gradle'
            }
        }
        stage('Test') {
            steps {
                sh 'groovy test.gradle'
            }
        }
    }

    post {
        always {
            junit '**/build/test-results/test/*.xml'
        }
    }
}
```

- Travis CI: Travis CI is a hosted continuous integration service used to build and test software projects hosted on GitHub. It provides various integrations with different programming languages, including Groovy.

```
// .travis.yml
language: groovy

script:
  - ./gradlew check
```

Build Automation Tools: Build automation is the process of automating the creation of a software build. This includes automating tasks such as compiling source code into binary code, packaging binary code, running tests, and deploying to production systems.

- Gradle: Gradle is a build automation tool that is open-source and supports Groovy as a first-class citizen. Gradle provides powerful support for the automation of testing processes.

```
// build.gradle
plugins {
    id 'groovy'
}

repositories {
    mavenCentral()
}

dependencies {
    testImplementation 'org.spockframework:spock-core:1.3-groovy-2.5'
}

test {
    useJUnitPlatform()
}
```

Test Frameworks: Several test frameworks provide capabilities to write tests in Groovy, allowing you to automate the testing process efficiently.

- Spock Framework: Spock is a test framework for Java and Groovy applications. It is highly expressive and allows for writing clear and maintainable tests.

```
// Example Spock Test
import spock.lang.Specification

class MyFirstSpec extends Specification {

    def "first test"() {
        expect: "math should work"
        1 + 1 == 2
    }
}
```

- JUnit: JUnit is a well-known testing framework for Java, it is also used in Groovy for writing repeatable tests. JUnit tests can be automated to run within a continuous integration pipeline.

```
// Example JUnit Test
import org.junit.Test
import static org.junit.Assert.assertEquals

class MyFirstJUnitTest {

    @Test
    void testAddition() {
        assertEquals(4, 2 + 2)
    }
}
```

Automation Execution and Scheduling: Automating the execution of tests is a fundamental part of test automation. This includes deciding when and how frequently the tests should execute.

- Cron Jobs: Unix-based systems use cron jobs to schedule scripts or commands to run at specific times. These can be configured to execute test scripts regularly.

```
# Cron job to run the test script every night at 2 AM
0 2 * * * /usr/bin/groovy /path/to/tests.groovy
```

- Scheduled Tasks in Jenkins: Jenkins offers functionality to schedule jobs through a built-in management interface.

```
// Jenkins pipeline script with cron trigger
pipeline {
    triggers { cron('H 2 * * *') }
    stages {
        stage('Build') {
            steps {
                sh 'groovy build.gradle'
            }
        }
        stage('Test') {
            steps {
                sh 'groovy test.gradle'
            }
        }
    }
}
```

Reporting: Creating and reviewing test reports is a key aspect of test automation, providing insights into pass/failure rates and supporting regression analysis.

- JUnit Reports: JUnit provides XML formatted test reports that can be parsed by continuous integration systems to produce human-readable reports.

```
// Test task in build.gradle for JUnit Report
test {
    reports {
        junitXml.enabled = true
        html.enabled = true
    }
}
```

- Spock Reports: Spock framework integrates with various reporting tools to give developers insights into the testing process.

```
// Adding Spock Reports to build.gradle
dependencies {
    testImplementation 'org.spockframework:spock-reports:2.0'
}
```

Code Coverage: Automated test coverage tools help determine what percentage of the code is executed during tests, highlighting untested parts that need additional attention.

- Jacoco: JaCoCo is a code coverage library for Java, which also works seamlessly with Groovy.

```
// Adding Jacoco plugin to build.gradle
plugins {
    id 'jacoco'
}

jacocoTestReport {
    reports {
        xml.enabled true
        csv.enabled false
        html.destination file("${buildDir}/jacocoHtml")
    }
}

check {
    dependsOn jacocoTestReport
}
```

Automating tests in Groovy requires utilizing various tools and frameworks effectively. Each tool and technique should be chosen based on the specific needs of the project, ensuring that the test suite is reliable, efficient, and maintainable.

10.8 Debugging Groovy Applications

Debugging is a critical aspect of software development, involving the identification and resolution of defects or issues within a program. In Groovy, debugging can be performed using various tools and techniques that facilitate the isolation, examination, and fixing of bugs.

Using println Statements

One of the simplest methods of debugging involves inserting println statements into the code to print variable values and program state. While rudimentary, this approach can be effective for quick inspections.

```
def exampleFunction(int a, int b) {
    println "Entering exampleFunction with a=${a}, b=${b}"
    def result = a + b
    println "Result of a + b=${result}"
    return result
}
```

Upon execution, the printed statements will display in the console, allowing for inspection of the variables a, b, and $result$.

```
Entering exampleFunction with a=5, b=10
Result of a + b=15
```

Using Groovy's Built-in Debugging Support with IDEs

Modern Integrated Development Environments (IDEs) like IntelliJ IDEA or Eclipse offer sophisticated debugging tools for Groovy applications:

- **Breakpoints:** These are markers set in the code where execution will pause, enabling developers to inspect variables and program flow.
- **Watch Expressions:** Developers can monitor the values of specific expressions or variables when a breakpoint is hit.
- **Step Through Execution:** This functionality includes stepping into methods (step-into), stepping over methods (step-over), and stepping out of methods (step-out).

For instance, while debugging in IntelliJ IDEA, one can set a breakpoint by clicking in the gutter next to the line number. Execution will pause at this line, allowing inspection in the Debug tool window.

Debugger Initialization in IntelliJ IDEA

To start the debugger in IntelliJ IDEA:

1. Open the Groovy script or class file.
2. Set breakpoints by clicking in the gutter.
3. Click on the Debug button (typically displayed as a bug icon).
4. The Debugger tool window appears, displaying variables and allowing the developer to step through the code.

Using the Groovy Console

The Groovy Console is a powerful tool for debugging Groovy scripts interactively:

- It provides an environment to execute Groovy scripts with immediate feedback.

- The console displays results of Groovy expressions, which helps identify errors quickly.
- Scripts can be tested incrementally, which facilitates pinpointing issues.

To use the Groovy Console:

1. Launch the Groovy Console, typically found within the Groovy package.
2. Write or load the Groovy script into the editor pane.
3. Execute the script by clicking the Run button.
4. Inspect the output and potential error messages in the output pane.

Consider the following example script executed in the Groovy Console:

```
def x = 10
def y = 20
def sum = x + y
println "Sum of x and y is: ${sum}"
```

Upon execution, the output pane will display:

```
Sum of x and y is: 30
```

Groovy's Logging Frameworks

For more structured and manageable debugging, Groovy supports various logging frameworks such as Log4j or SLF4J. Logging provides a way to output detailed debugging information without scattering println statements throughout the code.

Here is an example using SLF4J with Logback:

```
import org.slf4j.Logger
import org.slf4j.LoggerFactory

class Example {
    private static final Logger log = LoggerFactory.getLogger(Example.class)

    static void main(String[] args) {
        log.debug("Starting Example.main")
        int a = 5
        int b = 10
        log.info("Adding a=${a} and b=${b}")
        int result = a + b
        log.debug("Sum of a and b is ${result}")
        log.debug("Ending Example.main")
    }
}
```

To use SLF4J with Logback:

1. Add dependencies in the build.gradle file:

```
dependencies {
    implementation 'org.slf4j:slf4j-api:1.7.30'
    implementation 'ch.qos.logback:logback-classic:1.2.3'
}
```

2. Create a logback.xml configuration file to customize logging outputs.

3. Run the Groovy application, and the log messages will appear according to the configuration.

Exception Handling and Stack Traces

Exception handling is crucial in debugging as it allows programs to handle unexpected conditions gracefully. When exceptions occur, inspecting stack traces provides insights into the point of failure.

```
try {
    // Code that may throw an exception
    def result = 10 / 0
} catch (ArithmeticException e) {
    println "Caught an ArithmeticException: ${e.message}"
    e.printStackTrace()
}
```

Executing the above code will yield:

```
Caught an ArithmeticException: / by zero
java.lang.ArithmeticException: / by zero
    at Example.main(Example.groovy:2)
```

Inspecting the stack trace helps identify the exact line causing the exception, facilitating quicker resolution.

Efficient debugging practices are essential for developing robust Groovy applications, enabling developers to isolate and resolve issues effectively while maintaining code quality and performance.

10.9 Using the Groovy Console for Debugging

The Groovy Console is an invaluable tool for debugging Groovy applications. It provides an interactive environment for executing Groovy scripts, allowing developers to test snippets of code and observe their behavior in real-time. This section illustrates how to leverage the Groovy Console for effective debugging.

The Groovy Console can be launched from the command line. Ensure that Groovy is properly installed and configured on your system. To start the console, execute the following command:

```
groovyConsole
```

Upon launching, the Groovy Console window appears, providing a text editor area where you can write Groovy scripts. Let us break down the process of using this console for debugging into several key aspects:

- **Executing Code Snippets:** Write any Groovy code snippet directly in the editor pane and execute it by pressing the Ctrl+R (Windows/Linux) or Cmd+R (Mac) shortcut or by selecting Script > Run from the menu. The output will be displayed in the output pane at the bottom.

```
def greet(name) {
    return "Hello, $name!"
}

println(greet("World"))
```

  After running the above script, the console displays the output:

```
Hello, World!
```

- **Inspecting Variables:** The console allows inspection of variables by printing their values to the output pane. This feature is useful for tracking variable states at different execution points.

```
def sum(a, b) {
    return a + b
}

def result = sum(5, 7)
println(result)
```

  The console shows:

```
12
```

- **Evaluating Expressions:** The console lets you evaluate mathematical and logical expressions, assisting in verifying algorithm correctness.

```
def a = 10
def b = 20
```

```
println("a + b = ${a + b}")
println("a * b = ${a * b}")
println("Is a less than b? ${a < b}")
```

The output is:

```
a + b = 30
a * b = 200
Is a less than b? true
```

- **Debugging with println:** Inserting numerous println statements can trace the code execution flow. This technique helps identify where incorrect values or unexpected behaviors begin.

```
def factorial(n) {
    println("Calculating factorial of $n")
    if (n <= 1) return 1
    return n * factorial(n - 1)
}
println(factorial(5))
```

The detailed output indicates the recursion process:

```
Calculating factorial of 5
Calculating factorial of 4
Calculating factorial of 3
Calculating factorial of 2
Calculating factorial of 1
120
```

- **Exception Handling:** Capturing and printing exceptions allows you to understand errors and their origin.

```
try {
    def numbers = [1, 2, 3]
    println(numbers[5])
} catch (Exception e) {
    println("An error occurred: ${e.message}")
}
```

The console reports:

```
An error occurred: Index 5 out of bounds for length 3
```

- **Script Properties and Configuration:** You can configure the script properties within the console, such as setting custom classpaths or properties. These options are available under Script > Configure Script.

```
@Grab(group='org.apache.commons', module='commons-lang3', version='3.12.0'
    )
import org.apache.commons.lang3.StringUtils

println(StringUtils.upperCase("groovy"))
```

The result:

```
GROOVY
```

Utilizing the Groovy Console is particularly beneficial during the development phase, enabling rapid feedback and issue isolation.

10.10 Best Practices for Testing and Debugging

Effective testing and debugging are paramount to ensuring the reliability and maintainability of your Groovy applications. By adhering to best practices, you can significantly enhance the quality of your code. This section delineates a detailed set of best practices for testing and debugging within the Groovy ecosystem, leveraging the principles and tools discussed earlier in this chapter.

1. Write Clear and Concise Tests

Each test should focus on a single functionality or a specific behavior of the code. Avoid writing tests that perform multiple assertions as they become harder to maintain and debug. Consider the following example:

```
class Calculator {
    int add(int a, int b) { a + b }
    int subtract(int a, int b) { a - b }
}

class CalculatorTest {
    @Test
    void testAddition() {
        def calculator = new Calculator()
        assert calculator.add(3, 5) == 8
    }

    @Test
    void testSubtraction() {
        def calculator = new Calculator()
        assert calculator.subtract(10, 4) == 6
    }
}
```

In the above example, tests for addition and subtraction are separated, making it clear what each test is verifying and simplifying issue isolation.

2. Follow the Principle of Least Surprise

Your test code should be easy to understand and follow the principle of least surprise. This means using meaningful names for tests, classes, and variables, and avoiding overly complex or deeply nested structures that may confuse future maintainers.

3. Mock and Stub Judiciously

While mocking and stubbing are powerful techniques to isolate units of code, they should be used judiciously. Overusing mocks can lead to brittle tests that break upon refactoring and obscure the true behavior of your code. Aim to mock external dependencies and interactions rather than the core functionality of your application.

Consider the example:

```
class UserService {
    UserRepository userRepository

    User findUserById(Long id) {
        userRepository.findById(id)
    }
}

interface UserRepository {
    Optional<User> findById(Long id)
}

class MockingExampleTest {
    @Mock
    UserRepository userRepository

    @InjectMocks
    UserService userService = new UserService()

    @Test
    void testFindUserById() {
        def user = new User(id: 1, name: 'John Doe')
        given(userRepository.findById(1)).willReturn(Optional.of(user))

        def result = userService.findUserById(1)

        assert result == user
    }
}
```

4. Ensure Test Coverage But Avoid Redundancy

Use tools to measure test coverage and ensure critical paths are tested, but avoid striving for 100% coverage as it often leads to unnecessary testing of simple functions that might change rarely. Focus on covering edge cases and areas that have been historically prone to bugs.

5. Employ Automated Testing Strategies

Automated tests should be part of your continuous integration pipeline to catch regressions early. Utilize tools like Jenkins, Travis CI, or

GitHub Actions to run your test suite on each commit or pull request. Automation frees up developer time and ensures consistency in testing.

6. Use the Groovy Console for Rapid Debugging

The Groovy Console provides an interactive environment for testing snippets of code quickly. This can be invaluable for debugging complex code by allowing exploratory testing and immediate feedback. Consider parsing JSON data:

```
def json = '{ "name": "John", "age": 30 }'
def data = new groovy.json.JsonSlurper().parseText(json)
assert data.name == 'John'
```

Running this in the Groovy Console helps in swiftly testing and iterating on the code.

7. Use Effective Logging

Incorporate logging within your application to capture the state during execution. This is essential for diagnosing issues that are hard to reproduce. Groovy's log annotation can simplify logging:

```
@groovy.util.logging.Log
class Example {
    void someMethod() {
        log.info "Method executed"
    }
}
```

8. Debugging With IDE Tools

Modern IDEs like IntelliJ IDEA or Eclipse provide powerful debugging tools. Set breakpoints, inspect variables, and use step-through debugging to understand the execution flow. Ensure that the IDE is properly configured to recognize Groovy sources and dependencies.

```
IDE Setup Example:
1. Open IntelliJ IDEA.
2. Import your project.
3. Navigate to the code you wish to debug.
4. Set breakpoints by clicking the left margin.
5. Run the debugger using the 'Debug' button.
```

9. Leverage Test Data Factories

Creating consistent and realistic test data can reduce flakiness in tests. Use object mother patterns or data factories to create test data. This ensures that your tests are reproducible and easy to extend.

Example of a test data factory:

```
class UserFactory {
    static User createUser(Map overrides = [:]) {
```

```
        return new User(overrides + [id: 1, name: 'Default Name', age: 30])
    }
}

class UserServiceTest {
    @Test
    void testFindUser() {
        def testUser = UserFactory.createUser(name: 'John Doe')
        // Proceed with the test using testUser
    }
}
```

10. Adopt Code Reviews for Tests

Involve your team in reviewing test code just as rigorously as application code. Code reviews for tests help catch missing cases, logical errors, and improve overall test quality.

Adhering to these best practices will foster a culture of quality and reliability in your development process, making your Groovy applications robust and easier to maintain.

Made in the USA
Monee, IL
05 November 2026

67845313R00164